The Information Behavior of a New Generation

Children and Teens in the 21st Century

Edited by Jamshid Beheshti and Andrew Large

THE SCARECROW PRESS, INC.
Lanham • Toronto • Plymouth, UK
2013

Published by Scarecrow Press, Inc.
A wholly owned subsidiary of The Rowman & Littlefield Publishing Group, Inc.
4501 Forbes Boulevard, Suite 200, Lanham, Maryland 20706
www.rowman.com

10 Thornbury Road, Plymouth PL6 7PP, United Kingdom

British Library Cataloguing in Publication Information Available

Library of Congress Cataloging-in-Publication Data

The information behavior of a new generation : children and teens in the 21st century / edited by Jamshid Beheshti and Andrew Large.
p. cm.
Includes bibliographical references and index.
ISBN 978-0-8108-8594-3 (cloth) — ISBN 978-0-8108-8595-0 (ebook)
1. Information behavior. 2. Information literacy. 3. Human information processing in children. 4. Children—Effect of technological innovations on. 5. Teenagers—Effect of technological innovations on. 6. Internet and children. 7. Internet and teenagers. 8. Technology and children. 9. Technology and youth. I. Beheshti, Jamshid, 1952–, editor of compilation. II. Large, J. A., editor of compilation.
ZA3075I5325 2013
027.62'6—dc23
2012024646

The paper used in this publication meets the minimum requirements of American National Standard for Information Sciences Permanence of Paper for Printed Library Materials, ANSI/NISO Z39.48-1992.

Printed in the United States of America.

Contents

Introduction

Andrew Large and Jamshid Beheshti

The information behavior of young people over the past 30 or so years has increasingly engaged the attention of researchers, both because the young are information creators and users in their own right and, of course, because they will shortly become adults; behaviors acquired at a young age will help form those exhibited later in life. Such research interest has undoubtedly been stimulated by the opportunities afforded children and teenagers through information technologies, greatly expanding their ability not only to access and exchange information but also to create their own information. A second impetus has been provided by the focus in elementary as well as secondary education on inquiry-based learning, where students are actively encouraged to seek information individually and as members of small groups in order to undertake projects.

These developments have prompted the publication of several books devoted to young people's information behavior; so why do we need another one? One response would be that the information technologies so central to information behavior have themselves continued to advance. The most obvious current example is social networking, into which children and teens have immersed themselves with enthusiasm, as several of the chapters in this collection will explain. But a second rationale for this particular book is the broad remit it gives to the examination of information behavior. The authors themselves are drawn from the disciplines of education, educational psychology, and computer science as well as from library and information science. The resulting content reflects this variety, encompassing theory-based as well as practice-based discussions of information behavior that are viewed through a wide-angle lens.

Before reviewing the content of the individual chapters, we need to first explain the editorial policy of *Information Behavior of a New Generation: Children and Teens in the 21st Century*. First, we have not sought to impose a monolithic structure on the contributors. All authors were provided with guidelines as to the expected general content of their chapters, but within these constraints they were free to exercise their own judgment and follow their own trail, so to speak. A good example is the concept of the "digital native." Is this an appropriate term to assign to children who have grown up surrounded by digital technologies and who, as a consequence, behave differently from those who once inhabited the pre-diluvian world of paper and pen, and where technology at most meant a typewriter? We believe it is legitimate to hold conflicting views on this term, so the authors have been left to make up their own minds.

A second issue for a book concerned with information behavior in the digital age is the geopolitical coverage given to the topic. As several authors say, digital information has now reached young people in practically all corners of the world, though the degree and kind of penetration still varies significantly. The contributors' home base of Canada and the United States, their personal familiarity with events in these regions, and their linguistic skills all mitigate any attempt to claim global coverage. In practice, although from time to time reference is made to events in the broader world, this book focuses upon the North American continent and asserts no wider aspirations.

A third issue to be confronted was the definition of a child. At what age does a child pass into adulthood? At what age does a child exhibit "information behavior"? And should teenagers be grouped with children, with adults, or assigned a category in their own right? Our decision has been to leave such decisions up to the individual authors. This has resulted in some chapters discussing the information behavior of very young children, while others focus upon those of school age. Many authors have discussed both children and teens, and in at least one case this discussion has been extended into adult life because the author thought it important to draw links between information behavior at various times in the life process.

In a similar fashion, authors have been left to choose their own presentation style, with the exception of standardization for such things as numbers, place names, and spellings (where the U.S. standard has been adopted). As a consequence, for example, the first-person singular, first-person plural, and the impersonal passive constructions have all been chosen. Some chapters, at least to the editors' ears, have adopted a more formal, "academic" voice, while others have opted for a more informal style. As editors we preferred to let our contributors assume their own voices, and indeed the resulting variety might even render the book both more readable and more enjoyable.

Information Behavior of a New Generation: Children and Teens in the 21st Century begins with two chapters that focus upon theoretical issues and establish the foundation for the remaining chapters. In his chapter "Concepts, Propositions, Models, and Theories in Information Behavior Research," Charles Cole explores the meanings of these four terms and relates them to research on information behavior. He argues that they represent a sort of research communication tool that allows researchers to understand what others have previously done in the field, and, in turn, to effectively communicate to others the patterns they find in their own research data. James Byrnes and Matthew Bernacki, in their chapter "Cognitive Development and Information Behavior," express their surprise that researchers like themselves in the field of cognitive development have not conducted many studies of information behavior or developed specific theories to explain or predict age differences in the tendencies to seek, interpret, or use information. As they comment, the studies have been done primarily by scholars in the discipline of library and information science who do not have extensive training in cognitive developmental theory. They therefore have chosen to describe well-established age trends in the components of cognition (e.g., knowledge, working memory, etc.) and to consider whether age changes in these components would likely lead to age changes in information behavior. They conclude that it would be premature to draw firm conclusions on what to expect when children, adolescents, or adults seek information, make sense of it, or use it in particular situations. They do argue, however, that the predictions they make in the chapter are reasonable and many are likely to be born out in practical studies, and they suggest several approaches that researchers interested in information behavior could take to advance our understanding of this phenomenon.

Leanne Bowler and Valerie Nesset have constructed their chapter "Information Literacy" around two studies that they conducted, one with young elementary school children and the other with pre-university college students. Their objective is to explore the level of information literacy among today's young people. After discussing the concept of information literacy and models of information behavior that relate to information literacy, Nesset reports on her research into the information behavior of students in grade three (between the ages of eight and nine) when undertaking a project set by their teacher. From her study she has derived her own model of information behavior that she calls the Preparing, Searching, and Using (PSU) Model. Bowler worked with older students, her focus on the role of metacognition— the undercurrent of thinking about one's own thinking, as she defines this term—which she argues is essential to information literacy. She looked at the information search processes of 10 adolescents between the ages of 16 and 18 as they searched for, evaluated, and used information to complete a research paper.

The previous chapter focused upon information behavior in a formal learning environment: the school or college. June Abbas and Denise Agosto, in their chapter titled "Everyday Life Information Behavior of Young People," shift our attention to the information behavior of young people in less formal settings as they surf for information of various kinds. Building upon their own research, as well as that of others, they try to construct a picture of how today's youth seeks, shares, and creates information in the digital environment. They argue that young people today grapple with the developmental issues that have been encountered by all youth as they grow to be adults but that they do so now in the context of a modern, technologically dependent society. They encounter the same issues that young people have always dealt with, but they now have more sources and channels in which to find information to help with their everyday life needs.

In "Digital Age Libraries and Youth: Learning Labs, Literacy Leaders, Radical Resources," Eliza Dresang asks how libraries have adapted to the information behavior of young people in our "digitally saturated environment." She argues that adults have become more aware of young people's capabilities and their ability to participate in planning facilities, programs, and services. She points to flagship initiatives that are highlighting the role that libraries can play as learning labs, and the place that libraries can occupy as leaders in literacy. Above all, she emphasizes the importance of relationships between adults and youth in determining success.

Denise Agosto and June Abbas turn to "Youth and Online Social Networking" in their chapter. They emphasize the significance of such networks for the young and the varied means for which they are used. They review a wide range of studies from different disciplines and domains that paint a multifaceted picture of why and how young people use online social networks. They conclude that young people are increasingly able to successfully combine their online and offline lives, but that face-to-face communication remains the most popular form of discourse among youth peer groups. They also emphasize that while online communication is significant and expanding, the extent of its use by young people does vary, and no simple model will fit everyone. They also argue that it is important to study youth separately from adults as there appear to be differences in the ways these two groups use online social networking.

Giovanni Vincenti's chapter focuses on "Gaming and Virtual Environments." He discusses the risks to which young people can be exposed when using computers, before turning specifically to game-based learning. Educators have the choice between creating custom-made products or opting for off-the-shelf software, each with their pros and cons. Examples of "serious games" are presented, and the role of multi-user virtual environments is explored. Vincenti ends with a consideration of applications and designs for small- as well as large-screen displays.

In her chapter on the "Enhanced Quality of Life for Young Adults with Intellectual Disabilities," Dana Hanson-Baldauf looks at a population that she argues has been underserved by the library and information community and neglected by the research community. She believes that although young people with intellectual disabilities face an unwelcome and uncertain future, they can be empowered by meaningful information skills and resources. As students they experience segregation and bullying, often dropping out of school. She argues for more research, service, and outreach to empower these young people, especially at an early age.

The theme of bullying is again taken up in the next chapter by Shaheen Shariff, "Defining the Line on Cyber Bullying." Cyber bullying and cyber lurking are two negative aspects of the digital environment. Shaheen highlights the dangers, as well as clarifying the legal risks, that young people take as they seek, view, create, and distribute digital information. She does this through several case studies drawn from Canada and the United States, as well as a number of research studies. She says young people need to be engaged in developing boundaries to guide online policy and practice in collaborative ways, and they need to think about their online activities in order to recognize the point at which fun and entertainment transmute into harm at another's expense.

Jamshid Beheshti and Andrew Large then look at "Systems." The information and communication technologies (ICT) environment is evolving rapidly and young people are now major players in all its aspects. The chapter discusses children and youth as information technology users across a wide variety of platforms, the problems they encounter, and the solutions that are being pursued. In this discussion the role of children in the design process itself is illustrated with examples from a variety of research projects and the technologies that have emerged from them. Virtual environments are seen as a productive way of engendering user engagement and facilitating usability, and again, examples are used to reinforce the argument. The chapter ends with a brief résumé of studies that are exploring new directions that children may be traversing before too long.

The concluding chapter, again by Beheshti and Large, summarizes the arguments presented by the earlier chapters and looks toward the future information behaviors of children and teens. It asks whether current models will remain applicable as information technologies continue to evolve; children increasingly become content providers as well as seekers; and digital text, images, and sound are ubiquitous.

As editors we owe a debt of thanks to all the authors who have been so obliging in all respects, and especially the most important one: timelines! We are also grateful to our publisher, Scarecrow Press, for the freedom afforded us in assembling this book. We have collaborated for 20 years in research broadly related to children's information behavior, and have written many articles, chapters, and conference papers on different aspects of this field. For several years we toyed with the idea of writing a book about our thoughts and findings without taking action. The diversification of the topic finally convinced us that rather than attempting a book ourselves, we should instead seek help from some of our many colleagues, and this is the outcome. We hope that *Information Behavior of a New Generation: Children and Teens in the 21st Century* makes its own contribution to this fascinating topic in which we have invested so much of our lives.

Chapter One

Concepts, Propositions, Models, and Theories in Information Behavior Research

Charles Cole

This chapter is about concepts, propositions, models, and theories in information behavior research. Information behavior is the modern (post-2000) label for information seeking, needs, and uses (Case 2007). According to Wilson's nested circle model (the reader is referred to Wilson 1999, 263, Figure 11), information behavior is all purposive and non-purposive information-related behavior. Inside the large information behavior circle, information seeking is purposive behavior only, while the smallest nested circle is information search, which describes the specific behavior that occurs during the user's interaction with an information system. We argue in this chapter that information behavior research's contribution to the design of effective information systems is to incorporate information behavior's more holistic notion of concepts, proposition, models, and theory into the interaction between information systems and humans—including children—during information search.

Concepts, propositions, models, and theories are human constructs whose purpose is to extend private thinking into the public realm so that collaborative progress in research can occur. In effect, they are constructs that enable humans to harness brain power in discerning, analyzing, and understanding natural and human phenomena. In the more practical realm, concepts, models, and theories are research communication tools providing formulaic vehicles for researchers to understand what others have previously done in the field, and, in turn, to effectively communicate to others the patterns they themselves find in their research data.

1

It is the theme of this chapter that conceptualizing, creating proposition statements, modeling, and theorizing about natural and human phenomena is hardwired, allowing us to interact with and understand our natural and social environment and our place in that environment. In a more specific sense, we hold that it is instinctive of humans to categorize incoming sense data, to seek patterns in it, which allows humans to make sense of and give meaning to the world in which we exist.

We begin this chapter by presenting brief definitions of a concept, a proposition, a model, and a theory. In the second part, we describe the paradigm shift in information behavior research. We describe the old paradigm design model, the new paradigm, and then the new paradigmatic core. In the third part, the chapter gives specific information behavior examples of concepts, propositions, models, and theories, highlighting Dervin's theory of sense-making and Kuhlthau's Information Search Process (ISP) Model for students researching a course assignment. The chapter concludes by suggesting paths to follow for concepts, models, and theories for children's information behavior.

DEFINITIONS

We make the claim in this chapter that concepts and propositions on the one hand, and models and theories on the other, are micro- and macro-level manifestations, respectively, of human thinking. Models and theories create symbolic systems into which specific instances of thinking—concepts and propositions—can be inserted, thus giving the concepts and propositions wider, predictive, and explanatory power. We will briefly define these notions here, but we develop them further with illustrative examples from information behavior research in subsequent sections of the chapter.

A concept is "a generalized idea or notion" (Oxford Dictionary 1984, 147). An example of a concept is information. It could fit into larger models of information seeking, or a larger theory of sense-making. The problem with information science concepts is that there are no commonly agreed-upon definitions. For example, although a range of definitions for the concept "information" has been identified by Buckland (1991), there is no real agreement, putting the concept in a sort of vague, amorphous conceptualized state somewhere between data and knowledge.

A proposition is a statement made up of at least two concepts with some sort of relation suggested in the statement. For example, for the proposition "Information need is the start state for information seeking," the concepts are information need and information seeking, and there is a suggestion of a cause and effect relation in the statement.

We define here the term "conceptual framework" to distinguish it from a model or theory. A conceptual framework can be created from a variety of sources, including going outside the discipline—in the case of information behavior— to theories and models from psychology, sociology, and so on. A conceptual framework is often the beginning framework for a research study, resulting from a review of the literature. The conceptual framework can be formed from bits and pieces of various studies in the literature review, or it can be based on the selection of a particular model that closely matches the aspirations of the research study. In Cole (M. J. Cole et al. 2011), for example, a reading model served as a conceptual framework or starting point for a larger-scope information acquisition / information retrieval model in complex information environments.

A conceptual framework is a useful starting point for a research study; but it can also be joined with the results or findings from the research study to create, for example, a model or theory. In this way, the state of the research area before the study, which the conceptual framework represents, is made to evolve as the result of the study. By summing up previous research in a conceptual framework and directly tying the study to advancing it (by verifying/confirming, expanding, or falsifying an aspect or aspects of the framework), the researcher's intention is to serve a discipline-level purpose. In the mid-1990s, Chatman criticized information needs and uses research for being "focused on the application of conceptual frameworks rather than on the generation of specific theories" (Chatman 1996, 190). We will return to this issue in subsequent sections.

A model is a descriptive, sometimes predictive, summary of a research area that joins the findings from a research study to the conceptual framework determined via the study's literature review. The study's findings could, for example, modify the established understanding (as determined in the literature review) of the concepts and their relations, which had been previously established in the conceptual framework for the study. The model should take the conceptual framework further. A study can also have as its purpose the evaluation or testing of a model, which would either strengthen or refute the model.

A model is an interim tool or stage in a new or immature research discipline, before a theory can be established, serving as a "working strategy" for hypothesis testing (Jarvelin and Wilson 2003). However, according to Wilson (1999, 251), most of the models in information behavior do "not directly suggest hypotheses to be tested," although Bates (2005, 3) is more sanguine on the efficacy of information behavior models. Both Wilson and Bates agree that models are an essential descriptive, even predictive tool, an essential step to the development of theories.

A theory is, according to Bates (2005, 2), "a system of assumptions, principles, and relationships posited to explain a specified set of phenomena." The difference between a model and a theory is also one of scope or ambition (e.g., Reese and Overton 1970; Lerner 1998). A theory is broader in scope and has predictive/explanatory power, whereas a model is smaller in scope, its ambition being limited to describing or representing a phenomenon. The distinguishing mark of a theory is its explanatory power, that is, it gets at under-the-surface characteristics of the phenomenon. The following sections of the chapter will further develop this theme of description versus explanation in theories and models.

PARADIGM SHIFT

Information science has long been criticized for its lack of theories, models, and commonly agreed-upon definitions for its central concepts (Pettigrew, Fidel, and Bruce 2001); this is true for both information science in general (Jarvelin and Vakkari 1990) and information seeking in particular (Jarvelin and Vakkari 1993). However, a chronological analysis of the utilization of conceptual and theoretical frameworks in information-seeking research shows that modeling and theorizing have progressed from 1984 to 1998 (Julien 1996; Julien and Duggan 2000; see also, McKechnie, Pettigrew, and Joyce 2001; Pettigrew and McKechnie 2001), although Wilson has characterized models in information behavior research as being in a "pre-theoretical stage," which he defined as not "specifying relationships among theoretical propositions" (Wilson 1999, 250).

We make the argument that with the recent push for models and theories in information-behavior research, galvanized by the collection of writings on theories of information behavior in Fisher, Erdelez, and McKechnie (2005), there has been a paradigm shift from description to explanation in information-behavior research, in the Kuhn (1962) sense of the term. We will focus on two reasons for this paradigm shift:

1. the maturation of the research discipline and
2. the perturbations to the traditional methods of providing information service caused by the Internet.

The first reason for the field's recent interest in models and theories indicates that information-behavior research is maturing, becoming more sophisticated as a research field. Strong theories and well-defined, generally agreed-upon concept definitions, conceptual frameworks, models, and theories form a snapshot of a research area or discipline at a given point in time. Subsequent researchers can then refer to the theories and concepts in their work, which will either support these theories and concepts or disprove them. It is believed that only in this way can a research area or discipline progress in a rigorous and scientific manner. Also, the push for theories indicates that the discipline has moved beyond straightforward descriptions of phenomena to the ability to "predict" and "explain" natural and human phenomena (Bates 2005; Neuman 2006). In Figure 1.1, the research continuum is illustrated, starting from Descriptive research on the left-hand side of the figure to Explanatory research on the right hand side (see Neuman 2006).

A second reason for the paradigm shift in information behavior research is the Internet, which has not only revolutionized how people seek, find, and use information, but also expanded the utilization of information to a wider portion of the population, including children and disadvantaged groups in society. The last section of this chapter will discuss the Internet and the implications it has for information behavior research becoming useful for children's information behavior while utilizing in-classroom and mobile device Internet connections.

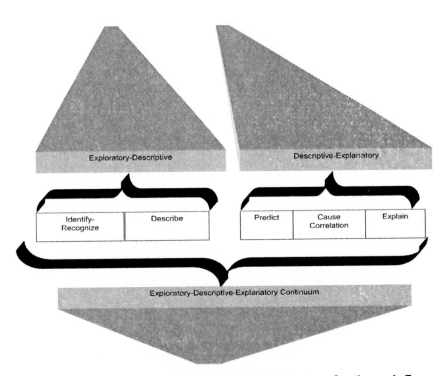

Figure 1.1. Exploratory-Descriptive-Prediction-Explanatory Continuum in Research

OLD PARADIGM

In this section, we conceptualize our view of the parameters of the new paradigm in information behavior research by first describing the old paradigm. It is important to identify the declared objectives of the old paradigm and then compare them to the objectives of the new paradigm. It is our thesis that the objectives have changed due to the advent of the Internet and the aforementioned maturation of the discipline toward explanatory versus descriptive research.

Information behavior comes out of the information seeking, needs, and uses research tradition formalized in the 1960s by annual chapters in ARIST (starting with Menzel 1966). Information seeking research was concerned with description, primarily relying on quantifying information use and information need by associating these phenomena with the utilization of sources of information access (i.e., catalogue usage, index and abstract usage, number of reference questions, etc.). Part of this can be explained by the practitioner-orientation of pre-2000 information behavior research (Julien, Pecoskie, and Reid 2011). We summarize these traditional, library-oriented concerns as empirical studies of a user group's frequency of use or preference for, or satisfaction with, "channels" (sources) of information, in a needs assessment study (Kunz, Rittel, and Schwuchow 1977, 10–11; see also Case 2007, 149).

It is important to underline that, because of its emphasis on "use" of accessing channels or tools to potential sources of information, the old paradigm's objectives are interested in entirely different concepts of "information" (as "thing"), "information need" (i.e., as in the user's query), and "information seeking" (frequency of using an accessing tool) than the new paradigm; in effect, these old paradigm concepts seem one step removed from the actual user; it is almost as if they were interested in an idealized model of the user rather than the real thing (i.e., the real human). Ellis (1993) called this an "information man" conception of the real user.

In the design of information systems, the old paradigm model is represented by Figure 1.2. The central concept of the old paradigm is that information "use" refers to the user's use of sources or channels of information access. In turn, the traditional model utilized in the development of information retrieval systems is articulated by Shannon's (1949) communication system diagram, called the "look-up" model (White and Roth 2009), which we define as a user's command input to an information system to start it or make it work, with the system output being a factual-type response (Oddy 1977; Taylor 1968; Jansen and Rieh 2010).

Information system design is premised on the Shannon model illustrated in the upper half of Figure 1.2. The user (A) sends a message to the information system at the receiver (B) end of the channel. The sender's message is

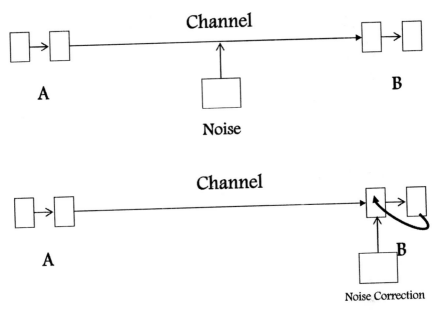

Figure 1.2.   Upper half of the figure: Shannon's communication model, from sender of message (A) to receiver of message (B). Lower half of the figure: the old paradigm classic information retrieval model

the system user's information need. In order to send it over the channel, the user must transform the information need into a query to the system (the small box at the A end of the channel in Figure 1.2), which is a command form of the need (see Taylor 1968). The Shannon model, it is important to point out, is primarily interested in the signal (not the message itself), and especially the signal degradation during transmission due to noise. The Shannon model is transposed, in the bottom half of Figure 1.2, into what Bates (1989) calls the classic information retrieval model. It is assumed in this "looking up" information view of information search, and this "information man" view of the user, that the user's information need at the sender end (A in the figure) is adequately represented by the user's query (in the sender transducer box in the figure); but there is a technical problem requiring "noise correction" in the receiver transducer box where the user's query is matched with the information system's index representation of the information documents/Web pages/sites in the receiver database.

On the receiver end of the channel, there are many ways to look at the system or receiver transducer box. In the case of Google, the keywords in the user's query are transmitted to the system index in the receiver transducer box, which is the system's representation of the information in the database, so the transducer matches the user's query terms with terms in the predetermined index of the database effectuated by Google's crawler. In the lower half of Figure 1.2, on the far right-hand side, the curved arrow starting from the destination box and going to the receiver's transducer indicates the index representation of the information documents or Web pages/sites in the database, where the user's query signal is matched with the appropriate index terms. When the index terms are activated by the user's query signal, the Internet addresses attached to each term in the index are retrieved and assembled by the system in the results list.

If the results list is topically relevant to the user (Harter 1986), from the system's point of view, the interaction was deemed a success in the 1990s by "system-oriented" evaluation studies such as a Text REtrieval Conference, or TREC (Ingwersen and Jarvelin 2005, 177). Topical relevance is not the same as information "use," however. Topical relevance indicates only potential "use" of the found information. The essential assumption of this traditional model is that the user's query to the system, made up of keywords meant to represent this individual's information need, effectively represents the individual's information need. In fact, there are many reasons why a citation in the results list that the system deems a "successful" match to the user's information need because it is topically relevant to the user's query may not be the information the user actually needs.

NEW PARADIGM

With the advent of the Internet, the information behavior research's holistic perspective, and its concentration on the real user instead of a once removed "information man," are now being brought to bear on information system design to improve information search performance. The new paradigm in information behavior research brings the user's information need, seeking, and finding into much closer alignment with the user's actual use of the information instead of his or her use of information sources or channels.

The new paradigm conceptualization of information use is, according to Wilson (2000), the physical and mental acts humans employ to incorporate found information into their knowledge base or knowledge structure. As noted in Spink and Cole (2006, 28).

> This semantic clarification—one of the aims of creating an integrated model of human information behavior—produces the effect of being able to distinguish potential use (as in: I looked at that source but didn't find anything) from real use, which we define here in the cognitive sense of use as causing cognitive transformation. (See also Todd 1999.)

We note that the paradigm shift to the new definition of information use, in the Kuhn (1962) sense of the term, did not occur all at once, but initially started as an "anomalous" disruptive seed in the old paradigm. There were several strains in this seed. For one, information science's concept of "information" shifted from being conceptualized as a "thing" that filled a "bucket" (the user's information need) (Dervin and Nilan 1986) to a "process" that in Brookes's "fundamental equation of information science" was defined as "that which modifies a user's knowledge structure" ($K[S] + \Delta I = K[S + \Delta S]$) (Brookes 1980, 131). However, we will concentrate here on the central thrust of the paradigm shift, which has been termed the new "paradigmatic core" in information-seeking research (Pettigrew, Fidel, and Bruce 2001).

The essence of the new paradigmatic core in information-behavior research is the concern for the perceptual-cognitive and sociological processes underlying why and how individuals need, seek, find, and use information. Kuhlthau (1993) exemplifies this change. "Kuhlthau was attempting to capture the whole experience of the information seeker" (Pettigrew, Fidel, and Bruce 2001, 5). The label change from the old paradigm's information seeking, needs, and uses to the new paradigm's information behavior reflects this broader, new paradigm objective. According to Fisher, Erdelez, and McKechnie (2005), Wilson (1999, 249) encapsulated the label change, defining information behavior as "the totality of human behavior in relation to sources and channels of information, including both active and passive information seeking, and information use." In 2002, Case (2002, 2007) wrote an influential textbook that expounded the broadening of information seeking, needs, and uses research to include the wider notion of information behavior.

Pettigrew, Fidel, and Bruce (2001) review the shift from old paradigm to new, dividing the new paradigmatic core into cognitive, sociological, and multifaceted approaches. The cognitive approach emphasizes the user's "self" controlling and directing information behavior—that is, the user's cognitive behavior during information and memory processes. The sociological approach, on the other hand, focuses on the "individual's social, professional, or information seeking setting" (Pettigrew, Fidel, and Bruce 2001, 54). We will refer to the third stream in new paradigm information research, the multifaceted approach, at the end of this section.

The cognitive approach posits humans processing a phenomenon in their physical and social environment, mediated by knowledge structures; these are packets of knowledge based on the person's past experience with the phenomenon, stored in the individual's memory, also referred to as the individual's prior knowledge or tacit knowledge (Vakkari 1999). Knowledge structures both process information from the environment and store it in memory for subsequent use by the individual, but most importantly they guide the person's subsequent information behavior. Early key researchers in the development of the cognitive approach are Belkin (1990), Brookes (1980), Dervin and Nilan (1986), Ingwersen (1996), and Taylor (1968).

The sociological approach to information behavior emphasizes the user's situation or social context for information seeking. When we think of an information-based task, many elements of needing, seeking, and finding information for a task are imposed on the user by the task. This is because most if not all tasks are initiated and evaluated by someone else, so the information need of the individual is partly formulaic or organizationally driven, for example, a school essay. All information-based tasks, even the creation of works of art, have imposed information elements, to a greater or lesser extent, which are dictated by the user's "life world" (Wilson 1981).

Chatman's (1996, 1999) studies of the information situation of outsider groups such as janitors and women prisoners constitute a prototypical sociological approach to information behavior research. The individual's life within a group dictates his or her information need, seeking, finding, and use rather than the self-derived information need, taking precedence over the unfulfilled or kept-hidden (secret) need. Thus her theory of information poverty as a determinant of information behavior has explanatory power, which we will analyze at greater length in a subsequent section (see "Propositions").

A primary difference in the new cognitive and sociological approaches to information behavior research is how much information need is positioned as a mostly internally derived phenomenon that is created by mediating structures that are recalled from memory storage by the user to interact with information in the user's physical or social environment. The sociological approach concentrates on information behavior barriers that are both socially and psychologically created, but it emphasizes the sociologically imposed nature of information need and the sociological barriers that prohibit the user from exercising his or her real information need. This is a valid observation about information need indicating that information behavior research should obey both psychological and sociological constraints—that is, the information user must be conceptualized as operating in the real world.

The multifaceted approach in information behavior research assumes there is greater complexity than can be explained by either the cognitive or sociological approaches alone. Pettigrew, Fidel, and Bruce (2001) give as an example Dervin's (1999) Sense-Making theory, which we describe below. The nexus between cognitive and sociological approaches to information behavior research has a long tradition in information science research, which Cool (2001) distills down to the concept of the user's situation while seeking information. "On a theoretical level," she states, "the concept of situation has a potential for bringing together both individual cognitive-level and social level analyses of human information behavior" (Cool 2001, 31).

The concept of an information seeker/user's "situation" at the time of seeking information is a uniquely information science perspective on information behavior with deep historical roots. It is also referred to as "problematic situation" (Wersig and Windel 1985; see also Belkin and Vickery 1985), which is defined as users recognizing there are gaps in their mental model of "her or his environment, knowledge, situation and goals" that require information behavior in order to achieve these goals (Belkin and Vickery 1985, 14). While the concept of the user's "situation," or "problematic situation" has a sociological starting point—that is, the person's situation or problem in a social or physical environment—the concept's center is the person's psychological mechanisms for dealing with the problematic situation. This slight shift or nuance is vital: it is the user's interpretation of the problem, situation, or problematic situation rather than the actual problematic situation itself that information behavior research is interested in.

In the next four sections, we illustrate specific concepts, propositions, models, and theories in new paradigm information behavior research, highlighting specific information behavior research from both the cognitive and sociological approaches. We end with the multifaceted approach of Dervin's Sense-Making theory.

CONCEPTS

An extreme cognitive approach to concept formation underlies the Associative Index Model (AIM) for Information Search on the Internet of Cole, Julien, and Leide (2010). AIM posits the notion that information retrieval systems can facilitate concept formation in the user during information search. AIM forms only part of a larger theory of information need during information search, which includes a strong sociological input component (Cole 2011, 2012).

AIM's central premise is that concept formation is a natural human activity that transforms sensory input from the human physical and human environment into the language of thinking. A concept is an abstract notion of human experience, the end point of a process during which we apply human powers of observation to analyze and generalize about patterns we discern in the natural and social phenomena that surround us.

In Figure 1.3, we summarize human processing of sensory input perceived in our social or natural environment (for a complete description, see Cole 2012). According to Harnad's (1987a, b) categorical perception theory, our sensory system discerns environmental input and decodes it by categorizing the input. It is then labeled as a concept by the human cognitive system and inserted into the conceptual or symbolic system of that individual, thus giving context or meaning to the initiating sensory input. Full conceptualization of the initiating environmental stimulus, according to Harnad (1987a), takes place only when the concept is successfully inserted into the person's symbolic system.

In Figure 1.3, dotted arrows from the encoded conceptual/symbolic system indicate a heavy involvement of the human cognitive system in the perceptual decoding of social and natural environmental input. That is, the individual's past experience with the specific environmental input being processed is recalled from memory to participate in the decoding.

The human symbolic system is the "language" of thinking, which Bialystok and Olson (1987) conjecture is in propositional code. Thus the objective of concept formation is to create "symbols for the propositional system to be able to operate on" (Harnad 1987b, 21). The objective of AIM is to enable categorization and conceptualization of the IR system's results list for the domain novice user by (a) facilitating the formation of the user's symbolic system for the task at hand, then (b) actualizing the user's symbolic system for IR system manipulation (i.e., to treat it as the user's query to the system).

PROPOSITIONS

In contrast to the cognitive approach of concepts illustrated in the previous section, we highlight Chatman's (1996, 1999) extreme sociological approach to information behavior to illustrate propositions. The sociological perspective in information behavior looks at all the types of human activity that require information and asks, What is the sociological context in which these

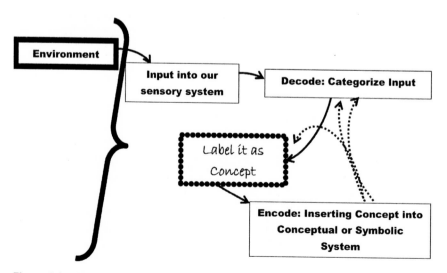

Figure 1.3.   Human perceptual-cognitive processing system

information needs, seeking, and use arise? These researchers study a human activity in depth but start from the social environment from which the problem, task, or other such societal-controlled information behavior arises.

As is the case with many information scientists, Chatman was struck by how many groups within our information society utilize little or no information in their work and everyday lives—the so-called information poor. One way of looking at information poverty is that society puts up barriers to their information access and use (e.g., Harris and Dewdney 1994), but Chatman studied how groups within society erect their own barriers to information finding and use, creating their own small world that is cut off from the information flows of the larger society. For example, Chatman (1996) described the "small world" of janitors where a janitor deliberately kept out information from outsiders, even though that information might have been of value to the individual janitor.

Chatman's studies have come to be known as models of rigorous qualitative behavior research, particularly for her advocacy of theory-making. Essential to her theory-making is the careful creation of propositions. Propositions, in turn, are made up of concepts that are linked by some sort of relationship (e.g., cause and effect).

We illustrate Chatman's proposition building by starting with her concepts. Chatman (1996) focuses on the creation of innovative concepts for her theory-making. She started by (a) identifying a problem that could be addressed by information behavior research. In her case, she identified the problem of the impoverished life of members of sub-groups within society and its link to information poverty. She then (b) imported theories from other disciplines to create a starting conceptual framework for the collection and analysis of qualitative data. She (c) actively sought out anomalies in her data, which (d) led to her four concepts.

Chatman's four concepts that define the impoverished life world of the study groups are secrecy, deception, risk taking, and situational relevance. All of these concepts have to do with self-protective behaviors on the part of members of the groups she studied, how they protect themselves against information that is threatening their small world, or in order to maintain something in their small world life that is essential.

Chatman created six propositions from these concepts to construct her Theory of Information Poverty. We will focus on her third proposition only: "Information poverty is determined by self-protective behaviors, which are used in response to social norms" (Chatman 1996, 197). This is a very explicit proposition made up of three concepts: information poverty, self-protective behavior, and social norms. There are two relationships among the three concepts:

- social norms "cause" self-protective behaviors, and

• self-protective behaviors "cause" information poverty.

Propositions, because of their directness, facilitate testing of the proposition, leading to its possible refutation, which then refutes the theory itself (see also Popper 1975). According to Chatman (1996, 198), "The value of propositions to theory construction lies in their ability to be tested, thereby strengthening or weakening the theory."

A proposition can be tested for validity and reliability by designing a subsequent study based on the proposition. Turning the proposition into a research question serves as a starting position in qualitative and/or exploratory research for the collection and analysis of data. In quantitative research, the researcher tests a proposition by turning each of its component concepts into a variable by selecting an "indicator" for each concept (also sometimes called a "construct"). "An indicator is any empirical manifestation of a construct, that is, some overt behavior that can be counted or rated, or perhaps a set of responses to a test or other standardized stimulus" (Smith and Glass 1987, 84). As an example, for the proposition, Computers in the classroom improve students' learning of mathematics, the concept "student learning" can be measured via its indicator, the instructor's mark on the student's mathematics test.

MODELS

We have thus far defined a model as a descriptive framework relating a set of natural or human phenomena. As defined earlier, a model is narrower in scope and ambition than a theory; it has none or very little of the explanatory power a theory has. However, there is some ambiguity in what constitutes a model and what constitutes a theory. For example, here we utilize Kuhlthau's ISP Model as an example of a model, but it is sometimes referred to as an information behavior theory (e.g., Pettigrew, Fidel, and Bruce 2001, 46).

Kuhlthau's Information Search Process (ISP) Model is one of the most cited information-seeking models in information science. Although called a "search process" model, Kuhlthau's model is actually an information-seeking model but was created before Wilson (1999) determined the generally accepted distinction between information seeking (all purposive information-seeking behavior) and information search (user-IR system interaction).

In Figure 1.4, Kuhlthau's ISP Model describes a six-stage model of students performing the task of researching and preparing a school assignment, starting from Stage 1, the Initiation stage when the student receives first notice of the assignment from the instructor, to the presentation of the finished project in Stage 6. The key stages we would like to focus on here are

Stages 3 and Stage 4. In Stage 3, the students in Kuhlthau's studies have selected the assignment topic and now must explore the topic area to find a focus for the assignment, which occurs in Stage 4.

Kuhlthau's model is descriptive of the stages a student goes through from start to finish of performing a task such as a school assignment. It utilizes the Feelings, Thoughts, and Actions of the members of the study group as description attributes. In Cole, Julien, and Leide (2010), we have suggested the ISP Model's predictive power in terms of Information Search Type, by adding a row to the bottom of Figure 1.4. This added row indicates the type of search the person will conduct in terms of each stage. The ISP Model thus predicts the type of information search the user will conduct in each stage. In Stage 3, the exploration stage, the student will conduct browsing searches, or what we call an Unknown Item Search (Cole, Julien, and Leide 2010), while in Stage 5, the post-focus collection stage, the student will engage in a Known Item Search or a Known Form of Answer Search.

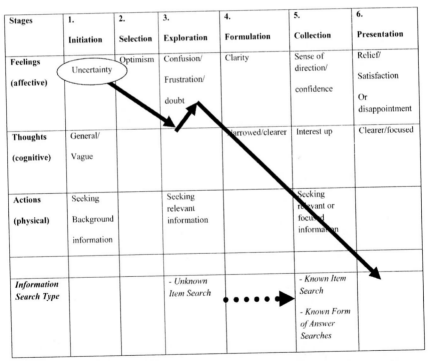

Stages	1. Initiation	2. Selection	3. Exploration	4. Formulation	5. Collection	6. Presentation
Feelings (affective)	Uncertainty	Optimism	Confusion/ Frustration/ doubt	Clarity	Sense of direction/ confidence	Relief/ Satisfaction Or disappointment
Thoughts (cognitive)	General/ Vague			Narrowed/clearer	Interest up	Clearer/focused
Actions (physical)	Seeking Background information		Seeking relevant information		Seeking relevant or focused information	
Information Search Type			- Unknown Item Search		- Known Item Search - Known Form of Answer Searches	

Figure 1.4. Kuhlthau's (1993) six-stage ISP model in upper part of figure (Feelings, Thoughts, and Actions), with the bottom row added by Cole, Julien, and Leide (2010) containing the type of search for Stage 3 (Exploration) and, after the Stage 4 focus formulation (indicated by the dotted arrow), the type of search in Stage 5 (Collection)

Charles Cole

We wish to highlight here the fine line between the descriptive-predictive power of a model and the explanatory power of a theory. What separates a model that can predict information behavior from a theory that explains it?

Kuhlthau's ISP Model describes and predicts that the individual's feelings of "uncertainty" will decrease from Stage 1 to Stage 3 but increase in Stage 3, before steadily declining again for the rest of the stages (Kuhlthau, Heinstrom, and Todd 2008). In Stage 3, the ISP Model describes the individual exploring the selected topic via seeking information. Does this explain why the feelings of uncertainty increase in Stage 3? It almost does but, we would argue, not quite. It is still only describing and predicting information behavior. But The ISP Model, like all good models, comes right to the edge between prediction and explanation. (In Cole [2012], we "explain" the Kuhlthau ISP Model's described-predicted rise in uncertainty in Stage 3 by indicating the individual is undergoing a continuous series of information processes that establish, in fits and starts, the individual's guiding information need. It is this starting of information processes that causes the Stage 3 rise in both cognitive and affective uncertainty.)

THEORIES

Theory-making is a way of observing, categorizing, and conceptualizing the world we live in, which has epistemological and ontological implications we have not discussed in this chapter. In library information systems, epistemological and ontological starting positions for theory-making are discussed at a higher level of abstraction—as theoretical approaches, approaches to theory-making, or metatheories (see Bates 2005). Five such abstractions are as follows:

- bibliometrics
- socio-cognitivism
- evolutionary (psychology)
- critical theory
- constructionism

Pettigrew and McKechnie (2001) list a wide range of definitions of theory (see also, Bates 2005). Summarizing them, and based on the previous section in this chapter, we define a theory as a body of propositions describing, predicting, and explaining relationships between an observed, categorized, and conceptualized set of natural and social phenomena. There are wide-ranging theories like Marxism, which may be described as a type of grand theory (Glaser and Strauss, 1967). However, following Chatman (1996, 190), information behavior research is almost exclusively concerned with more narrowly focused theories. These are called substantive theories (theories based on empirical findings from studies of one substantive area or practice) or formal theories (several substantive theories combined into a more generalized theory); both are sometimes referred to as "middle range" theories (Glaser and Strauss 1967, 32–24; see also Boudon 1991).

With the proviso of the previously discussed ambiguities in the definition of theory, particularly what separates a model from a theory, we give Pettigrew and McKechnie's (2001, 69) listing of the 11 most highly cited theories in information behavior research:

- Bates's Berry Picking
- Belkin and colleagues' ASK
- Dervin's Sense-Making
- Ellis's Information Seeking
- Harter's Psychological Relevance
- Ingwersen's Cognitive IR Theory
- Kuhlthau's Information Search Process Model
- Salton's Vector Space Model
- Schamber and colleagues' Theory of Relevance
- Taylor's Information Needs and Negotiation
- Wilson's Situation Relevance

According to Pettigrew and McKechnie (2001), in the new paradigm, the two most cited theories in information seeking are Kuhlthau's ISP Model and Dervin's Sense-Making approach. We have presented Kuhlthau's ISP Model in the previous section. Here, as an example of a theory in information behavior research, we summarize Dervin's Sense-Making theory.

Dervin's Sense-Making theory is a broad perspective, all-encompassing theory that looks at human information behavior at both an information behavior and existential level. Humans seek information because the world has persistent gaps—the "assumption of discontinuity," as Dervin calls it (Dervin 2003b, 270), which is our "continuing human dilemma" (Dervin 2003a, 332). We bridge the gaps by seeking and finding information to re-establish our sense of the world and our place in the world. Fortunately or unfortunately, there is an "absence of complete instruction from the environment" (Dervin, Jacobson, and Nilan 1982, 429). As a result, we are never able to be "completely instructed" (Dervin 2003a, 329), leading us to constantly construct, deconstruct, and reconstruct our sense of the world and our place in it via information behaviors. According to Dervin, "SMM [Sense-Making Methodology] positions ordinary human beings as theorists, able to identify both the nouns of their worlds and the linkages between—the verbs" (Dervin 2008, 11).

This constant theorizing is "a mandate of the human condition" (Dervin 1999, 733). The upside of this constant mandate is that from the point of view of our species, and our ability to discern and adapt to changes in our physical and social environment, "it offers enormous survival value" (Dervin 2003a, 325).

Dervin's Sense-Making theory has enormous explanatory power for human information behavior and the design of information systems. It explains, for example, our need to multitask while conducting an information search. It explains Bates's (1989) Berry-Picking model of information search, which posits humans picking up information bit by bit during an information search session, with in-between bouts of thinking, contemplation, and note-taking, frequently on a subconscious or visceral level.

CHILDREN: CONCEPTS, PROPOSITIONS, MODELS, AND THEORIES

A major part of the new paradigm in information behavior research is the Internet and the new opportunities it affords Internet-based information system designers to facilitate information seeking not only for the traditional users of information and information systems in their work and everyday life, but also new groups of people such as school children. The Internet has made multiple sources of information available to school children, taking the place of the single textbook and memorization-based learning exercises in school. School children now seek, find, and select information from among multiple potential sources made available to them via the Internet. Multiple information sources require sophisticated information behavior and skills in terms of selecting and evaluating the authority and appropriateness of these information sources for the child's task at hand. This sophisticated skill set was formerly taught only to university students. Now, with the Internet and multiple sources of information, information utilization skills such as critical thinking, the formulation of propositions and thesis statements, and so on, have been pushed down at least to high school and middle school students.

How do high school and middle school students utilize information? How is this different from university students and adults performing school and work tasks? School students need help in utilizing information effectively. As a result, information science has become concerned with developing new concepts, propositions, models, and theories of information behavior so that they can be applied to information system design for school-aged information users.

Do students in middle school and high school categorize and conceptualize natural and social phenomena in their environment differently than adults? Can they create relations between concepts to form propositional statements, thus forming the basis of theory-making? It is possible that children make theories about the world, and can shift their constant theory-making in their everyday lives, in the Dervin sense of the term, to information search utilizing an information system such as the Internet for a school task, but it is possible their brains do not yet function at this highly symbolic level. However, an information system could create metaphors of theory-making that children conduct in their everyday life, in order to function in it, so that they can perform the symbolic theorizing necessary to be a critical thinker in the subjects they learn in school. However, this proposition remains to be tested.

REFERENCES

Bates, Marcia J. 1989. "The Design of Browsing and Berrypicking Techniques for the Online Search Interface." *Online Review* 13 (5): 407–424.

Bates, Marcia J. 2005. "An Introduction to Metatheories, Theories, and Models." In *Theories of Information Behavior*, edited by Karen E. Fisher, Sanda Erdelez, and Lynne E. F. McKechnie, 1–25. Medford, NJ: Information Today, Inc.

Belkin, Nicholas J. 1990. "The Cognitive Viewpoint in Information Science." *Journal of Information Science* 16 (1): 11–15.

Belkin, Nicholas J., and Aline Vickery. 1985. *Interaction in Information Systems: A Review of Research from Document Retrieval to Knowledge-based Systems.* Boston Spa, UK: British Library.

Bialystok, Ellen, and David R. Olson. 1987. "Spatial Categories: The Perception and Conceptualization of Spatial Relations." In *Categorical Perception: The Groundwork of Cognition*, edited by Steven Harnad, 511–531. Cambridge, UK: Cambridge University Press.

Boudon, Raymond. 1991. "Review: What Middle-Range Theories Are." *Contemporary Sociology* 20 (4): 519–522.

Brookes, Bertram C. 1980. "The Foundations of Information Science. Part I. Philosophical Aspects." *Journal of Information Science* 2: 125–133.

Buckland, Michael K. 1991. "Information as Thing." *Journal of the American Society for Information Science* 42 (5): 351–360.

Case, Donald O. 2002. *Looking for Information: A Survey of Research on Information Seeking, Needs, and Behavior.* Amsterdam: Academic Press.

Case, Donald O. 2007. *Looking for Information : A Survey of Research on Information Seeking, Needs, and Behavior.* London, UK: Academic Press.

Chatman, Elfreda A. 1996. "The Impoverished Life-World of Outsiders." *Journal of the American Society for Information Science* 47 (3): 193–206.

Chatman, Elfreda A. 1999. "A Theory of Life in the Round." *Journal of the American Society for Information Science* 50 (3): 207–217.

Cole, Charles. 2011. "A Theory of Information Need for IR that Connects Information to Knowledge." *Journal of the American Society for Information Science and Technology* 62 (7): 1216–1231.

Cole, Charles. 2012. *Information Need: A Theory Connecting Information Search to Knowledge Formation.* Medford, NJ: Information Today Inc.

Cole, Charles, Charles-Antoine Julien, and John E. Leide. 2010. "An Associative Index Model for Hypertext Internet Search Based on Vannevar Bush's Memex Machine: An Exploratory Case Study." *Information Research* 15 (3): paper 435. Retrieved on August 8, 2011, from http://InformationR.net/ir/15-1/paper435.html.

Cole, Michael J., Jacek Gwizdka, Chang Liu, Ralf Bierig, Nicholas J. Belkin, and Xiangmin Zhang. 2011. "Task and User Effects on Reading Patterns in Information Search." *Interacting with Computers* 23: 346–362.

Cool, Colleen. 2001. "The Concept of Situation in Information Science. *Annual Review of Information Science and Technology* 35: 5–42.

Dervin, Brenda. 1999. "On Studying Information Seeking Methodologically: The Implications of Connecting Metatheory to Method." *Information Processing and Management* 35 (6): 727–750.

Dervin, Brenda. 2003a. "Chaos, Order, and Sense-Making: A Proposed Theory for Information Design." In *Sense-Making Methodology Reader: Selected Writings of Brenda Dervin*, edited by Brenda Dervin, Lois Foreman-Wernet, and Eric Lauterbach, 325–340. Cresskill, NJ: Hampton Press Inc.

Dervin, Brenda. 2003b. "From the Mind's Eye of the User: The Sense-Making Qualitative-Quantitative Methodology." In *Sense-Making Methodology Reader: Selected Writings of Brenda Dervin*, edited by Brenda Dervin, Lois Foreman-Wernet, and Eric Lauterbach, 269–292. Cresskill, NJ: Hampton Press Inc.

Dervin, Brenda. 2008. "Interviewing as Dialectical Practice: Sense-Making Methodology as Exemplar." *International Association for Media and Communication Research (IAMCR), IAMCR 2008, Annual Meeting, July 20–25, 2008, Stockholm, Sweden*, 1–34.

Dervin, Brenda, Thomas L. Jacobson, and Michael S. Nilan. 1982. "Measuring Aspects of Information Seeking: A Test of Quantitative/Qualitative Methodology." *Communication Yearbook* 6: 419–444.

Dervin, Brenda, and Michael Nilan. 1986. "Information Needs and Uses." *Annual Review of Information Science and Technology* 21: 3–33.

Ellis, David O. 1993. "Modeling the Information Seeking Patterns of Academic Researchers: A Grounded Theory Approach." *Library Quarterly* 63 (4): 469–486.

Fisher, Karen E., Sanda Erdelez, and Lynne E. F. McKechnie (Eds.). 2005. *Theories of Information Behavior*. Medford, NJ: Information Today, Inc.

Glaser, Barney G., and Anselm L. Strauss. 1967. *The Discovery of Grounded Theory: Strategies for Qualitative Research*. Chicago, IL: Aldine Publishing Company.

Harnad, Steven. 1987a. "Category Induction and Representation." In *Categorical Perception: The Groundwork of Cognition*, edited by Steven Harnad, 535–565. Cambridge, UK: Cambridge University Press.

Harnad, Steven. 1987b. "Psychophysical and Cognitive Aspects of Categorical Perception: A Critical Overview." In *Categorical Perception: The Groundwork of Cognition*, edited by Steven Harnad, 1–25. Cambridge, UK: Cambridge University Press.

Harris, Roma, and Patricia Dewdney. 1994. *Barriers to Information: How Formal Help Systems Fail Battered Women*. Westport, CO: Greenwood Press.

Harter, Stephen P. 1986. *Online Information Retrieval: Concepts, Principles, and Techniques*. San Diego, CA: Academic Press Inc.

Ingwersen, Peter. 1996. "Cognitive Perspective of Information Retrieval Interaction: Elements of a Cognitive IR Theory." *Journal of Documentation* 52 (11): 3–50.

Ingwersen, Peter, and Kalervo Jarvelin, 2005. *The Turn: Integration of Information Seeking and Information Retrieval in Context*. Dordrecht, Netherlands: Springer.

Jansen, Bernard J., and Soo Young Rieh. 2010. "The Seventeen Theoretical Constructs of Information Search and Information Retrieval." *Journal of the American Society for Information Science and Technology* 61 (8): 1517–1534.

Jarvelin, Kalervo, and Pertti Vakkari. 1990. "Content Analysis of Research Articles in Library and Information Science." *Library and Information Science Research* 12 (4): 395–421.

Jarvelin, Kalervo, and Pertti Vakkari. 1993. "The Evolution of Library and Information Science 1965–1985. A Content Analysis of Journal Articles." *Information Processing and Management* 29 (1): 129–144.

Jarvelin, Kalervo, and Tom D. Wilson. 2003. "On Conceptual Models for Information Seeking and Retrieval Research." *Information Research* 9 (1): paper 163, accessed August 8, 2011, http://InformationR.net/ir/9-1/paper163.html.

Julien, Heidi. 1996. "A Content Analysis of Recent Information Needs and Uses Literature." *Library and Information Science Research* 18 (1): 53–65.

Julien, Heidi, and Lawrence J. Duggan. 2000. "A Longitudinal Analysis of the Information Needs and Uses Literature." *Library and Information Science Research* 22 (3): 291–309.

Julien, Heidi, Jen L. Pecoskie, and Kathleen Reid. 2011. "Trends in Information Behavior Research: A Content Analysis." *Library and Information Science Research* 33 (1): 19–24.

Kuhlthau, Carole. 1993. *Seeking Meaning: A Process Approach to Library and Information Services.* Norwood, NJ: Ablex Publishing Company.

Kuhlthau, Carole, Jannica Heinstrom, and Ross J. Todd. 2008. "The 'Information Search Process' Revisited: Is the Model Still Useful?" *Information Research* 13 (4). Accessed August 8, 2011, http://informationr.net/ir/13-4/paper355.html.

Kuhn, Thomas S. 1962. *The Structure of Scientific Revolutions.* Chicago, IL: The University of Chicago Press.

Kunz, Werner, Horst W. J. Rittel, and Werner Schwuchow. 1977. *Methods of Analysis and Evaluation of Information Needs: A Critical Review.* Munich: Verlag Dokumentation.

Lerner, Richard M. 1998. "Theories of Human Development: Contemporary Perspectives." In *Handbook of Child Psychology: Theoretical Models of Human Development.* Vol. 1, edited by Richard M. Lerner and William Damon, 1–24. New York: Wiley.

McKechnie, Lynne E. F., Karen E. Pettigrew, and Steven L. Joyce. 2001. "The Origins and Contextual Use of Theory in Human Information Behaviour Research." *The New Review of Information Behaviour Research: Studies of Information Seeking in Context* 2: 47–63.

Menzel, Herbert. 1966. "Information Needs and Uses in Science and Technology." In *Annual Review of Information Science and Technology*, edited by Carlos A. Cuadra, 1: 41–69.

Neuman, W. Lawrence. 2006. *Social Research Methods: Qualitative and Quantitative Approaches*, Sixth Edition. Boston, MA: Allyn and Bacon.

Oddy, Robert N. 1977. "Information Retrieval Through Man-Machine Dialogue." *Journal of Documentation* 33 (1): 1–14.

Oxford Dictionary of Current English. 1984. Oxford: Oxford University Press.

Pettigrew, Karen E., Raya Fidel, and Harry Bruce. 2001. *Annual Review of Information Science and Technology* 35: 43–78.

Pettigrew, Karen E., and Lynne E. F. McKechnie. 2001. "The Use of Theory in Information Science Research." *Journal of the American Society for Information Science and Technology* 52 (1): 62–73.

Popper, Karl. 1975. *Objective Knowledge: An Evolutionary Approach.* Oxford: Clarendon Press.

Reese, Hayne W., and Willis F. Overton. 1970. "Models of Development and Theories of Development." In *Lifespan Development Psychology: Research and Theory*, edited by Larry R. Goulet and Paul B. Baltes, 115–145. New York: Academic Press.

Shannon, Claude E. 1949. "The Mathematical Theory of Communication." In *The Mathematical Theory of Communication*, by Claude E. Shannon and Warren Weaver, 3–91. Urbana, IL: The University of Illinois Press.

Smith, Mary Lee, and Gene V. Glass. 1987. *Research and Evaluation in Education and the Social Sciences.* Englewood Cliffs, NJ: Prentice-Hall.

Spink, Amanda, and Charles Cole. 2006. "Human Information Behavior: Integrating Diverse Approaches and Information Use." *Journal of the American Society for Information Science and Technology* 57 (1): 25–35.

Taylor, Robert S. 1968. "Question-Negotiation and Information Seeking in Libraries." *College and Research Libraries* 29 (3): 178–194.

Todd, Ross J. 1999. "Back to Our Beginnings: Information Utilization, Bertram Brookes and the Fundamental Equation of Information Science." *Information Processing and Management* 35 (6): 851–870.

Vakkari, Pertti. 1999. "Task Complexity, Problem Structure and Information Actions: Integrating Studies on Information Seeking and Retrieval." *Information Processing and Management* 35 (6): 819–837.

Wersig, Gernot and G. Windel. 1985. "Information Science Needs a Theory of 'Information Actions.'" *Social Science Information Studies* 5: 11–23.

White, Robert W., and Resa A. Roth. 2009. *Exploratory Search: Beyond the Query-Response Paradigm. Synthesis Lectures on Information Concepts, Retrieval and Services.* San Rafael, CA: Morgan and Claypool.

22

Charles Cole

Wilson, Tom D. 1981. "On User Studies and Information Needs." *Journal of Documentation* 37 (1): 3–15.

Wilson, Tom D. 1999. "Models in Information Behavior Research." *Journal of Documentation* 55 (3): 249–270.

Wilson, Tom D. 2000. "Human Information Behavior." *Informing Science* 3 (2): 49–55.

Chapter Two

Cognitive Development and Information Behavior

James P. Byrnes and Matthew L. Bernacki

Inasmuch as information behavior (IB) is a pervasive and important aspect of people's lives, it is somewhat surprising that researchers in the field of cognitive development (such as the present authors) have not conducted many studies of IB, nor have they developed specific theories to explain or predict age differences in the tendencies to seek, interpret, or use information. The few studies that have explored possible age differences in IB have been conducted primarily by scholars in the IB field, who tend not to have extensive training in cognitive developmental theory. This unfortunate disjunction between the two fields of cognitive development and IB, combined with the limited number of age comparisons of IB, means that it is not possible to write a traditional developmental review in which one summarizes a large body of studies, explains age changes in terms of theoretical constructs, and proposes a set of guidelines for practitioners that are firmly rooted in a reliable empirical and theoretical base. As a result, a different approach has to be taken. Alternative approaches include (1) appealing to general theories of cognitive development that can be applied to any domain including IB (e.g., Piaget's theory, Vygotsky's theory, and so on), or (2) describing well-established age trends in the *components* of cognition (e.g., knowledge, working memory, etc.) and considering whether age changes in these components would be likely to lead to age changes in IB.

The latter approach is adopted in this chapter for two reasons. The first is that domain-general theories no longer predominate in the field of cognitive development and appealing to them would send the false impression to IB researchers (and other readers of this book) that these theories are widely espoused and utilized by mainstream developmentalists. The second is that these theories are too general to provide adequate guidance to IB researchers regarding what to expect when individuals of various ages are placed in a context conducive to IB. Thus, instead of organizing this cognitive developmental analysis by theory, it is organized by cognitive component and discusses general theories only when they have something to say about particular components. In what follows, we not only describe the nature of each component of cognition, but also consider whether age changes in these components might precipitate age changes in IB.

WHAT IS COGNITION AND HOW DOES IT DEVELOP?

As Bjorklund (2011) notes, the term *cognition* is used to refer to aspects of the mind that play a central role in the acquisition, modification, or manipulation of knowledge in particular contexts. Examples of these aspects of mind include language, memory, concepts, and reasoning. When researchers study the development of cognition, they often focus on age-related quantitative and qualitative improvements in children's language, memory, and so on. In what follows, we describe age changes in aspects of cognition that are likely to lead to age changes in IB. For expository purposes, it is useful to organize the discussion around whether the components reflect structural aspects of cognition or functional aspects.

Age Changes in Structural Aspects of Cognition

In a structural analysis of some physical or mental system, the focus is on the component parts of the system and how the parts are organized and interrelated. In a functional analysis, in contrast, the emphasis is on activities, operations, and processes within the systems that are implemented to achieve certain goals (Byrnes 1992). The structural and functional perspectives within some domains are intrinsically related to each other because the component parts both determine and place constraints on the way the system can carry out tasks or operations. For example, the fact that the human heart has several kinds of chambers arranged in a particular way (a structural analysis) determines how blood can circulate through the body (a functional analysis). In the case of cognition, there are three structural features that subtend, constrain, or direct the performance of mental processes and behaviors: *knowledge, processing capacity,* and *affective orientations.* When people have more knowledge and more processing capacity, they can perform a wider array of mental tasks and carry out these tasks more accurately and efficiently. Affective orientations such as interest and values are primarily involved in determining the choices people make and the level of attention and effort allocated to specific kinds of information and tasks. In what follows, age changes in these three structural aspects are summarized in turn.

Age Changes in Knowledge

A number of studies have revealed that knowledge is not stored in the human mind as a large mass of isolated ideas. Rather, knowledge is organized along specific distinctions, kinds, or categories (Gelman 2009). For example, one basis for organization is content domain (e.g., mathematics, science, history, music, etc.). Most people have varying levels of expertise in different domains and their knowledge in one domain may have little bearing on their knowledge and performance in another domain. The claim that cognition is domain-specific is supported by many traditional studies in the field of psychology, and also by studies conducted by neuroscientists and evolutionary psychologists in the sense that cognitive skills within domains cluster in specific regions of the brain (Byrnes 2011; Barkow et al. 1995).

Within each content domain, moreover, elements of an adult's knowledge can be classified as being one of three types: declarative, procedural, or conceptual (Byrnes 2008). *Declarative knowledge,* or "knowing that," is knowledge of facts in each domain (e.g., that 9 is the answer to 3 x 3 = ?; that Harrisburg is the capital of the state of Pennsylvania in the United States; that hydrogen is the first element of the periodic table; etc.). In contrast, *procedural knowledge,* or "knowing how," is knowledge of actions, procedures, or strategies that can be implemented to achieve a goal or solve a problem (e.g., how to search for information on the web; how to add two fractions; how to fry an egg; how to ride a bike, etc.). Many educators and employers have bemoaned the fact that students often know their facts and procedures in particular domains, but are incapable of higher-level problem solving and creativity because they do not understand what they are doing. The third kind of knowledge, *conceptual knowledge,* helps to counteract the limitations of rote learned facts and procedures. It might be called "knowing why" because it reflects a deeper understanding of why facts are true and why procedures must be carried out in certain ways (e.g., why Harrisburg was selected as the capital, why the least common denominator method must be used to add fractions, and so on). Once again, the distinctions among declarative, procedural, and conceptual knowledge have been supported by both traditional psychological and neuroscientific studies (Byrnes 2011).

In addition to arguing for these distinctions, however, psychologists have created productive lines of research in which they specialize in characterizing and elaborating on the nature of one of these kinds of knowledge. For example, some have found it especially useful to elaborate on a specific kind of procedural knowledge that comes to play in recurring, culturally defined contexts. All cultures have in common the tendency to create participatory structures for events such as birthday parties, religious services, trips to the post office, and so on, in which people in each culture know how to behave and what to expect (Nelson 1986). To illustrate, consider the case of the so-called restaurant script (or, more formally, an *event representation* for restaurants). Most citizens of the United States expect that when they first enter a restaurant, they will be greeted by a hostess who will first ask, "How many?" She will then select the corresponding number of menus and escort them to a table. Soon, a waiter or waitress will appear and ask if they want drinks. Eventually they order a meal, begin to eat, and the waitress returns and asks how the meals are. The event continues with other sub-steps and ends when the couple pays the bill and leaves. Comparable descriptions could be made for a variety of other events such as weddings, university lectures, and so on. The scripts sometimes vary within subcultures of a population and across cultures. In some European countries, for example, there are no hostesses, couples seat themselves, and diners share tables in restaurants.

Besides the distinctions among content domains and types of knowledge, two other features of an adult's knowledge base that influence their behavior and thinking include its associative structure and hierarchical structure. The *associative structure* derives from the fact that items of information or elements of experiences tend to co-occur (Anderson 2009). For example, in the same recurring situations, a person's face often co-occurs with his or her name being said. Or, a teacher may repeatedly ask a class, "What is 3 x 3?" and the class responds as a group "9." When items co-occur, mental representations of these items become associated in a mutually evocative relationship; that is, when one thinks of one element of the associated pair (e.g., the mental representation of a person's face), the other member of the pair comes to mind (e.g., the mental representation of the person's name). The ability of one member of an associated representational pair to evoke the other depends, of course, on the frequency and recency of co-occurrence. Two aspects of experience that always co-occur over many years (e.g., your grandfather and his favorite fishing hat) create a very high likelihood of mutual evocation (see one, think of the other). If two aspects only co-occur for a short time and only for a few repetitions, items of a pair tend not to evoke each other (e.g., the name of someone you only met once). The associative structure of knowledge is true of all domains and all three kinds of knowledge.

The *hierarchical* structure of the knowledge base, in contrast, mainly pertains to conceptual knowledge, and within that, categorical knowledge. All domains have categories that can be subdivided into subcategories, and categories themselves are often subdivisions of their own superordinate categories (Gelman 2009). For example, most people's biological knowledge contains categories such as "dogs," superordinate categories such as "mammals," and subcategories such as "terrier." In music, there are notes, melodies, and musical keys, as well as categories of musical styles such as classical, R&B, rock, and indie (and representative artists within these styles). Moreover, across domains, individual phenomena can be represented and understood as instances of larger principles. For example, even though one homework problem in a physics textbook contains an inclined plane and the other includes a balance with a fulcrum, the solutions to both problems may appeal to the first law of thermodynamics (Chi et al. 1982). Similarly, the mathematical principle of inversion can be instantiated through an analysis of various pairs such as subtraction and addition, or derivative and integral.

So in the ideal case, the following would be true of the knowledge base of a well-educated adult: (a) it is extensive and contains all three kinds of knowledge (declarative, procedural, and conceptual) in many domains (e.g., mathematics, science, history, music, etc.), (b) it has an associative structure that maximizes the chances that related ideas within each domain will reliably evoke each other when needed, and (c) it is characterized by a hierarchical structure in which categories of information are arranged in ways that mirror the arrangements specified in professional disciplines, and organize facts, concepts, and procedures according to general principles in the fields.

In practice, however, the knowledge base of the average, college-educated adult is certainly more extensive than a child's but often barely meets the minimum requirements for being able to say that the average adult is conversant in particular fields (Byrnes 2008). More often than not, adults tend to be conversant in only one or two fields, and tend to have a knowledge profile opposite to that of a "renaissance man." In addition, national and international studies suggest that high school students and adults tend to have more declarative and procedural knowledge than conceptual, so their ability to articulate a deep understanding of fields is limited, as is their ability to show higher level forms of problem solving (Byrnes 2008, 2011). To the extent that facts and procedures are not rehearsed or utilized after the end of coursework in an area (e.g., the end of a semester in which one completes a college-level history course), moreover, there is fairly rapid decay of associations that makes recall of this information difficult in as little as a year later (Anderson 2009). Finally, adults harbor many misconceptions about key ideas in mathematics, science, and history, and tend not to organize information on the basis of principles (see Byrnes 2008 for a comprehensive review).

Nevertheless, many adults acquire a fair amount of *expertise* in one domain (usually their professional domain but also sometimes in an avocation). Studies of the development of expertise reveal the following:

- If an individual engages in three to four hours per day of deliberate practice of skills in some field for 10 years, and has access to more competent mentors who provide feedback on strategies and approaches that the individual does not realize are faulty, he or she often attains the level of expert. Deliberate practice involves intensive concentration, challenging oneself, and concern about improvement (Ericsson 2003);

- Experts learn from their mistakes (they make adjustments based on recognizing errors on their own or with the help of mentors);
- Experts are characterized by their extensive amount of declarative, procedural, and conceptual knowledge in their field that is organized around general principles;
- Through their extensive practice and experience, experts develop the capacity to recognize problems and solutions very rapidly;
- Early in the development of expertise, individuals are so immersed in the performance of activities in a domain that they cannot "see the big picture" or reflect upon their performance in a metacognitive way; after years of experience solving problems, however, they develop the capacity to take a bird's eye view of their performance;
- Experts can be contrasted with "experienced non-experts" who may have similar years of experience in some field, but do not progress as far along the expertise continuum due to factors such as (a) a lack of deliberateness in their practice (less concern about improvement or the need to improve; uncritical monitoring of performance), (b) lack of access to mentors with helpful advice, (c) the tendency to repeat mistakes, or (d) lower levels of aptitude in the field;
- In addition to being distinct from experienced non-experts, experts also differ from novices (beginners) in the following ways: (a) novices have an impoverished knowledge base (far fewer facts, procedures, and concepts; absence of principles), (b) novices are much slower in solving problems and recognizing situations, and (c) novices are not very metacognitive in their approach (Chi et al. 1988).

Children, adolescents, and adults can be said to fall on different points of the expertise continuum for different domains. Children nearly always fall near the novice end for all domains, but adults sometimes fall near the expert end if the first bullet point above is true of them for a specific domain. Otherwise, adults may fall near the middle of the continuum or even lower. Adolescents tend to fall somewhere in between children and adults for various domains. However, a particularly potent example of the importance of experience and practice rather than age per se in the development of expertise are various studies of 10-year-old children who are experts in domains such as chess or dinosaurs and solve problems and remember domain-relevant information substantially better than adults who are relative novices for the same domain (Chi 1978; Chi and Koeske 1983). To get a sense of this phenomenon, perhaps readers of this chapter can identify with stories of adults asking their children for help with their cellular phones.

Likely Effects of Knowledge Change on IB

Assuming that (a) adolescents are farther along the expertise continuum than children for some search domain, and (b) adults are farther along the continuum than adolescents, how might these three age groups be expected to differ in terms of the ways in which they seek information, make sense of information, and use information? The answer would depend, in part, on the nature of the situation. Open-ended, unstructured, and self-generated tasks (e.g., a person decides on his or her own to understand the U.S. Constitution better) would generally produce larger differences than highly constrained tasks provided by others (for example, use an online encyclopedia to determine who were the most liberal of Supreme Court justices in the last 30 years). All age groups would tend to seek information to increase their knowledge rather than confirm something they already know within a self-generated search, so older and younger individuals (or more accurately, more knowledgeable and less knowledgeable individuals) would naturally tend to look for different kinds of information. In addition, studies in the expertise literature reveal that experts are more likely than novices to constrain and provide more definition to an open-ended task, which would thereby make the search more focused and efficient (Voss et al. 1983).

But knowledge of a domain is also closely aligned with the vocabulary and conceptual structure of that domain (e.g., the main categories and hierarchical arrangement). It would be predicted, then, that individuals who are highly knowledgeable about a domain (e.g., adults) would be more likely to know the correct and most effective keywords to use in a search than less knowledgeable individuals (e.g., children), and would find the information they seek more quickly and efficiently. In support of this prediction, Byrnes and Guthrie (1992) found that college students who were more knowledgeable about human anatomical and physiological systems (e.g., the digestive system) found the correct answer to questions in both a traditionally organized text (e.g., in which text on salivary glands, the stomach, and small intestine could be found in the same chapter on the digestive system), and an experimenter-created version that crossed system boundaries (e.g., in which the gall bladder, stomach, and urinary bladder were all grouped in a contrived section called "temporary storage areas"). The experimenter-created version caused particular problems for the low-knowledge students. Azevedo and colleagues (see, e.g., Moos and Azevedo 2008) likewise found that more knowledgeable individuals located the correct answers to open-ended prompt questions more effectively than less knowledgeable individuals when searching for information in a hypermedia environment.

Differential levels of knowledge would also lead to the prediction that more knowledgeable individuals would be more equipped to make sense of any information that they discover in their searches. As the level of difficulty of the material increases, the gap in performance between those with less knowledge and those with more should increase. Classical constructivist theories of cognition (e.g., Piaget, Vygotsky) argue that the level of understanding of 4-year-olds is qualitatively distinct from that of 8-year-olds, which is qualitatively distinct from 13-year-olds, which is qualitatively distinct from adults (Piaget and Inhelder 1969; Vygotsky 1978). Similar predictions would emerge from scholars who espouse expertise theory (Ericsson 2003) and advocates of the frameworks emphasizing the theory-like nature of children's and adults' cognition (so-called theory theory; Carey 2009). The primary difference among these theories is that the advocates of the more contemporary approaches believe that younger children (especially preschoolers) have more intellectual competence than Piaget or Vygotsky believed. Existing knowledge structures allow for an assimilative base for incoming information. The more abstract the content and the more it appeals to general principles, the more likely it would not be comprehended by searchers with less knowledge. So, children and adults may locate the same information, but adults would be more likely to understand it if it is complex and abstract.

It is not immediately clear whether age differences in knowledge would lead to the prediction that older searchers would be more likely to use information once it was retrieved. It would seem the key variable that predicts a higher likelihood of use is whether the searcher considers the information to have met their goals (it is useful for the original purpose). It is possible that information that is poorly comprehended could be misused (e.g., cited in a school paper as backing up an assertion when it does not; ignored entirely when it truly is the right information; etc.).

One final form of knowledge that could affect the manner in which information is sought, interpreted, or used pertains to the searcher's understanding of the information media or resources available. In the case of written materials, individuals who understand that a book has both a table of contents and an index, and how these components function, will utilize them more effectively than individuals who do not appreciate these components. For example, children looking up information on a particular science topic such as erosion may not know that a book has an index with an entry for erosion. They may scan chapter titles in the table of contents or scan through a book from front to back and never find the text on erosion. Similarly, individuals who do not know about Internet search engines (e.g., the elderly), how they work, and how they are helpful may flounder in a similar fashion. The first author knew an elderly gentleman who loved his computer (to read the obituaries!) but did not understand the difference between applications that worked within the confines of his PC (e.g., Microsoft Word) and applications that were on the web (e.g., Google). He never understood when he was on the web and when he was not. Both of these examples and empirical studies demonstrate that the ideal combination is someone who has both the content knowledge of some domain and knowledge of the structure, features, and benefits of the medium or resource (Lawless et al. 2007; Mitchell et al. 2005; Slone 2003). Librarians often have highly refined versions of the latter knowledge but not necessarily the content knowledge of an expert.

Age Changes in Processing Capacity

In addition to knowledge, a second structural aspect of the mind that can facilitate or impede knowledge acquisition and use is the processing capacity of *working memory*. Psychologists divide the human memory system into two components: permanent memory and working memory. Permanent memory is the storehouse of a person's knowledge. It was referred to earlier in this chapter as the knowledge base. Working memory, in contrast, refers to "a limited capacity system responsible for the simultaneous storage and manipulation of information during the performance of cognitive tasks" (Bayliss et al. 2003). Working memory (WM) is a concept that has supplanted the notion of short-term memory (STM) in contemporary Cognitive Psychology. STM highlights the storage function but not the processing function of WM. Baddeley and Logie (1999) suggest that WM is principally involved in tasks such as comprehending and mentally representing the immediate environment, retaining information about immediate past experiences, supporting the acquisition of new knowledge, solving problems, and formulating, relating, and acting on current goals. WM is considered a transient form of memory because information will fade from it within a few seconds if it is not maintained through rehearsal or transferred to permanent memory.

WM is assumed to contain two systems for rehearsing information and keeping it in mind in a temporary fashion. The *phonological loop* is used to maintain verbal information in WM by saying it to oneself over and over. For example, imagine the case in which one person gives another person her phone number but the listener cannot find a pen and paper to write it down. He may keep the number in mind by repeating it over and over. The *visuospatial sketchpad* works the same way for visual information. The existence of these two distinct rehearsal systems was originally confirmed in traditional laboratory experiments conducted by psychologists. Over the past 20 years, however, their existence has been corroborated in research using neuroimaging techniques. In particular, whereas tasks requiring spatial working memory activate regions of the right hemisphere, tasks requiring verbal working memory activate regions of the left hemisphere (see, e.g., Smith et al. 1996).

Psychologists also assume that WM contains both a short-term "buffer" that temporarily holds information and a "processing space" that is utilized when information in working memory is operated on (Halford et al. 1994). To understand this distinction, it is helpful to consider the following analogy. When people are engaged in a home repair project, they usually need some space to do their work (e.g., a corner of their basement, garage, or tool shed). This part of your home is like your memory's "processing space." Note that materials cannot be stored in the processing space of your home, because you would be unable to move about and do your project. Hence, there is also a need for space that temporarily holds materials until they can be worked on (e.g., a room or closet adjacent to the room for working on projects). The latter is like the buffer.

At one time, moreover, psychologists used to think that the phonological loop had a fixed capacity of between five and nine units (e.g., "the magic number 7"; Miller 1956). Thus, if someone has a "span" of, say, seven units and she heard someone call out six letters (one at a time), she could recall all six of them. In contrast, if this person heard someone call out 12 letters in sequence, she would probably fail to remember about five of them. These days, we recognize that it is not the number of items per se that influences what we recall; what matters is how many we can rehearse before the sensory trace for each item fades. For example, since we can say "wit, sum, harm, bag, top" in two seconds, we could recall all five of these words if they were called out. However, we typically cannot say "university, opportunity, expository, participation, auditorium" in two seconds, so we would probably only recall about two or three of these words (Baddeley 1990). Interestingly, this word length effect was replicated in a study of hearing-impaired individuals who used sign language. Some signs take a longer time to perform than others. Participants recalled fewer items when lists contained time-consuming signs than when lists contained shorter signs (Wilson and Emmorey 1998).

Baddeley likens the process of rehearsal to that of a circus performer spinning plates on top of sticks. Each time we rehearse, we "spin the plate" for that item of information to keep it going. If we have many items (e.g., 12) or items that take a lot of time to "spin" (e.g., five-syllable words), the "plates" for those items will stop before we can keep them going. A plate stopping is analogous to a sensory trace fading.

The visuo-spatial and verbal components of working memory are said to be "slave" systems to a *central executive* that is thought to be responsible for (a) managing the flow of information in and out of the two slave systems through selective attention and (b) planning, monitoring, and retrieving information about specific operations to be used in a particular task. Moreover, it is thought to offload some of its own short-term functions to the slave systems in order to free its own capacity for performing more complex tasks (Baddeley and Logie 1999). Studies have shown that whereas there is a degree of domain-specificity associated with working memory related to different codes (verbal versus spatial), there is a domain-general aspect to it that applies to any cognitive task that requires temporary storage and attentional processing of information (Barratt et al. 2004).

Barratt and colleagues (2004) argue that individual differences in working memory capacity (WMC) are extremely important because WMC relates to success on a wide variety of skills such as reading comprehension, math problem solving, learning, cognitive inhibition, and resistance to distraction. They suggest that the central component of WMC is the ability to control attention in order to activate, maintain, or suppress knowledge representations. In a common task used to measure WMC, a person may be asked to read a series of sentences and then recall the last word of each of the sentences. People who can recall more of these words are said to have a larger WMC. Those students with a larger WMC perform better in school than students with less WMC. Although some scholars have suggested that working memory and intelligence are the same, a recent meta-analysis showed that these constructs tend to correlate $r = .48$, which is far less than the perfect correlation of $r = 1.0$ (Ackerman et al. 2005). Thus, working memory and intelligence are related, but nevertheless distinct.

Whereas cognitive psychologists have investigated the nature of WM and its subdivisions, developmental psychologists have studied the development of WM. With respect to the phonological loop and the visuo-spatial sketchpad, children would not be able to utilize the phonological loop until they develop language skills (between the ages of one and five). Of course, having this ability available for use as a rehearsal system and actually using it in this way are two separate things. As for the visuo-spatial sketchpad, the vast majority of studies have focused on children older than six, though a few have examined this component in four-year-olds using standard sorts of spatial WM tasks (see, e.g., Luciana and Nelson 1998), and also in infants using variants of Piaget's "A-not-B" task (Schwartz and Reznick 1999). In the latter (which was originally designed to be a measure of Piaget's construct of object permanence), one successively hides an object in two locations. Young infants usually make the error of looking under the first location. By nine months, however, infants often look under the last location. Hence, it would appear that the spatial component of WM comes "on line" earlier than the verbal component. These findings for WM in infancy are similar to those found for studies of short-term memory (STM). One study found that less than 25 percent of five-month-olds and seven-month-olds could hold as many as three to four items in STM. By nine months, nearly half could hold this many items in memory (Rose et al. 2001). Infant memory was tested by showing a succession of four pictures to infants and seeing how many they recognized on later trials.

After the infancy period, various cross-sectional studies have shown largely linear increases with age on both verbal WM and spatial WM tasks (see, e.g., Luciana et al. 2005; Swanson 1999). For example, Swanson (1999) reported that 10-year-olds show a greater WM span than 6-year-olds (effect size or $d = .37$), and 24-year-olds show a greater WM span than 10-year-olds

($d = .63$). Performance only started to decline after age 45. Riggs, McTaggart, Simpson, and Freeman (2006) found that the capacity of visual WM seemed to double between the ages of 5 and 10. Such age-related increases in performance reflect increases in the ability to (a) process information quickly, (b) store larger chunks of information temporarily, and (c) shift attention (Cowan et al. 1999). Using structural equation modeling, Gathercole, Pickering, Ambridge, and Wearing (2004) found good evidence for the tripartite model of WM described earlier (i.e., the phonological loop, visuo-spatial sketchpad, and central executive) in children as young as six years old. They also found large, comparable increases with age in each of these three components.

Likely Effects of Processing Capacity Increases on IB

How might increases in WM processing capacity lead to age differences in the manner in which information is sought, interpreted, and used? People seek information because it helps them accomplish a goal that they have set for themselves or have been given by others (e.g., teachers). Processing capacity would only make a difference in information seeking for complex goals that require the coordination and prioritization of multiple sub-goals (see, e.g., Klahr 1985). For simple goals, age differences in knowledge would matter more than age differences in WM. In a related sense, WM capacity would also be important in situations in which individuals are trying to make sense of complex, multifaceted information. These tasks would be considered by cognitive scientists to have a high *cognitive load* (Sweller 1988) and may challenge the processing capacity of the individual's WM. Inevitably, searchers resort to intentional truncation of the information to deal with the cognitive overload and to make the task more manageable. This truncation will often be unprincipled and random. To truly understand and integrate a large number of items of information (e.g., on a website discussing health issues), it is important to focus on key ideas and arrange them in conceptually canonical ways. To do this, an individual can apply a *schema*, which is a mental representation or organizational structure that enables an individual to integrate information in a meaningful way. Using a schema increases the *germane* cognitive load of a task and can help the individual attend to useful information, thus enabling the individual to achieve a goal (Sweller et al. 1998).

If adults are able to process the majority of items of information but children can only process a small subset of these items, age differences in their ability to complete complex tasks would be expected. In addition, differences in knowledge make it likely that adults possessing more knowledge would have more available schemas that could be applied to organize new information. Research with children and adults by O'Hare, Lu, Houston, and colleagues (2008) demonstrates that there are developmental differences in children's and adults' capacities to handle cognitive load. Results of fMRIs of individuals completing a complex working memory task showed activity in children's prefrontal cortex, and in the cerebellar, frontal, and parietal regions of adults' brains. These findings suggest that the brain regions individuals recruit to conduct complex tasks differ by age. Accordingly, children and adults may demonstrate differences in IB when engaging in complex tasks that relate to these differences in cognitive resources.

Age Changes in Affective Orientations

In addition to representing information in the form of declarative, procedural, or conceptual knowledge, the human mind assigns various kinds of affective orientations to knowledge. For example, I may know that a close friend passed away (declarative knowledge), but consider this fact upsetting and depressing (affective orientation). Or, I may find it very interesting (affective orientation) that the ancient Egyptians and Mayans used sophisticated mathematics to construct their pyramids (declarative knowledge). When psychologists refer to the affective orientation called *values*, they mean the assessment that the information is considered important to an individual or, more colloquially, that the individual "cares about" the information. Psychologists are not referring to the lay construct that might be championed by conservative or religious groups (e.g., "family values," being raised with "good values," etc.). People care about such things as being on time, having a tidy home, getting accepted into a prestigious college, their appearance, their health, and so on. There is some overlap between the constructs of interests and values (in fact, some scholars argue interest is a subcategory of values), but it is possible for people to be interested in things that really do not matter to them and are not very important in their life (e.g., celebrity gossip). Conversely, many things that are very important to a person would not be considered interesting per se (e.g., a person who obsesses about her grades in school would probably not say that the topic of good grades is interesting in the normal sense of this word).

Affective orientations probably have their largest effect on behavior when tasks are open-ended and self-generated. For example, students who really care about getting admitted to an Ivy League college in the United States might spend an inordinate amount of time searching the Internet for sites devoted to tips for getting into Ivy League schools. Similarly, a spouse who finds the idea of being divorced disturbing and considers it very important to not break a marriage vow might spend a considerable amount of time looking for and reading self-help books on how to fix a troubled marriage. When given free rein, values and interests are likely to drive searches in a variety of disparate directions (unless there was a set of topics that most people rated very high on interest and importance). In contrast, when goals are assigned by others, it is likely that interest and values would mainly affect the amount of time devoted to completing the task and the level of attention allocated (i.e., low-interest topics would make it hard to stay focused and not be distracted).

Adults, adolescents, and children obviously care about different things. Given free rein to search, they would seek out different kinds of information and spend a different amount of time on sites if they happen to end up on the same sites or are directed to these sites through assignments. Age differences in values would also likely affect the extent to which information is used. For example, adults tend to care more about their health than younger people, so adults may be more likely to use information about unhealthy behaviors to change their behaviors than young people. A handful of developmental studies of interests and values show that children start out reporting strong interest in a variety of topics including math and reading. Over time, however, there are fairly constant drops in interest in school-related topics, and comparable drops in the importance of many of these topics (Wigfield and Eccles 1992), but interest in social relations and peers increases with age (Wentzel and Wigfield 1998).

Summary of Structural Aspects

Knowledge, processing capacity, and values all change with age and these changes are likely to lead to age differences in the kinds of information sought, how information is interpreted, and whether information is used. However, studies of academic achievement show that knowledge explains 50 to 60 percent of the variance in knowledge growth across an academic year, processing capacity explains 10 to 15 percent, and interest and values explain an additional 10 percent of the variance. It is possible that a comparable ordering of importance could occur in studies of IB. That is, if adults, adolescents, and children all differ in terms of their knowledge, processing capacity, and affective orientations, these differences could collectively produce large differences in their IB but knowledge differences might be the most important or potent source of differences.

Age Changes in Functional Aspects of Cognition

As noted above, a functional analysis of cognition pertains to the activities, operations, and goal-directed behavior of people. That is, it focuses on what people do and how they reason rather than what they know. Defined as such, IB would be an example of the functional aspect of cognition because it is goal directed. As noted earlier in this chapter, functional behaviors of any type are constrained by, or dependent upon, corresponding structural components in the same domain. For example, in order for functional memory processes such as retrieval (what is recalled in a particular situation) to operate in an optimal manner, these processes must interact with properly arranged knowledge stored in memory (including its associative and hierarchical structure). Similarly, in order for people to use the memorization strategy of grouping an unorganized array of to-be-learned items into categories (e.g., grouping the items tree, hamburger, car, truck, ice cream, rose bush, bus, tulip, banana into the categories of plants, food, and vehicles), they have to have the categories stored in memory. When readers infer that the text, "She heard the flapping of wings under the porch and saw that the poor creature was injured," is referring to a bird and that the female character feels sorry for it, they are basing such functional inferences on their structural knowledge base. One cannot infer that the bird is the implicit reference unless one knows that birds have wings.

As one further example of a structural-functional linkage, consider the case of decision making. When people evaluate their options in a particular situation (e.g., what to wear to work, whether to exercise today, which applicant to hire for a job, etc.), they rely on their causal knowledge to project what will likely happen if a particular option is selected, and on their affective orientations toward these projected outcomes. Although the consequences of some decisions are not terribly serious if causal projections are wrong (e.g., if I choose the wrong tie to wear to work), some decisions are consequential (career decisions, marital decisions, etc.) and it is important that causal inferences are correct. In addition, however, decisions are also based on our assessments related to our values and emotions. Emotions and values pull us toward certain outcomes and repel us away from others (Byrnes 2005). For example, I may know that speeding will get me to my destination faster than driving more slowly (a causal inference), but I also value my life and my driving record, and I would feel guilty if caught by the police. Thus, I usually choose to not speed.

The foregoing analysis suggests that there would be a straightforward developmental relationship between changes in structural aspects of cognition and changes in corresponding functional aspects. For example, as soon as children's knowledge becomes hierarchically arranged (it does not start out that way), children should start using the organizational memory strategy. Similarly, as soon as they have the requisite knowledge needed to support inference-making while reading, they will make the appropriate inference. Or, as soon as they have the requisite causal knowledge and values, they will make good decisions.

It turns out that such predictions often turn out to be false. Children have hierarchically arranged knowledge well before (e.g., age 5 or 6) they use the grouping memory strategy (e.g., age 8 to 10; Bjorklund 2011). Similarly, many studies have shown that children have the knowledge needed for inference-making while reading, but nevertheless fail to make the inferences (Paris et al. 1991). And studies of adolescent and adult decision making show that there is often a disconnect between what people know and value, and the decisions they make in the heat of the moment (Byrnes 2005).

How can these and related findings be explained? In many cases, such developmental delays and situational failures reflect a problem of self-regulation. Self-regulated learning (SRL) has the following attributes (Bernacki et al. 2011):

SRL is metacognitive, in the sense that learners engage in effective forms of planning, organizing, task analysis, goal-setting, and monitoring of progress; they understand the task and recognize their own limitations as learners.

SRL is strategic, in the sense that learners utilize effective domain-general (e.g., help-seeking, note-taking) and domain-specific strategies (e.g., reading strategies) that help them overcome processing limitations, overcome emotional distress, and/or promote better comprehension and retention of material.

SRL is adaptive, in the sense that learners adjust appropriately to changes in circumstances and demonstrate an emotional and motivational profile that is associated with achievement (e.g., a calibrated sense of ability, self-efficacy, being concerned about the right kind of things).

SRL is engaged, in the sense that learners are focused and remain focused on learning the material and are able to avoid being distracted.

SRL is self-initiating, in the sense that learners do not need others to urge them to begin tasks, remain focused, organize themselves, use strategies, and so on. They engage in self-regulatory behaviors on their own because they want to be successful and understand how these behaviors help them be more successful.

Azevedo and colleagues (see, e.g., Azevedo and Cromley 2004; Azevedo et al. 2005; Azevedo et al. 2008) have found in a number of studies that college students who demonstrate more of the attributes of SRL than their less self-regulated peers are more likely to locate information when placed in a hypermedia learning environment (e.g., a commercially available computerized encyclopedia). However, these studies also have found that few college students demonstrate more than limited amounts of self-regulation of their learning on their own, but can be trained to become more self-regulated using technology-based scaffolds (Azevedo et al. 2011). Those trained in SRL strategies acquire more information and find what they need more efficiently.

Although few developmental studies of SRL have been conducted in which adults, adolescents, and children are placed in the same complex learning situation, the following trends are likely to emerge given the results of studies of individual aspects of SRL: with age, children are more likely to demonstrate higher levels of metacognition, engage in more adaptive use of strategies, initiate tasks without prodding, and resist distraction during learning (Bernacki et al. 2011; Bjorklund 2011; Byrnes 2008). However, the differences between children, adolescents, and adults are relative rather than large per se. As noted above, many college students fail to demonstrate the kinds of SRL behaviors they need to appropriately find and make sense of information required to complete school-related tasks.

The literature documenting problems of metacognition, adaptive strategy use, self-initiation, and resistance to distraction is considerably more extensive than the literature explaining why it is that the level of SRL is not very impressive even in adults. In other words, we know that SRL increases with age and that certain kinds of technology can elicit it (Bernacki et al. 2011), but we do not have definitive answers regarding why it increases, why it increases so modestly, and why individual differences exist in adult learners (i.e., why some demonstrate high levels of SRL but some do not).

We can, however, appeal to Vygotsky's theory (1978) for clues as to likely developmental mechanisms that could promote increases in SRL. Vygotsky argued that successful development consists of the progressive internalization of skills within collaborative learning opportunities between a child who lacks the skills and someone who already has the skills (e.g., a parent, teacher, or more capable peer). Because the child starts out as a novice in a skill such as using a search engine to locate information, it is necessary for the more capable individual to be rather heavy handed in providing advice and feedback. However, as the child gains skill, it is important for the more capable individual to be less and less directive, and provide less and less structure and feedback over time. If this "fading" is implemented appropriately, the child eventually learns how to perform the skill on his or her own. In other words, the skill progresses from being completely "other regulated" at the beginning to being completely "self-regulated" at the end.

Vygotsky's theory would predict that college students do not demonstrate a high level of SRL because their parents and teachers failed to promote SRL in the manner described. For example, parents may operate in a heavy-handed way, reminding their children of deadlines, essentially doing the task for the child. Teachers may likewise walk students through the task, monitor them, and remain heavy handed. If this is the case, the removal of parent or teacher input would lead to students floundering on their own because they never internalized the skills and never relied on their own metacognition and strategies to figure out how to proceed effectively.

CONCLUSIONS AND IMPLICATIONS

In this chapter, we have relied on findings regarding age changes in the structural and functional aspects of cognition to speculate about the likely consequences of these age changes for IB. Although these findings on cognitive development are well established, it would be premature to draw firm conclusions from them regarding the implications for practitioners on what to expect when children, adolescents, and adults are asked to seek information, make sense of it, or use it in particular situations. We think the predictions expressed in this chapter are certainly reasonable and many are likely to be borne out, but part of the fun of conducting research is discovering that predictions can sometimes be wrong (at least for us). Thus, we would encourage researchers interested in IB to conduct the following kinds of studies:

- Create or administer credible measures of existing knowledge to groups of information seekers who vary along the expertise continuum for some domain; correlate the level of knowledge with the IB of these groups; more expert individuals should show more facility with keywords, should rely on the hierarchical structure of knowledge in the domain to facilitate their searches, and find the information they need more efficiently than those with less knowledge. It would also be interesting to contrast true experts, experienced non-experts, novices, and expert searchers who are not expert in the domain (e.g., librarians) to see who locates and makes sense of the information fastest or most efficiently; given the extreme domain-specificity of expertise, it is important to conduct such studies in multiple domains to identify common patterns.
- In follow-up studies, add measures of information processing capacity to determine the extent to which information overload affects IB, over and above the effects of knowledge. These might include measures of an individual's working memory capacity and the amount and type of cognitive load experienced during a search task.
- Add measures that assess the extent to which searchers consider the topic of the search interesting and important to them (and the importance of doing well on the assignment or completing it with accurate information); there are reasons to expect that knowledge, processing capacity, and affective orientations would all make independent contributions to performance; if age differences exist in knowledge, processing capacity, and affective orientations, these differences should lead to age differences in IB.
- Finally, it would be important to assess participants' self-regulated learning behaviors since SRL has been clearly related to search behavior in college students. Conducting think-aloud protocols (Greene et al. 2011)

and logging participants' search behavior could supply the data needed to examine why searchers who have the requisite content knowledge nevertheless do not engage in optimal forms of search behavior.

REFERENCES

Ackerman, Phillip, Margaret Beier, and Mary Boyle. 2005. "Working Memory and Intelligence: The Same or Different Constructs?" *Psychological Bulletin* 131: 30–60.

Anderson, John. 2009. *Cognitive Psychology and Its Implications* (7th edition). New York: Freeman.

Azevedo, Roger, and Jennifer Cromley. 2004. "Does Training On Self-Regulated Learning Facilitate Students' Learning with Hypermedia?" *Journal of Educational Psychology* 96 (3): 523–535. DOI: 10.1037/0022-0663.96.3.523.

Azevedo, Roger, Jennifer Cromley, Fielding Winters, Daniel Moos, and Jeffrey Greene. 2005. "Adaptive Human Scaffolding Facilitates Adolescents' Self-Regulated Learning with Hypermedia." *Instructional Science* 33 (5): 381–412.

Azevedo, Roger, Amy Johnson, Amber Chauncey, and Arthur Graesser. 2011. "Use of Hypermedia to Assess and Convey Self-Regulated Learning." In *Handbook of Self-Regulation of Learning and Performance*, edited by Barry J. Zimmerman and Dale H. Schunk. New York: Routledge.

Azevedo, Roger, Daniel Moos, Jeffrey Greene, Fielding Winters, and Jennifer Cromley. 2008. "Why Is Externally-Facilitated Regulated Learning More Effective than Self-Regulated Learning with Hypermedia?" *Educational Technology Research and Development* 56 (1): 45–72.

Baddeley, Alan. 1990. *Human Memory: Theory and Practice*. Boston: Allyn and Bacon.

Baddeley, Alan, and Robert Logie. 1999. "Working Memory: The Multiple-Component Model." In *Models of Working Memory: Mechanisms of Active Maintenance and Executive Control*, edited by Akira Miyake and Priti Shah, 28–61. New York: Cambridge University Press.

Barkow, Jerome, Leda Cosmides, and John Tooby. 1995. *The Adapted Mind: Evolutionary Psychology and the Generation of Culture*. New York: Oxford University Press.

Barratt, Lisa, Michele Tugade, and Randall Engle. 2004. "Individual Differences in Working Memory Capacity and Dual-Process Theories of Mind." *Psychological Bulletin* 130: 553–573.

Bayliss, Donna, Christopher Jarrold, Deborah Gunn, and Alan Baddeley. 2003. "The Complexities of Complex Span: Explaining Individual Differences in Working Memory in Children and Adults." *Journal of Experimental Psychology: General* 132: 71–92.

Bernacki, Matthew, Anita Aguilar, and James P. Byrnes. 2011. "Self-Regulated Learning and Technology-Enhanced Learning Environments: An Opportunity-Propensity Analysis." In *Fostering Self-Regulated Learning through ICT*, edited by Giuliana Dettori and Donatella Persico, 1–27. Hershey, PA: Information Science Reference.

Bjorklund, David. 2011. *Children's Thinking: Cognitive Development and Individual Differences* (5th edition). Belmont, CA: Wadsworth Publishers.

Byrnes, James P. 1992. "Combining and Categorizing Theories of Cognitive Development and Learning." *Educational Psychology Review* 4: 309–343.

Byrnes, James P. 2005. "Self-Regulated Decision-Making in Children and Adolescents." In *The Development of Judgment and Decision-Making in Children and Adolescents*, edited by J. E. Jacobs and P. A. Klaczynski, 5–38. Mahwah, NJ: Erlbaum.

Byrnes, James P. 2008. *Cognitive Development and Learning in Instructional Contexts* (3rd edition). Needham Heights, MA: Allyn and Bacon.

Byrnes, James P. 2011. "How Neuroscience Contributes to Our Understanding of Learning and Development in Typically Developing and Special-Needs Students." In *APA Educational Psychology Handbook, Vol. 1: Theories, Constructs, and Critical Issues*, edited by Karen Harris, Steve Graham, and Tim Urdan, 561–595. Washington, DC: American Psychological Association.

Byrnes, James P., and John Guthrie. 1992. "Prior Conceptual Knowledge and Textbook Search." *Contemporary Educational Psychology* 17: 8–29.

Carey, Susan. 2009. *The Origin of Concepts*. New York: Oxford University Press.

Chi, Michelene. 1978. "Knowledge Structures and Memory Development." In *Children's Thinking: What Develops?* edited by Robert Siegler, 73–96. Hillsdale, NJ: Erlbaum.

Chi, Michelene, Robert Glaser, and Marshall Farr. 1988. *The Nature of Expertise*. Mahwah, NJ: Erlbaum.

Chi, Michelene, Robert Glaser, and Ernest Rees. 1982. "Expertise in Problem Solving." In *Advances in the Psychology of Human Intelligence* (vol. 1), edited by Robert Sternberg, 7–75. Hillsdale, NJ: Erlbaum.

Chi, Michelene, and Randi Koeske. 1983. "Network Representation of a Child's Dinosaur Knowledge." *Developmental Psychology* 19: 29–39.

Cowan, Nelson, Lara Nugent, Emily Elliott, Igor Ponomarev, and J. Scott Saults. 1999. "The Role of Attention in the Development of Short-Term Memory: Age Differences in the Verbal Span of Apprehension." *Child Development* 70: 1082–1097.

Ericsson, K. Anders. 2003. "The Acquisition of Expert Performance as Problem Solving: Construction and Modification of Mediating Mechanisms through Deliberate Practice." In *The Psychology of Problem Solving*, edited by Janet Davidson and Robert Sternberg, 31–83. New York: Cambridge University Press.

Gathercole, Susan, Susan Pickering, Benjamin Ambridge, and Hannah Wearing. 2004. "The Structure of Working Memory from 4 to 15 Years of Age." *Developmental Psychology* 40: 177–190.

Gelman, Susan. 2009. "Learning from Others: Children's Construction of Concepts." *Annual Review of Psychology* 60: 115–140.

Greene, Jeffrey, Jane Robertson, and Lara-Jean Costa. 2011. "Assessing Self-Regulated Learning Using Think-Aloud Methods." In *Handbook of Self-Regulation of Learning and Performance*, edited by Zimmerman and Schunk, 313–328. New York: Routledge.

Halford, Graeme, Murray Mayberry, Anthony O'Hare, and Paul Grant. 1994. "The Development of Memory and Processing Capacity." *Child Development* 65: 1338–1356.

Klahr, David. 1985. "Solving Problems with Ambiguous Subgoal Ordering: Preschoolers' Performance." *Child Development* 56: 940–952.

Lawless, Kimberly, P.G. Schrader, and Hayley Mayall. 2007. "Acquisition of Information Online: Knowledge, Navigation and Learning Outcomes." *Journal of Literacy Research* 39 (3): 289–306.

Luciana, Monica, Heather Conklin, Catalina Hooper, and Rebecca Yarger. 2005. "The Development of Nonverbal Working Memory and Executive Control Processes in Adolescence." *Child Development* 76: 697–712.

Luciana, Monica, and Charles Nelson. 1998. "The Functional Emergence of Prefrontally Guided Working Memory Systems in Four- to Eight-Year-Old Children." *Neuropsychologia* 36: 273–293.

Miller, George. 1956. "The Magical Number Seven, Plus or Minus Two: Some Limits on Our Capacity for Processing Information." *Psychological Review* 63: 81–97.

Mitchell, Timothy, Sherry Chen, and Robert Macredie. 2005. "Hypermedia Learning and Prior Knowledge: Domain Expertise vs. System Expertise." *Journal of Computer Assisted Learning* 21 (1): 53–64.

Moos, Daniel, and Roger Azevedo. 2008. "Self-Regulated Learning with Hypermedia: The Role of Prior Domain Knowledge." *Contemporary Educational Psychology* 33 (2): 270–298.

Nelson, Katherine. 1986. *Event Knowledge: Structure and Function in Development*. Mahwah, NJ: Lawrence Erlbaum.

O'Hare, Elizabeth, Lisa Lu, Suzanne Houston, Susan Bookheimer, and Elizabeth Sowell. 2008. "Neurodevelopmental Changes in Verbal Working Memory Load-Dependency: An fMRI Investigation." *Neuroimage* 42 (4): 1678–1685. doi:10.1016/j.neuroimage.2008.05.057.

Paris, Scott, Barbara Wasik, and Julianne Turner. 1991. "The Development of Strategic Readers." In *Handbook of Reading Research* (vol. II), edited by Rebecca Barr, Michael Kamil, Peter Mosenthal, and P. David Pearson, 609–640. New York: Longman.

Piaget, Jean, and Bärbel Inhelder. 1969. *The Psychology of the Child*. New York: Basic Books.

Riggs, Kevin, James McTaggart, Andrew Simpson, and Richard Freeman. 2006. "Changes in the Capacity of Visual Working Memory in 5- to 10-Year-Olds." *Journal of Experimental Child Psychology* 95: 18–26.

Rose, Susan, Judith Feldman, and Jeffrey Jankowski. 2001. "Visual Short-Term Memory in the First Year of Life: Capacity and Recency Effects." *Developmental Psychology* 37: 539–549.

Schwartz, Bena, and J. Stephen Reznick. 1999. "Measuring Infant Spatial Working Memory Using a Modified Delayed-Response Procedure." *Memory* 7: 1–17.

Slone, Debra. 2003. "Internet Search Approaches: The Influence of Age, Search Goals, and Experience." *Library and Information Science Research* 25 (4): 403–418.

Smith, Edward, John Jonides, and Robert Koeppe. 1996. "Dissociating Verbal and Spatial Working Memory Using PET." *Cerebral Cortex* 6: 11–20.

Swanson, H. Lee. 1999. "What Develops in Working Memory? A Life Span Perspective." *Developmental Psychology* 35: 986–1000.

Sweller, John. 1988. "Cognitive Load during Problem Solving: Effects on Learning." *Cognitive Science* 12(2): 257–285.

Sweller, John, Jeroen Van Merrienboer, and Fred Paas. 1998. "Cognitive Architecture and Instructional Design." *Educational Psychology Review* 10 (3): 251–296.

Voss, James, Sherman Tyler, and Laurie Yengo. 1983. "Individual Differences in the Solving of Social Science Problems." In *Individual Differences in Cognition* (vol. I), edited by Rona Dillon and Ronald Schmeck, 205–232. New York: Academic Press.

Vygotsky, Lev. 1978. *Mind in Society*. Cambridge, MA: Harvard University Press.

Wentzel, Kathryn, and Allan Wigfield. 1998. "Academic and Social Motivational Influences on Students' Academic Performance." *Educational Psychology Review* 10: 155–175.

Wigfield, Allan, and Jacquelynne Eccles. 1992. "The Development of Achievement Task Values: A Theoretical Analysis." *Developmental Review* 12: 265–310.

Wilson, Margaret, and Karen Emmorey. 1998. "A 'Word Length Effect' for Sign Language: Further Evidence for the Role of Language in Structuring Working Memory." *Memory and Cognition* 26: 584–590.

Chapter Three

Information Literacy

Leanne Bowler and Valerie Nesset

In the age of information and communications technology, information literacy is a prerequisite to lifelong learning and engagement in the community. The twenty-first century child is growing up in a media-saturated world, where information is ubiquitous, multi-modal, interactive, and increasingly, designed to persuade. It is no longer adequate to simply access information. Young people need to know how to critically and ethically evaluate, synthesize, use, create, and share information.

In this chapter we attempt to answer the question "How information literate is the new digital generation?" To answer it, we begin with a synopsis of common definitions and models of information literacy. We then take a look at what the research in youth information-seeking behavior says about how young people are navigating their information worlds. We present in some detail two case studies that demonstrate youth information literacy along the developmental spectrum, one study that looked at children, aged eight to nine, in a grade-3 class (Nesset 2009, 2011), the other which investigated older teens, aged sixteen to eighteen, in their final school year before entering university (Bowler 2010a, 2010b, 2010c). The chapter concludes with a look toward the future of research in information literacy, particularly with regard to the convergence of information and media literacies in the participatory culture of new media.

WHAT IS INFORMATION LITERACY?

The concept of information literacy emerged in the late twentieth century, as digital, networked information became accessible to the broad population. The information explosion prompted librarians to revisit their traditional

45

stance on library instruction. Basic library skills such as how to search the library catalog or use a periodical index were simply not adequate in the new information environment. A broader understanding of information skills emerged, one that went beyond basic retrieval to include the problem-solving skills related to the evaluation and use of information. An early definition of information described an information literate person as one who has "learned how to learn" and is "able to recognize when information is needed and ha[s] the ability to locate, evaluate, and use effectively the needed information" (ALA 1989). Early on, information literacy was seen as something quite different from basic library (or bibliographic) instruction. Calling information literacy a "new liberal art" because it reflects a humanistic approach to learning, Shapiro and Hughes argue that information literacy is actually a collection of literacies, including *tool literacy, resource literacy, social structure literacy, publishing literacy, critical literacy*, and an ability to adapt to new technology (called *emerging technology literacy*) (Shapiro and Hughes 1996). Bruce (2000a) identifies seven "faces" or experiences of information literacy: the IT experience, the information sources experience, the information-process experience, the information control experience, the knowledge construction experience, the knowledge extension experience, and the wisdom experience (p. 216). Each experience builds upon the others to produce an information product and/or increase the individual's knowledge base so that he or she can apply it to later situations.

The earliest definitions of and standards for information literacy were developed for the college environment. Many educational jurisdictions and school library associations around the world subsequently developed definitions and standards to reflect the K–12 context. *Information Power: Building Partnerships for Learning* (AASL 1998), prepared by the American Association of School Librarians, highlighted nine information literacy standards that young people needed in order to access, evaluate, and use information in a socially responsible manner. The standards reflected the shift from library skills instruction to the broader framework implied by information literacy, where information skills are seen as both a problem-solving process and a state of mind. As Bruce (2000b) states, "My own research leads me to conclude that information literacy is an appreciation of the complex of ways of interacting with information. It is a way of thinking and reasoning about aspects of subject matter."

A decade after *Information Power*, AASL's *Standards for the Twentieth Century Learner* reflects the participatory environment of Web 2.0 and emerging mobile technologies (AASL 2007). The standards are grouped into four broad areas of competencies: (1) inquire, think critically, and gain knowledge; (2) draw conclusions, make informed decisions, apply knowledge to new situations, and create new knowledge; (3) share knowledge and participate ethically and productively as members of our democratic society;

and (4) pursue personal and aesthetic growth. The new standards have a strong social component and recognize that "multiple literacies, including digital, visual, textual, and technological, have now joined information literacy as crucial skills for this century" (AASL 2007, 3). The standards include explicit references to safe and ethical behaviors in personal electronic communication and interaction, and bring to the fore the metacognitive practices implicit in information literacy, highlighting self-assessment strategies such as self-questioning personal knowledge, monitoring information-seeking processes, and seeking feedback from teachers and peers to guide one's own inquiry process.

MODELS OF THE INFORMATION LITERACY PROCESS

Elemental to information literacy is the idea that information problem-solving is a process, a series of actions along a continuum that starts with information users identifying an information need and ends with them using, creating, and sharing new knowledge derived from their exchanges with information. The notion of "process" implies sequence, a "moving picture" that takes place over a period of time, rather than a "still photograph" of one search incident (Dervin and Nilan 1986, 14). What this means for information literacy instruction is that discrete information skills need to be situated within the context of a broader information problem. Various models of the problem-solving processes have attempted to do this, their purpose to serve as a template for instruction in information literacy (Eisenberg and Berkowitz 1990; Kuhlthau 1991, 2004; Harada and Tepe 1998; Irving 1985; Stripling and Pitts 1988; Todd 1998; Yucht 1997; Losey 2007). Process models also suggest "best practices" for students engaged in information seeking and problem solving and as such, act as a metacognitive support. For example, Stripling and Pitts's ten-step model for research projects (1988) provides a series of questions students should ask themselves in order to prompt self-reflection, each question matched to a particular phase in the research project. At Level 3 in the model, when the task at hand is to narrow the topic, students must ask themselves "Is my topic a good one?"

Perhaps the best known process model is Kuhlthau's information search process (ISP) model. The ISP model is one of the few grounded in a significant body of empirical study (Kuhlthau 1988a, 1988b). Initially based on an investigation of gifted high school students, it was validated in a series of five studies over a span of six years, using both small- and large-scale sample sizes, in a diverse range of settings, within a variety of populations. The ISP model identifies seven stages, each stage representing specific tasks in the information search process: (1) task initiation, (2) topic selection, (3) prefocus exploration, (4) focus formulation, (5) information collection, (6) search closure (presentation), and (7) reflection and self-assessment (Kuhlthau 2004).

Kuhlthau's ISP was tightly focused on the search aspect of information (hence, it is typically considered a model of information-seeking behavior), but many of the process models actually go beyond the search and include steps for communicating ideas via products such as a research paper. Unlike models of information-seeking behavior, the broader process models do not necessarily identify actual behaviors and/or processes but instead typically present an idealized set of steps (usually written in the form of questions) to encourage metacognition on the part of the student. They may also rely on a set of skills and/or standards and often emphasize the experience. Three such examples are the Big6, PLUS, and EXIT models. Eisenberg and Berkowitz's Big6 model (1990) prescribes six stages in the framework for solving information-based problems: (1) task definition, (2) information-seeking strategies (selecting sources), (3) location and access (finding sources and the information in sources), (4) use of information (extracting relevant information), (5) synthesis (organize and present information), and (6) evaluation (judging the product and process). Herring's (1996) PLUS (Purpose, Location, Use, Self-Evaluation) model makes many suggestions for guiding the students through the information research process (e.g., concept-mapping, using indexes and subject directories, communicating information, and self-evaluating). The EXIT (Extending Interactions with Text) model (Wray and Lewis 1995) is based on the idea that "any model aiming to describe the process of interacting with expository texts must account for its transactional nature and build in a strong element of the reader contributing to the constructed meaning" (p. 3). The model also emphasizes the importance of learning material by making connections with prior knowledge: "Learning which does not make connections with our prior knowledge is learning at the level of rote only, and is soon forgotten once deliberate attempts to remember it have stopped" (p. 4). Relying heavily on the work of Marland (1981), the EXIT model identifies ten steps (posed as questions to encourage metacognitive thinking) crucial to the information process. The first few questions concentrate on thinking about how to go about looking for information, the next several focus on actions associated with information seeking, and the last question deals with the presentation of the information.

HOW INFORMATION LITERATE IS THE NEW DIGITAL GENERATION

Despite their reputation as digital wizards, research shows that young people, for the most part, are merely adequate when it comes to information seeking and use and, in fact, could use some guidance (Watson 1998; Fidel et al. 1999; Agosto 2002; Branch 2003; Chen 2003; Shenton and Dixon 2003; Todd 2003; Neilsen 2005; Dresang 2005; Valenza 2006; Chung and Neuman 2007; Williamson et al. 2007; CIBER, 2008).

INFORMATION SEEKING AND USE

Research has revealed that children exhibit a lack of strategic thinking and planning when seeking the necessary information to complete an assigned task (Cooper 2002; Hirsh 1997; Kuhlthau 1991, 1993, 2004; Large and Beheshti 2000; Moore 2000; Schacter, Chung, and Dorr 1998). The Centre for Information Behavior and the Evaluation of Research (CIBER) produced a study designed to forecast the behavior of future researchers. The idea that young people are expert searchers, the authors suggest, is "a dangerous myth" (2008, 20). The study analyzed the published literature related to young people's information behavior over the past twenty-five years and conducted a deep log analysis of web-based searches, comparing different age groups' use of the same platform. Findings from this study tell us that while today's young people overwhelmingly prefer to use the web as their principal information source, their information search skills have not improved over time.

Children's information needs differ from those of adults (Kuhlthau 1988a, 1988b; Shenton and Dixon 2003; Walter 1994). In the digital domain, it has been confirmed that a correlation exists between children's information needs and their information-seeking behaviors and that these behaviors are different from those of adults (Bilal and Kirby 2001, 2002; Cooper 2002; Revelle et al. 2002). Research has also established that information-seeking behavior can vary depending on the level of domain knowledge (Bilal 2000; Hirsh 1996, 1997; Lawless, Mills and Brown 2002) and the amount of prior searching experience (Slone 2003).

PLAGIARISM

One of the greatest problems with information use, at least in the school setting, is plagiarism. The ease with which digital information can be copied and pasted has meant a focus on the ethics of intellectual property in the classroom and strategies for avoiding plagiarism. The idea that someone owns information is often new to young people. Furthermore, the cognitive effort needed to synthesize information from multiple sources can be too difficult for many young people without proper scaffolding from the teacher or librarian. Some students are simply unmotivated to make the effort. So even though the young may be aware of intellectual property rights and the concept of ethical use of information, the problem of plagiarism persists (McGregor and Streitenberger 1998; Williamson et al. 2007). McGregor and Streitenberger's study (1998) was one of the first to look at the relationship between plagiarism and information use among students in the K–12 environment. They found that senior high school students who had received an admonition from the teacher not to copy adopted a round-about strategy, simply paraphrasing the text without citing the source, leading McGregor and Streitenberger to label the students as "scribes" rather than active learners who synthesize the information into new knowledge.

Williamson and McGregor's study (2006) explored plagiarism among a group of secondary school students, in a study that framed their model for understanding the influences on information use and plagiarism. The model identifies five themes that "bear upon student information use, especially the level of plagiarism" such as "people, practices, attitudes, technology and prior learning" (under "A model for understanding influences on information use and plagiarism"). The study showed that people played a role in helping to synthesize information. For example, the mother of one participant read out parts of a book that she felt were relevant to his school project. Note taking was identified by participants as an important strategy for dealing with information overload. A positive attitude, engagement with the topic, and motivation to persist factored into the relationship between information use and plagiarism.

Building on this model, Williamson and colleagues (2007), in their Smart Information Use project, investigated the creative and effective use of information to minimize plagiarism among secondary students in four Australian schools. Students were found to be overconfident in their information literacy skills. Those students who copied extensively tended to do so, not surprisingly, from Internet-based sources rather than from non-Internet sources. Interestingly, although several of the students used note taking during their information gathering process, a strategy that is meant to help synthesize information from multiple sources into a coherent whole, the notes in fact did not deter the students from using copied text. Williamson and colleagues suggest that students need explicit instruction in note taking and strategies that encourage creative thinking in order to alleviate plagiarism. Teaching materials developed by the four schools during the *Smart Information Use* project are available on the project's website (http://smartinformatio-nuse.synthasite.com/).

TWO CASE STUDIES IN YOUTH INFORMATION LITERACY

In this section we present two case studies that looked at the information literacy skills of young people in the context of an inquiry-based learning assignment at school. The case studies present an interesting contrast in child development, the first study investigating children's information behavior in the early elementary years of school, the second study working with a group of older teens as they transition into the adult world.

Proposed Evidence-Based Model for Information Literacy Instruction for Elementary School Students

Younger elementary school students remain an understudied group, yet educational research shows that in today's constructivist classroom these young students are actively engaging in information seeking and use from the earliest grades. Inquiry learning initiatives such as project-based learning (sometimes referred to as resource-based learning) require that students interact directly with information in a variety of formats. Nesset's research investigates how these young students are navigating such environments. Using a qualitative methodology that included six data collection methods (pre- and post-questionnaires; participant observation; semi-structured interviews; screen and voice capture of search sessions; journals; and working and submission copies of the final projects), she followed two classes of grade-3 students (aged eight to nine years—fifty-two students in total, twelve of whom were studied in depth) in a project-based learning classroom (Nesset 2009). Nesset's findings revealed that the overall process could be divided into three stages: preparing, searching, and using, and that all three stages are of equal importance. The findings also revealed that in the classroom environment, young students search for information in both print and digital domains. From these findings emerged a three-stage process model, the PSU (Preparing, Searching, and Using). This model does not fit neatly into either the category of information-seeking behavior where models tend to concentrate on the searching stage, or into models of information literacy that typically do not identify and discuss behaviors and largely ignore the searching stage. Instead it forms a bridge between the two types of models.

A simplified version of the PSU model was developed for instruction with younger children. Titled the BAT (Beginning, Acting, and Telling), this version presents only the stages and the actions associated with them within a stylized depiction of a bat (Figure 3.1).

The *Preparing/Beginning* stage is largely instructional in that the teacher develops and guides the activities of the students to help them acquire the knowledge necessary to successfully navigate the searching and using stages. In the model, these activities are grouped under two main categories: reading

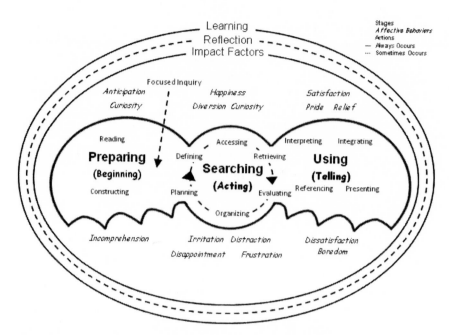

Figure 3.1. Preparing, Searching, and Using (PSU) and Beginning, Acting, and Telling (BAT) models

and constructing. Reading activities promote better reading and comprehension of text (thereby increasing subject knowledge) as well as the learning of more advanced terminology (which can then be used to construct search queries in the next stage). In the study, the teacher introduced vocabulary exercises, reading aloud and silently, and creative writing and drawing. Constructing activities not only help the students to increase their knowledge of the subject matter but also to develop critical thinking skills. In the study they took the form of a significant adult reading aloud from informational sources, guest speakers, guided group activities where the children worked in teams to investigate and present information about particular aspects of the broader topic, and concept-mapping exercises.

The *Searching/Acting* stage is the only stage where the students take the initiative and act completely on their own. In this stage the students searched for information in print and online. In the digital environment, it was observed that the students who were able to make use of visual cues or "signposts" (e.g., bolded font related to a search term, embedded images within chunked, relevant text) and could skim the text, could more quickly and efficiently evaluate the relevance of a website (Nesset 2011). It is in this stage that several behaviors are identified: *planning*, where the student may make decisions about the scope of the assignment, how the information will be presented, and so on; *defining*, which is related to planning—the act of defining ensures that the students understand exactly what is expected of them and helps them to focus their efforts on the task at hand (e.g., deciding which search engine and search queries to use, etc.); *accessing/finding*, which is the user's first visual presentation of the surrogates or pointers (e.g., results lists) to actual information items; *retrieving/gathering*, where the student interacts with the actual information item; *evaluating*, where the student examines and evaluates the retrieved information in more depth; and finally, *organizing*, an action in which the student organizes the materials in a way that makes sense to him or her in preparation for the final stage of using.

In the *Using/Telling* stage the students actually interacted with and then presented the information found and organized during the searching stage. Since it is in this stage that the students reviewed the retrieved information in more depth, some of them revisited one or both of the previous stages in order to fill in gaps. When this was done, however, the student was much more focused and therefore able to more easily and quickly find the missing information. Actions associated with this stage were *interpreting* or rereading and reevaluating the information found and then rewriting it in the students' own words (and thus making it their own); *integrating*, in which the students incorporated the interpreted information in a way that satisfied the guidelines of the assignment (in this case, a scrapbook and oral presentation); *referencing* or acknowledging the sources used; and *presenting* the material. In this stage the students did much of the work on their own, but some instruction was involved in areas of spelling and grammar and to reinforce the importance of acknowledging other people's work. Many of the children commented on how hard it was to write the information in their own words —one boy summing it up beautifully when he stated, "they [authors] use all the best words." The students did appear to recognize, however, that it was unacceptable to simply copy and paste information—that doing so was akin to "cheating." They considered that changing a few words was enough to avoid plagiarism and this awareness only applied to the print domain. The students in the study did not appear to fully understand that websites were like books in terms of referencing. If the information was online (even if printed out later), it was not considered the same; they did not think to record the title and/or author of a website as they would have done with a printed book. The children never were able to give reasons for this perception but the stock answer of "my information came from 'the Google'" indicates that they were not aware of the difference between a search engine and a website (for more on this, see Nesset 2007).

While identification of actions is an important part of the PSU, the acknowledgement of affective behaviors also plays a major role. Previous research has indicated the importance of affective behaviors, especially with younger students (see, for example, Cooper 2002). In the PSU, what were identified as more positive affective behaviors are located above the stages; the more negative are found below. It should be noted, however, that what was observed as a negative behavior in this study (e.g., distraction—this happened when students examined websites completely unrelated to the task at hand—for example, the two boys who spent most of their time examining sites devoted to the X-Men character Wolverine, instead of investigating sites about the animal, the wolverine) in other contexts could act as a positive influence (e.g., when distraction results in the serendipitous discovery of a relevant site). The reason they are included in the model is to help make educators and students aware of the potential pitfalls or conversely, the efficacy of engaging in particular affective behaviors.

The model is surrounded by three ovals. The *Impact Factors* oval is included to demonstrate that there are external factors that impact on the overall process. Factors such as search engine and website design, classification schemes, currency of resources, and so on can facilitate or hinder a student's progress through the stages. The *Learning* oval indicates that some learning takes place throughout the process, whether or not that learning is what the teacher intended. A good example of this is again, the two boys who spent their time examining X-Men sites. While they did not learn about their assigned animal, they did learn about using search engines and evaluating results lists. The dashed *Reflection* oval signifies the fact that while sometimes present, the students did not always reflect on their work, a metacognitive activity that has been shown to improve performance.

This study shed light on many aspects of young students' practices when searching for and using information in an educational context. The model that has been developed emphasizes the importance of making students aware not only of the stages and actions involved in the information process but also potential affective behaviors that are associated with each stage (for example, curiosity or frustration) and impact factors (e.g., website design and readability level, search engine ranking procedures) over which they may have limited or no control. Making students aware of these aspects of the information process encourages metacognition and promotes the learning of information literacy skills. The research highlights the need to teach basic information literacy skills at an early age so that bad habits never form; furthermore, the students can build upon these basic skills over the course of their K–12 education so that they become second nature. This would go a long way in mitigating the angst and struggle many undergraduate students experience when entering their programs of study.

Further research will involve the investigation of the model within a classroom setting. The PSU model and its offshoot, the BAT, will be posted in all of the school libraries within the Buffalo District Public School System. Two classes at the elementary level will be followed as they use the model to do research for a class project. It is hoped that this model will not only result in better research practices on the part of the students, but will also act as a catalyst for collaboration between school librarians and classroom teachers who together can share their expertise and experience to further inform information literacy instruction.

ADOLESCENT METACOGNITIVE KNOWLEDGE DURING THE INFORMATION SEARCH PROCESS

The American Association of School Librarians *Standards for the Twentieth Century Learner*, (AASL 2007) highlights the importance of self-monitoring, self-evaluation, and the use of cognitive strategies to self-regulate learning. These are skills related to *metacognition*, the under-current of thinking about one's own thinking that is essential to information literacy, the package of competencies needed to negotiate complex, open-ended information systems. Metacognition, "thinking responsibly" about our thinking, is seen by educators as a critically important life skill required for "successful academic studies, in demand in the workplace, needed for good citizenship, and valued in the development of the whole person" (Foster et al. 2002, 24). The knowledge that underlies it is called *metacognitive knowledge*, which is knowledge about cognition in general as well as awareness of and knowledge about one's own cognition, the cognitive demands of a task, and the strategies to employ when unsuccessful (Anderson and Krathwohl 2001).

Bowler's study investigated adolescent metacognitive knowledge in order to paint a rich picture of both the gaps and strengths in teenage metacognition. (Bowler 2010a, 2010b, 2010c). The study was conducted in two Montreal-area, English-language, junior colleges, commonly called CEGEP. (The term CEGEP stands for "Collège d'enseignement général et professionnel" or, "College of General and Professional Education.") Although CEGEP is considered to be post-secondary education, the first year is roughly equivalent to grade 12 because high school in Quebec ends at grade 11. While CEGEP students negotiate the same complex world of information as adolescents in the rest of North America, they do so in a new learning environment, many having just graduated from high school the year before. This puts an interesting twist on their search behavior because the CEGEP library and information systems available through the library are generally new to them. As well, the position of teacher-librarian, at the time of the study, did not exist in Quebec public high schools or in most private high schools, and therefore information skills instruction at the high school level was limited. The students who participated in this study were, in a sense, a tabula rasa—a clean slate as it were —and, at least in terms of library experience, they may have had little else to guide them but their metacognitive knowledge.

The study applied a research approach adapted from cognitive science. Called cognitive ethnography, it is a way to study thinking from a socio-cultural perspective—cognition in its natural habitat or, thinking "in the wild" (Hutchins 1995). Bowler's study took a similar approach, although it focused on metacognition—the thinking behind the thinking—rather than the broader perspective of cognition. For this reason, the method used has been called a "metacognitive ethnography."

The study looked at the information search process of ten adolescents, all academic achievers and between the ages of sixteen and eighteen years, as they searched for, evaluated, and used information to complete a semi-imposed, inquiry-based research paper, using any variety of information sources. The study used a combination of *Think Aloud* and *Think After* verbal protocols in order to provide as many venues as possible for the expression of thoughts, feelings, and actions experienced by the participants during the search process. In this way, the data could be triangulated. Five types of data collection protocols were used in this study: (1) a series of three telephone interviews; (2) written and/or audio journals kept by the participants over the course of the semester; (3) an in-person interview immediately following the final submission of the essay; (4) a visualizing exercise (a timeline); and (5) a follow-up interview conducted several months later. Each instrument tried to capture three conceptual categories: the actions taken during the search process, the thinking underlying these, and the feelings experienced at each stage in the process. Metacognitive knowledge was specifically targeted with questions related to *why* and *self-prompting questions*. Analysis was inductive and grounded in the data, using the words and actions of the ten participants to tell the story of their journey through the information search process. Atlas.ti 5.2 qualitative data analysis software was used to organize, code, and sort the data into interpretive categories.

The participants demonstrated a wide range of metacognitive resources which they used to complete their information-seeking task. They were hindered in their searches by a lack of procedural knowledge related to information problem solving as well as a lack of conceptual knowledge in the domain of history. The study found that these roadblocks were mediated by metacognitive knowledge that was used as much as an emergency strategy as it was a deliberate line of attack. It is perhaps not a surprise that there was some evidence of metacognitive knowledge in this study, given that the participants were academic achievers and nearing the tail-end of their adolescence. However, while the young people in this study did show evidence of thinking ahead and planning, their use of metacognitive knowledge was as often as not reactive, rather than predictive, exhibiting a short metacognitive horizon—a paradox perhaps for a knowledge that is associated with planning. The metacognitive knowledge of the adolescents in this study was surprisingly varied and wide-ranging. The study uncovered thirteen attributes of adolescent metacognitive knowledge related to the information search process. The attributes represent both the strengths and gaps in the participants' metacognitive knowledge—the knowledge they had *and* the knowledge they should have had to help solve their information problem. In keeping with the ethnographic approach of this study and its focus on the totality of the participants' information experiences, the thirteen attributes have been drawn together to create a taxonomy of adolescent metacognitive knowledge. The attributes of the taxonomy are defined below:

Balancing. Knowing that the cognitive task of making choices, sometimes between two desirable options, helps to move you forward in the search process. Awareness that information seekers must weigh the options and make compromises.

Building a base. Knowing that the strategic use of exploratory tactics can help build foundational domain knowledge.

Changing course. Knowing that new tactics and strategies must be applied because the search is stalled or less fruitful than expected. It is dependent on the ability to assess one's status during the search process.

Communicating. Knowing that talking to people is a useful cognitive strategy. Involves the use of people as information mediators and information sources during the search process.

Connecting. Knowing how and when to implement tactics and strategies that will help the specific act of linking pieces of information. Requires an understanding that knowledge building is a process of construction.

Knowing that you don't know. Being able to identify a gap in the knowledge base not being able to say what that gap is.

Knowing your strengths and weaknesses. Ability to put a name to what one knows and then take advantage of it.

Parallel thinking. Consciously reviewing the past and predicting the future—even as one acts in the present.

Pulling back and reflecting. Being aware of the metacognitive benefits of reflecting, reviewing and just stepping away from the problem.

Scaffolding. Knowing when and how to apply cognitive supports, or reinforcements, that will to help map out a conceptualization of the information environment.

Understanding curiosity. Regulating the conflict between the need to discover versus the need to fulfill the requirements of the information task.

Understanding memory. Understanding the role of memory in information seeking. Knowing that it is difficult to remember everything, knowing how one's *own* memory works, and knowing how and when to use specific strategies in order to help one remember where information is located so that it can be retrieved later.

Understanding time and effort. Understanding the connection between effort and results. Awareness of the cognitive demands of information seeking.

The taxonomy is not a process model. What emerged from this study was not a neat pathway of metacognitive knowledge during the information search process, but rather, a multi-faceted, circuitous, sometimes tangled pattern. While the participants often thought and acted in metacognitive ways, they did so at a micro level as problems emerged and not necessarily as a tool for envisioning a fully formed outcome. A lack of an overall pattern may be a weakness of the students in this study but it may also be a weakness common to *all* information seekers, each of us being novices every time we approach a new domain of knowledge. If this is the case, then a healthy array of tools in the metacognitive knowledge toolkit is the most useful asset to have when exploring unknown territory.

What do the results of this study mean for information literacy instruction? Teaching students how to use search tools like indexes, search engines, and catalogs, while important, is not enough. Underlying the ability to "recognize when information is needed and have the ability to locate, evaluate, and use effectively the needed information" (ALA 1989) is a deeper layer of thinking that acts to guide decisions during the search process. Librarians need to teach students how to think about their own thinking. Kuhlthau (1994) suggested that teaching students about uncertainty—telling them that it is a normal part of the search process, that it should be expected, and that it is an indicator of work to be done—would help to keep them engaged in the search process. So an important task for librarians, according to Kuhlthau, is to raise in information seekers a self-awareness about their own cognitive state and to teach this alongside the traditional skills of locating and evaluating information. As this study shows, there are many types of "self-awareness" that students need to be taught.

The next step in this line of research is to explore the role of metacognition in the context of new media. Many questions remain: How do young people monitor and regulate their thinking processes when they search for, use, and create information in networked, multimodal, and immersive environments? What habits of mind do they need to navigate and create effectively in these worlds? Are there developmental differences?

CONCLUSION

We often associate information literacy and young people with school-based information tasks. Indeed, much of the research we have presented in this chapter is rooted squarely in the educational world of schools. But the information behavior of young people extends beyond the borders of their schools. Our understanding of information literacy and its connection to youth information behavior must continue to evolve in order to reflect the everyday life concerns of young people. Some research has been done in this area (see, for example, the work of Agosto and Hughes-Hassell, 2005, 2006, for a model of everyday life information seeking of urban teens), but much work remains. As well, new and emerging information technologies and ecologies will continue to impact our understanding of the information skills needed to navigate complex information environments effectively. The advent of social media and handheld mobile devices are a prime example of information technologies that were not reflected in the earliest articulation of information literacy.

The task for those who teach and conduct research in the area of information literacy will be to build, expand, and make relevant a concept that emerged from a world where print technology still ruled and which must now find relevance in the participatory culture of new media. Young people are not just consumers of information; they are now active creators. A new range of social skills, cultural competencies, and habits of mind must be built into the models that guide teaching and research in information literacy.

Some attempts to re-conceptualize information literacy have begun. UNESCO now uses the term *Information and Media Literacy* (combining information and media into one construct), stating that "information and media literacy enables people to interpret and make informed judgments as users of information and media, as well as to become skillful creators and producers of information and media messages in their own right" (UNESCO 2011). More dramatically, media scholars have argued that the information and media skills traditionally taught in schools are insufficient for the twenty-first century. Henry Jenkins, director of the Comparative Media Studies Program at the Massachusetts Institute of Technology, has identified eleven core skills that young people need in order to be "full, active, creative, and ethical participants in this emerging participatory culture" of new media (Jenkins et al. 2006, 4). They are *play, performance, simulation, appropriation, multitasking, distributed cognition, collective intelligence, judgment, transmedia navigation, networking,* and *negotiation.* Some of the core skills in Jenkins's framework look similar to information literacy, albeit framed in a new media context (*Judging*, for example). But others conflict with the traditional standards and values that are embedded in information literacy instruction. *Appropriation* is "the ability to meaningfully sample and remix media content" (Jenkins et al. 2006, 4). So while librarians are teaching students *not* to copy, media scholars are saying students should learn to copy better. Some of Jenkins's core skills also seem to conflict with recommendations from the research in information literacy. For example, Jenkins's *multitasking*, the ability to scan one's environment and shift focus as needed to salient details, seems to be the antithesis of Bowler's *pulling back and re-*

flecting (2009), which is a metacognitive knowledge related to the awareness of the cognitive benefits of reflecting, reviewing and stepping away from a problem. These confusions indicate that much work needs to be done in terms of integrating information and media literacies into a unified model.

Paradoxically, even as the information environment continues to grow, fed in part by the voices and media productions of young people, there is a concomitant narrowing of perspectives in the information that they retrieve. Pariser (2011) writes of the filter bubble and how intelligent search engines and social media sites are tailoring, or personalizing, search results, such that what we retrieve is really just a reflection of ourselves. Traditional information literacy argued for the skills needed to synthesize multiple points of view. In the new information environment, young people may first need to become aware that information mediated by technology represents less of the wide world than they think and is really a mirror image of their previous information behavior, which for young people with limited life experience might produce a very narrow perspective indeed. Personalization, combined with a massive increase in the digital data that young people leave behind, will have a lasting effect not only on the kind of information they encounter but also on their very identities as adults. As long as young people mediate much of their information behavior through technology, concerns about privacy and the legacy of their digital trail will exist. A critical understanding of the consequences of online information behavior needs to be embedded in any information literacy program in the twenty-first century so that today's digital youth can grow up to a world where the promise of open, diverse, and accessible information remains.

REFERENCES

Agosto, D. E. 2002. "A Model of Young People's Decision-Making in Using the Web." *Library and Information Science Research* 24 (4): 311–341.

Agosto, D. E., and S. Hughes-Hassell. 2005. "People, Places, and Questions: An Investigation of the Everyday Life Information-Seeking Behaviors of Urban Young Adults." *Library and Information Science Research* 27 (2): 141–163.

Agosto, D. E., and S. Hughes-Hassell. 2006. "Toward a Model of the Everyday Life Information-Seeking Needs of Urban Teens, Part 1: Theoretical Model." *Journal of the American Society for Information Science and Technology* 57 (10): 1394–1403.

American Association of School Librarians. 1998. *Information Power.* Chicago: American Library Association.

American Association of School Librarians. 2007. *Standards for the Twentieth Century Learner.* Chicago: American Library Association. Accessed July 24, 2011, http://www.ala.org/aasl/guidelinesandstandards/learningstandards/standards.

American Library Association. 1989. *Presidential Committee on Information Literacy. Final Report.* Chicago: American Library Association. Accessed July 24, 2011, http://www.ala.org/ala/mgrps/divs/acrl/publications/whitepapers/presidential.cfm.

Anderson, L.W., and D. R. Krathwohl, eds. 2001. *A Taxonomy for Learning, Teaching, and Assessing: A Revision of Bloom's Taxonomy of Educational Objectives.* Abridged edition. New York: Addison Wesley Longman.

Bilal, D. 2000. "Children's Use of the Yahooligans! Web Search Engine: 1. Cognitive, Physical and Affective Behaviors on Fact-Based Search Tasks." *Journal of the American Society for Information Science* 51 (7): 646–665.

Bilal, D., and J. Kirby. 2001. "Factors Influencing Children's and Adults' Information Seeking on the Web: Results of Two Studies." *Proceedings of the 64th ASIST Annual Meeting, November 4–8, 2001, Washington, DC,* 126–140. Medford, NJ: Information Today, Inc.

Bilal, D., and J. Kirby. 2002. "Differences and Similarities in Information Seeking: Children and Adults as Web Users." *Information Processing and Management* 38 (5): 649–670.

Bowler, L. 2009. "Adolescent Metacognitive Knowledge during the Information Search Process." *Proceedings of the American Society for Information Science and Technology* 46 (1): 1–4.

Bowler, L. 2010a. "The Self-Regulation of Curiosity and Interest during the Information Search Process of Adolescent Students." *Journal of the American Society for Information Science and Technology* 61 (7): 1332–1344.

Bowler, L. 2010b. "Talk as a Metacognitive Strategy during the Information Search Process of Adolescents." *Information Research* 15 (4), paper 449. Retrieved July 24, 2011, from http://InformationR.net/ir/15-4/paper449.html.

Bowler, L. 2010c. "A Taxonomy of Adolescent Metacognitive Knowledge during the Information Search Process." Library and Information Science Research 32 (1): 27–42.

Branch, J. 2003. "Instructional Intervention Is the Key: Supporting Adolescent Information Seeking." *School Libraries Worldwide* 9 (2): 47–61.

Bruce, C. 2000a. "Information Literacy Programs and Research: An International Review." *The Australian Library Journal* 49 (3): 209–218.

Bruce, C. 2000b. "Information Literacy Research: Dimensions of the Emerging Collective Consciousness." *Australian Academic and Research Libraries* 31 (2): 91–109.

Chen, S-H. L. 2003. "Searching the Online Catalog and the World Wide Web." *Journal of Educational Media and Library Sciences* 41 (1): 29–43.

Chung, J. S., and D. Neuman. 2007. "High School Students Information Seeking and Use for Class Projects." *Journal of the American Society for Information Science and Technology* 58 (10): 1503–1517.

Centre for Information Behaviour and the Evaluation of Research (CIBER). 2008. *Information Behavior of the Researcher of the Future: A CIBER Briefing Paper.* Retrieved January 21, 2008, from http://www.ucl.ac.uk/slais/research/ciber/downloads/.

Cooper, L. Z. 2002. "A Case Study of Information Seeking Behavior in 7-Year-Old Children in a Semistructured Situation." *Journal of the American Society for Information Science and Technology* 53 (11): 904–922.

Dervin, B., and M. Nilan. 1986. "Information Needs and Uses." *Annual Review of Information Science and Technology (ARIST)* 21: 3–25.

Dresang, E. 2005. "The Information-Seeking Behavior of Youth in the Digital Environment." *Library Trends* 54 (2): 187–196.

Eisenberg, M., and R. Berkowitz. 1990. *Information Problem Solving: The Big Six Skills Approach to Library and Information Skills Instruction.* Norwood, NJ: Ablex.

Fidel, R., R. K. Davies, M. H. Douglass, J. K. Holder, C. J. Hopkins, E. J. Kushner, et al. 1999. "A Visit to the Information Mall: Web Searching Behavior of the High School Students." *Journal of the American Society for Information Science* 50 (1): 24–37.

Foster, G., E., Sawicki, H. Schaeffer, and V. Zelinski. 2002. *I Think, Therefore I Learn!* Markham, Ontario: Pembroke Publishers.

Harada, V., and A. Tepe. 1998. "Pathways to Knowledge." *Teacher Librarian* 26 (2): 9—15.

Herring, J. 1996. *Teaching Information Skills in Schools.* London, England: Library Association Publishing.

Hirsh, S. G. 1996. *The Effect of Domain Knowledge on Elementary School Children's Information Retrieval Behavior on an Automated Library Catalog.* Unpublished doctoral dissertation. University of California, Los Angeles.

Hirsh, S. G. 1997. "How Do Children Find Information on Different Types of Tasks? Children's Use of the Science Library Catalog." *Library Trends* 45: 725–745.

Hutchins, E. 1995. *Cognition in the Wild.* Cambridge, MA: MIT Press.

Irving, A. 1985. *Study and Research Skills across the Curriculum*. London: Heinemann.

Jenkins, H., K. Clinton, R. Purushotma, A. J. Robinson, and M. Weigel. 2006. "Confronting the Challenges of Participatory Culture: Media Education for the 21st century." An Occasional Paper written for the MacArthur Foundation. Retrieved July 24, 2011, from http://digital-learning.macfound.org/atf/cf/%7B7E45C7E0-A3E0-4B89-AC9C-E807E1B0AE4E%7D/ JENKINS_WHITE_PAPER.PDF.

Kuhlthau, C. C. 1988a. "Developing a Model of the Library Search Process: Cognitive and Affective Aspects." *RQ* 28 (2): 232–242.

Kuhlthau, C. C. 1988b. "Meeting the Information Needs of Children and Young Adults: Basing Library Media Programs on Developmental States." *Journal of Youth Services in Libraries* 2 (1): 51–57.

Kuhlthau, C. C. 1991. "Inside the Search Process: Information Seeking from the User's Perspective." *Journal of the American Society for Information Science* 42 (5): 361–371.

Kuhlthau, C. C. 1993. "Implementing a Process Approach to Information Skills: A Study Identifying Indicators of Success in Library Media Programs." *School Library Media Quarterly* 22 (1): 11–18.

Kuhlthau, C. C. 1994. "Students and the Information Search Process: Zones of Intervention for Librarians." *Advances in Librarianship* 18: 57–72.

Kuhlthau, C. C. 2004. *Seeking Meaning*. Second edition. Westport, CT: Libraries Unlimited.

Large, A., and J. Beheshti. 2000. "The Web as a Classroom Resource: Reactions from the Users." *Journal of the American Society for Information Science and Technology* 51 (12): 1069–1080.

Lawless, K. A., R. Mills, and S. W. Brown. 2002. "Children's Hypertext Navigation Strategies." *Journal of Research on Technology in Education* 3 (3): 274–284.

Losey, B. 2007. *The Handy 5: Planning and Assessing Integrated Information Skills Instruction*. Second Edition. Lanham, Maryland: The Scarecrow Press.

Marland, M., ed. 1981. *Information Skills in the Secondary Curriculum*. London: Methuen Educational (Schools Council Curriculum Bulletin 9).

McGregor, J., and D. Streitenberger. 1998. "Do Scribes Learn? Copying and Information Use." *School Library Media Quarterly Online*, 1. Retrieved July 24, 2011, from http://www.webcitation.org/5JAOMNC4w.

Moore, P. 2000. "Primary School Children's Interaction with Library Media." *Teacher Librarian* 27 (3): 7–11.

Neilsen, J. 2005. *Usability of Websites for Teenagers*. Retrieved July 24, 2011, from http://www.useit.com/alertbox/teenagers.html.

Nesset, V. 2007. "Grade-Three Students' Use of Print and Electronic Resources." In C. Arsenault and K. Dalkir (Eds.), *Information Sharing in a Fragmented World: Crossing Boundaries: Proceedings of the Canadian Association for Information Science (CAIS)*. May 10–12, 2007, Montreal, QC.

Nesset, V. 2009. *The Information-Seeking Behaviour of Grade-Three Students in the Context of a Class Project*. Unpublished Dissertation. McGill University, Montreal, Quebec, Canada.

Nesset, V. 2011. "Following the Signs: Children's Use of Visual Cues for Facilitating Website Evaluation." *Proceedings of the Human Computer Interaction International 2011 Conference*, July 11–14, 2011, Orlando, FL. New York: Springer, 599–606.

Pariser, E. 2011. *The Filter Bubble: What the Internet is Hiding from You*. New York: Penguin Press.

Revelle, G., A. Druin, M. Platner, S. Weng, B. Bederson, J. P. Hourcade, and L. Sherman. 2002. "Young Children's Search Strategies and Construction of Search Queries." *Journal of Science Education and Technology* 11 (1): 48–57.

Schacter, J., G. Chung, and A. Dorr. 1998. "Children's Internet Searching on Complex Problems: Performance and Process Analysis." *Journal of the American Society for Information Science* 49 (9): 840–849.

Shapiro, J. J., and S. K. Hughes. 1996. "Information Literacy as a Liberal Art." *Educom Review* 31: 2. Retrieved July 24, 2011, from http://net.educause.edu/apps/er/review/reviewArticles/ 31231.html.

Shenton, A., and P. Dixon. 2003. "Just What Do They Want? What Do They Need? A Study of the Informational Needs of Children." *Children and Libraries* 1 (2): 36–42.

Slone, D. 2003. "Internet Search Approaches: The Influence of Age, Search Goals, and Experience." *Library and Information Science Research* 25 (4): 403–418.

Stripling, B. K., and J. M. Pitts. 1988. *Brainstorms and Blueprints: Teaching Library Research as a Thinking Process.* Englewood, CO: Libraries Unlimited.

Todd, R. 1998. "WWW, Critical Literacies and Learning Outcomes." *Teacher Librarian* 76 (2): 16–21.

Todd, R. 2003. "Adolescents of the Information Age: Patterns of Information Seeking and Use, and Implications for Information Professionals." *School Libraries Worldwide* 9 (2): 27–46.

UNESCO. 2011. *Media and Information Literacy.* Retrieved July 22, 2011 from http://portal. unesco.org/ci/en/ev.php-URL_ID=15886&URL_DO=DO_TOPIC&URL_SECTION=201. html#topPage.

Valenza, J. K. 2006. "They Might Be Gurus." *Teacher Librarian* 34 (1): 18–26.

Walter, V. A. 1994. "The Information Needs of Children." *Advances in Librarianship* 18: 111–129.

Watson, J. S. 1998. "'If You Don't Have It, You Can't Find It.' A Closer Look at Students' Perceptions of Using Technology." *Journal of the American Society for Information Science* 49 (11): 1024–1036.

Williamson, K., and J. H. McGregor. 2006. "Information Use and Secondary School Students: A Model for Understanding Plagiarism." *Information Research* 12 (1), paper 288. Retrieved July 24, 2011, from http://informationr.net/ir/12-1/paper288.html.

Williamson, K., J. McGregor, A. Archibald, and J. Sullivan. 2007. "Information Seeking and Use by Secondary Students: The Link between Good Practice and the Avoidance of Plagiarism." *School Library Media Research* 10, Retrieved July 24, 2011, from http://www.ala.org/ala/mgrps/divs/aasl/aaslpubsandjournals/slmrb/slmrcontents/volume10/williamson_informationseeking.cfm.

Wray, D., and M. Lewis. 1995. "Extending Interactions with Non-Fiction Texts: An EXIT into Understanding." *Reading* 29 (1): 2–9.

Yucht, A. 1997. *Flip It! An Information Skills Strategy for Student Researchers.* Worthington, OH: Linworth.

Chapter Four

Everyday Life Information Behavior of Young People

June Abbas and Denise E. Agosto

What is the everyday life information behavior of young people? What types of information needs do young people have in their daily lives and how do they resolve these needs? No doubt you have read popular media accounts, or witnessed for yourself, how young people are connected 24/7 through the use of different information and communication technologies (ICTs) such as the Internet and social network sites or cell phones, constantly sending and receiving text messages from their cell phones or other mobile devices, surfing the Web, or continuously checking and updating their status on their social network page. Just ask any parent with teens or tweens about their monthly phone bill. In fact, a recent study by the Pew Internet Research Center supports this perception. Lenhart and colleagues found that texting using a cell phone is the preferred channel of communication for young people between the ages of 12 and 17. For example, 75 percent of 12- to 17-year-olds own cell phones, with 88 percent of these teens being text messengers. Half of the teens sent 50 or more texts a day, or approximately 1,500 per month, and one in three sent more than 100 per day, or more than 3,000 per month (Lenhart, Ling, Campbell, and Purcell 2010, 2). Lenhart and colleagues also point out that while many teens are avid texters, a significant minority are not. One-fifth of teen texters send and receive only 1 to 10 texts a day, or 30 to 300 per month (3).

Young people are going online more, not just for entertainment but to find information and to create and share content. The Internet has become the resource of choice for many young people as they locate information for educational purposes, look for sources for personal reasons, and surf for recreational purposes (Lenhart, Simon, and Graziano 2001; Abbas, Kimball,

D'Elia and Bishop 2007a, 2007b). Large (2005) states, "[T]he Web should not be seen as an information source in itself but more of a gateway to millions of information sources from millions of information providers, most of which are not intended specifically for children, some of which might be considered unsuitable for them" (1069).

Lenhart, Purcell, Smith, and Zickuhr (2010) note that the Internet is nearly ubiquitous among teens and young adults. Since 2001, American young people have remained the most likely population to go online with 93 percent of teens aged 12 to 17 online, and 93 percent of young adults aged 18 to 29. Their study also found that 62 percent of teens get news about current events and politics online, and 48 percent have bought items online like books, clothes, or music. Thirty-one percent of online teens look for health, dieting, or physical fitness–related information online and 17 percent say they search online for information on sensitive health topics (4). Ito et al. (2008) state that young people are " 'always on,' in constant contact with their friends via texting, instant messaging, mobile phones, and Internet connections. This continuous presence requires ongoing maintenance and negotiation, through private communications like instant messaging or mobile phones, as well as in public ways through social network sites such as MySpace and Facebook" (1).

Dinet et al. (2003) report that young people seek information online for the following reasons: rapidity of access, the quantity of information, recency, the aesthetics of information, the accuracy and number of examples, the superiority of the Web to give information, and the possibility of learning to search for information by using the Web. Young people are also excited by the larger variety of information they can find online (Fidel et al. 1999; Large and Beheshti 2000). Being able to move beyond parental limits and to assert their autonomy also appeals to young people (Ling 2005). Boyd (2008) notes that youth enjoy actively participating in unregulated public spaces when they go online.

In terms of social network use, U.S. teens are particularly heavy users of social network sites. As of September 2009, 73 percent of online teens were social network users, as opposed to just 47 percent of online adults (Lenhart, Ling, Campbell, and Purcell 2010, 17). U.S. teens favor Facebook as the social network of choice, although there does seem to be some teen movement away from Facebook toward smaller, more specialized sites (Van Grove 2010). What is *little* known is the purposes these technologies serve for young people in supporting their everyday lives. Are teens using texting purely for communication and interaction with their friends and family, or are there other information-driven purposes at play? What is the role of the Internet, social networking sites, and ICTs in the everyday life information behaviors of young people?

Another popular perception that is very prevalent in the media and scholarly literature is that of the *digital native* who is characterized as being very technology savvy, able to multitask effectively; because such "natives" grew up using computers and the Internet, technology is an essential aspect of their everyday lives (Abram 2007; Frand 2000; Hoffman, Novak, and Venkatesh 2004; Lorenzetti 2007; Palfrey and Glasser 2008; Prensky 2001). Digital natives, a term coined by Prensky (2001), includes Millennials (individuals born between 1979 and 1994) and Gen Y or the Google generation (1993 to present). They have also been labeled Generation M to represent the perception that they are multimedia and multitasked and technologically addicted (Rideout, Foehr, and Roberts 2010; Roberts and Foehr 2008), or Generation@ referencing their lifestyles of buying, living, and playing online as staples of their lives (Hempel 2005). Regardless of the label we give them, these young people, according to the digital native supporters, are said to be "different to all generations before [them] because they think, behave, and learn differently as a result of continuous, pervasive exposure to modern technology" (Bennett and Maton 2010). They are also said to have a greater level of comfort using technology and more fluent skills than members of previous generations (e.g., Brown 2000; Costello, Lenholt, and Stryker 2004; Harris 2005; Oblinger 2003; Oblinger and Oblinger 2006).

Critics of this popular view of young people as digital natives, however, argue that in reality, the digital native concept is a limited view of what is actually a very complex, multifaceted daily use of technologies for many purposes that is developmentally appropriate for this group of young people (Dresang and Koh 2009; Harris 2011; Selwyn 2009). They also caution that we should not ascribe mythic technology guru abilities to this group of young people simply because they are among the first generation to grow up using computers and ICTs (Harris 2011; Thinyane 2010; Valenza 2007). Valenza (2007) reminds us that LIS research documents young people's feelings of confusion and frustration and less than effective approaches when interacting with information technologies. Bennett and Maton (2010) in their extensive review of the digital native literature conclude that "there is a significant lack of consensus over what effects digital technology is actually having on young people" (322). Furthermore, "it is clear from this recent research that there is significant variation in the ways in which young people use technology, suggesting that rather than being a homogeneous generation, there is a diversity of interests, motivations, and needs" (325).

If we accept these popular views of young people's everyday life information behavior, we really learn very little about the complex nature of the *everyday life information needs* of young people (what causes them to look for information about something and the types of information needs they experience), the sources young people use (or choose not to use) to find information that helps them solve an information need in their everyday life, or the spectrum of behaviors included in their information behaviors (barriers, sharing, contributing, serving as expert). We also do not learn the *motives* that contribute to their preferences for using specific sources, including technologies.

Putting popular perceptions aside, we should ask, "What has research uncovered about the everyday life information behaviors of young people?" Most of what we know about young people's everyday information needs and behavior can be attributed to research from library and information science (LIS), and also from health sciences studies. LIS research has focused on learning about what types of information needs young people experience in everyday contexts, the sources they choose to find information, and the purposes and behaviors that characterize their information-seeking behavior. Everyday life information seeking studies, or ELIS studies, have concentrated specifically on everyday life information behaviors of both adults and young people, rather than the needs and behaviors related to work, school, or academically based information seeking, though these often intersect with ELIS activities (Savolainen 1995; Agosto and Hughes-Hassell 2005). Additionally, research from communication, media studies, and education can also provide further understanding of the everyday life information behavior of young people. Recent work from communication studies and education (new media literacies) has revealed additional dimensions of youth everyday life information behavior that adds to the multifaceted picture we are creating and addresses some of the questions about why young people choose to participate in new media ecologies.

This chapter presents a review of the research related to the everyday life information behavior of young people, focusing primarily on tweens' (ages 9–12) and teens' (ages 13–18) everyday life information behavior. Only one everyday life information behavior study to date has included young children (ages 4–8) (Shenton and Dixon 2003, 2005, 2007). Research from communication studies and education (new media literacies) will also be included, as relevant, to help form a multifaceted, developmentally appropriate view of young people's everyday life information behavior. Research on young people's information seeking related to formulation of search strategies and obstacles encountered while searching, interface design, extent of use of specific technologies (ICTs, the Web, etc.), while relevant to the larger model of information behavior of young people, will not be included in this chapter. The chapter concludes with a discussion of further directions of research related to young people's ELIS.

EVERYDAY LIFE INFORMATION SEEKING (ELIS)

ELIS Defined

The Everyday Life Information Seeking (ELIS) framework as defined by Savolainen serves as the basis for much ELIS research. Savolainen proposed the framework as a means to address some of the shortcomings he saw in Dervin's sense-making model related to socio-cultural influences, but also to give legitimacy to research related to "nonwork" information seeking (Savolainen 1995, 260–261). In the ELIS framework, Savolainen introduced two concepts, "way of life" and "mastery of life," to help describe an individual's daily life information activities and how choices are made. Way of life refers to the "order of things," with "things" being the activities that take place in our daily lives, and "order" as the preference we ascribe to these things or activities (262). The second construct, "mastery of life," refers to an individual's manner of dealing with problem solving. Mastery of life, according to Savolainen, is the "caring activity" one takes to maintain a meaningful order of things in one's life. Mastery of life is "the general preparedness to approach everyday problems in certain ways in accordance with one's values" (264). An individual's mastery of life behavior may be either active or passive, meaning they actively address a problem when it arises or they choose to just let it pass by. Individuals develop their own mastery of life orientations through cultural and social experiences. These orientations can be cognitive or affective ("the degree of rational considerations in problem solving situations"), or optimistic or pessimistic (a person's expectations for solving problems) (265). Further, Savolainen sees the individual habits we form when monitoring daily events and seeking information, as well as the sources or channels we use to find information, as based on values, attitudes, and interests we have learned in socio-cultural contexts (267).

Simply put, everyday life information seeking occurs on a daily basis. Much of the information sought in our daily lives is for non-work-related, non-school-related purposes (Spink and Cole 2001; Agosto and Hughes-Hassell 2005). We seek information either consciously when we have a problem to solve, such as reviewing prices on something we wish to buy, or unconsciously as we scan the newspaper, or read blogs or websites. Savolainen's ELIS framework provides researchers with a means to examine everyday life information seeking, the sources and channels of information we use, and explains the possible orientations or problem-solving strategies we employ to make choices to maintain our way of life.

Everyday Life Information Seeking of Young People

A review of the research on young people's everyday life information seeking unfortunately reveals the paucity of studies in this area. Much of the information-seeking research focused on children and older youth has addressed how they interact with different information retrieval systems including the World Wide Web, the issues they encounter when retrieving information, the cognitive, affective, or developmental factors that affect their information seeking, system factors and usability studies of their use of systems for retrieval, and the processes they take to find information related to imposed information needs (those assigned to them by others, such as teachers): Abbas (2010) provides a more comprehensive review of research in these areas. Studies that focus primarily on the information needs that motivate young people to find information, how they resolve these needs or when they choose not to, the sources and channels they use to find information, and their general everyday life information behaviors are sparse. The role that technology and different ICTs might play within these activities is also an area that has not been fully explored, even though we see an increasing reliance on technology by young people in their everyday lives. Compared to studies of adults' ELIS, little research has focused on young people's everyday life information seeking, with even fewer studies on children below the age of 9 years (though see, for example, Shenton and Dixon 2003, 2005).

It is also important to note that not all studies focused on youth's everyday life information seeking use the ELIS framework. For example, Meyers, Fischer, and Marcoux (2009) employ Dervin's sense-making, Chatman's normative behavior, and Fischer's information grounds as frameworks to explore the everyday life information behaviors of tweens. Shenton and Dixon (2003, 2005) also used Dervin's sense-making as a guide for their study of children, tweens, and teens (ages 4–18). Many of the studies include discussion of adolescent information behavior research as it has informed our understanding of young people's ELIS and information needs. Each study, as will be explained below, has begun to paint a picture of the complex everyday life information activities of young people; however, as this process is so complex, researchers have also identified facets that could extend Savolainen's ELIS or other information seeking models to apply more specifically to the unique information needs and ELIS activities of young people.

Early Studies

The first ELIS studies of young people were undertaken in the early 1990s. Poston-Anderson and Edwards (1993) studied how adolescent girls used information to address life issues. When asked to recall problems or issues they had encountered in the last month, they identified two types of issues: relationships, and education and work (26). The teens in their study also identified informal information sources such as family, friends, and teachers as helpful, and did not think libraries would have the information they needed. The use of similar informal sources for information seeking was also found in a later study by the researchers (Edwards and Poston-Anderson 1996), who talked to adolescent girls about their information seeking related to jobs and education. The researchers found that teens engaged in little or no information seeking, but if they did use an informal source, it was most often their mothers, or to a lesser extent, their fathers. They did not approach friends or more formal sources when seeking this specific type of everyday life information.

Julien's study of adolescents seeking career information identified barriers that young people encounter when engaging in everyday life information seeking. Findings showed that many adolescents had an incomplete understanding of the decisions or questions to ask regarding career information or the decisions they would need to make in the future. The adolescents also felt anxious and overwhelmed and reported that they experienced troubles identifying sources and using information systems, or formulating questions to ask when seeking assistance with their needs (Julien 1999).

Shenton and Dixon conducted the first study that included young children (aged 4 to 8) in their sample of young people. Their study conducted in England with young people aged 4 to 18 explored their information universes, including their information needs and the actions they take in response to them. The overall goal of the study was to learn if young people's self-perceived attitudes and behaviors change over the course of their childhood (Shenton and Dixon 2003, 2005, 2007). Data were gathered from 188 students during 12 focus groups and in 121 individual interviews. Using Dervin's sense-making framework as a guide, participants were asked to recall a time when they needed help and to explain all that they remembered at that instance. Their findings indicate that young people choose informal sources as their preferred source when seeking information, but they also reported not wanting to ask teachers for assistance (Shenton and Dixon 2003, 2007). Shenton and Dixon also reported that young people often do not have their information needs met. They relate barriers that young people encountered. One, they chose to take no action:

- they did not want to expend the energy;
- they thought the materials they needed were not accessible;
- there was a reluctance to admit their need; or
- a fear of a hostile reaction from others.

Or two, they made an unsuccessful attempt to find the information, for example,

- the source was not appropriate to their topic or provided too general information;
- the level of the material was not age appropriate;
- the quality of the material and source was questionable;
- the material was unavailable; or
- their knowledge of the topic was inadequate. (Shenton and Dixon 2007)

Shenton and Dixon also developed a taxonomy of young people's information needs (included in the Taxonomies of Information Needs section later in this chapter).

ELIS and Youth Development

Two studies, one reported in Agosto and Hughes-Hassell (2006a, 2006b) and Hughes-Hassell and Agosto (2007), and the other in Fisher, Marcoux, Meyers, and Landry (2007) and Meyers, Fisher, and Marcoux (2007, 2009), point out the importance of keeping a young person's stage of development and resulting developmental needs in mind when assessing their everyday life information needs and seeking behaviors. According to Agosto and Hughes-Hassell (2006a) "cognitive, emotional, and physical aspects of the maturation process make growing up a difficult process for almost any teenager" (1394). Teens require different types of information (factual information, practical information, philosophical information) to help make this process smoother. Tweens (aged 9 to 13) also are undergoing significant physical, emotional, and cognitive development. They are transitioning from elementary to middle to high school. They are becoming more independent of parents, and peer relationships are of higher importance to them. Little is known about how these life changes influence their information needs and seeking behaviors, especially those outside of school-life contexts (Fisher, Marcoux, Meyers, and Landry 2007).

Agosto and Hughes-Hassell conducted the first study of urban teens' everyday life information seeking. Urban teens may experience different daily life challenges than teens or tweens living in nonurban contexts. Agosto and Hughes-Hassell state that "many inner-city teens face a harsh reality of poverty, prejudice, and a lack of strong role models, making this process [the maturation process] even more difficult than for teens living in more advantaged situations" (1394). Using Savolainen's ELIS framework, the researchers worked with 27 teens in an urban U.S. city. Sixteen of the participants were volunteers from a library leadership group, while 11 were members of the local Boys and Girls Club. Data were gathered in two stages. In stage one, four qualitative methods were used: (1) written surveys including demographic and computer use questions, (2) audio journals that recorded the kinds of issues encountered by the youth each day, as well as efforts to address their information needs, (3) written activity logs to record questions and sources used to find information, and (4) digital camera tours to record places they went for information. Researchers analyzed the data from the first stage and developed a coding scheme. The second stage involved the young people directly in the data "analysis" process, and researchers used this opportunity to learn more about their perspectives on everyday life information needs and seeking. In the second stage, the initial coding scheme was presented to the study participants during a series of semi-structured group interviews in which participants discussed the scheme, rearranged the codes, and made additions to the scheme. Further data were also gathered related to participants' everyday life information seeking during the interviews. This new data, combined with the new coding scheme, served as a basis for the re-analysis of all of the data.

The findings of this study indicate the complex richness of urban teens' everyday information needs and information-seeking activities. The coding scheme resulted in a list of 28 information needs topics. The researchers also used these topics to construct both an empirical and theoretical model of urban teens' ELIS topics. The typology and seven elements of the model are listed in the section below on Typologies of Information Needs. Their findings also showed the sources that urban teens use to find information, including for example, *people sources* (friends and family or school employees), *communication media* (face-to-face or telephone or computer), and *media sources* (computer, TV, books, etc.). For example, urban teens referred to human information sources predominantly when seeking everyday life information. This preference for consulting informal, human sources first is a common finding of other ELIS studies across age and socioeconomic divisions (e.g., Savolainen 2004; Shenton and Dixon 2003). The findings also show that urban teens tended to experience the same types of information needs previous researchers found with more advantaged, non-minority teens (Agosto and Hughes-Hassell 2006b, 1425).

The resulting theoretical model illustrates that the "essence of urban teens' ELIS is the gathering and processing of information to facilitate the multifaceted teen-to-adult maturation process" (Agosto and Hughes-Hassell 2006a, 1401) and that further studies of youth information seeking should be tied to developmental theory and to an understanding of the developmental reasons *why* teens engage in everyday life information behaviors.

Fisher, Meyers, Marcoux, and Landry conducted their study with urban tweens (aged 9 to 13). Guided by Dervin's sense-making, Chatman's normative behavior, and Fisher's information grounds, the researchers gathered data from 34 tweens using scenario-based focus groups and interviews conducted during "Tween Days." The goals of the study were to understand more about situations, settings, and sources Millennials or Gen Y tweens use to seek information and what factors support or hinder tween everyday life information seeking. They further hypothesized that tweens would engage in a variety of media-rich interpersonal information seeking using any available synchronous and asynchronous media (Meyers, Fisher, and Marcoux 2009).

The researchers also developed an innovative new methodology for gathering the data called the Tween Day. The Tween Day was a "play-date" that included social interaction, creative play, and multiple data collection methods that took place on one day, over a five-hour period. Focus groups, individual interviews, and a lab-based WebQuest activity enabled researchers to interact directly with the tweens and to gather data using multiple methods. Over the course of the study, Tween Days were conducted at three different locations: a university in the city, a faith-based ministry in a culturally diverse urban neighborhood, and an elementary school in a middle-class suburb (Meyers, Fisher, and Marcoux 2007).

The findings of their research emphasize yet another dimension of ELIS information behavior, the influence that social and affective factors have on both the process and outcomes of tween everyday information needs and seeking. Research questions 1 to 3 and 7, along with the findings of each, are briefly summarized here. Due to space constraints, research questions 4 to 6 and 8 are not included as they focus on how tweens manage their information and their criteria for assessing and sharing information. (See Fisher, Marcoux, Meyers, and Landry 2007; Meyers, Fisher, and Marcoux 2009.)

(RQ1): *What types of ELIS do tweens perceive themselves as needing?*

- Tweens reported needing information to support concrete, immediate, or short-term goals or activities.
- Tweens stressed the need to share and receive private or secret information.
- The urban ministry tweens differed in their concerns, reporting information related more to socioeconomic realities of living in a low-economic urban environment (e.g., dealing with bullies, dangerous strangers, drug and alcohol users, and personal safety) (Meyers, Fisher, and Marcoux 2009, 315). This type of information need confirms findings from Agosto and Hughes-Hassell's urban teens.

(RQ2): *How do tweens seek everyday information?*

- Interpersonal sources were very important and were often enhanced by telephones, instant messaging (IM), and email. Tweens might use multiple sources, but interpersonal sources such as asking parents or family or friends were the primary sources used.
- The Internet was used by those who had access, though perception of its utility varied across the three groups.

- Print sources were less important than electronic and interpersonal sources.

(RQ3): *What barriers do tweens encounter in seeking and using information?*

- Barriers perceived by tweens affected the types of questions they would ask.
- Tweens' age and maturity were barriers to their information seeking.
- Concerns for tweens' safety limited sources they could use to seek information.
- Tweens' mobility and access to information sources were reliant on adult transportation.
- Adult authority limited sources tweens could access for information.
- Oversight or monitoring by adults undermined tweens' comfort levels in sharing information.
- Not all tweens had the same level of access to computers, the Internet, or ICTs.
- Schedules and daily structure limited time tweens could spend seeking information.
- Social costs and perceptions such as feelings of embarrassment and loss of esteem were barriers to what questions they felt comfortable asking (Meyers, Fisher, and Marcoux 2009, 319–321).

(RQ7): *What are the roles of information grounds in tweens' lives?*

- Tweens reported a variety of places where they share information, usually with their peers. The most common were school (cafeteria, hallways, playground, and bus), shopping malls, athletic fields, parks, home, and their neighborhoods. The least common places were churches, libraries, restaurants, convenience stores, and public transit.
- There were important differences among the three sample populations. For example, the suburban tweens felt comfortable in their neighborhoods, while the urban ministry tweens were concerned with personal safety in some areas of their neighborhoods. The university urban/suburban tweens did not socialize in their neighborhoods except for tweens they knew from school (Meyers, Fisher, and Marcoux 2009, 328–330).

Fisher, Meyers, and Marcoux proposed the following five principles as a framework for information service to this age group, though these principles should also be kept in mind more generally in future ELIS research.

1. *Information seeking is a natural and necessary part of tweens' physical, social, and intellectual growth.* Tweens are naturally and insatiably curious, and they are constantly seeking information not for academic purposes but as an aid in their transition to young adulthood.
2. *All aspects of information behavior have social and affective nuances.* In most information-seeking incidents, informal human sources played important roles in the search process.
3. *Information literacy is developed and honed in informal social settings as well as in tandem with formal scholastic venues.* Tweens explore different information sources and often develop ideas about trust and authority through trial and error using these sources.
4. *Trust (cognitive authority and social costs) is a critical determinant of information seeking by tweens.* Tweens learn trust and authority through experimenting with different interpersonal sources. Tweens may sacrifice information quality to reduce their own social costs (embarrassment or loss of social status).
5. *Informal social settings provide key opportunities for exchange of information.* Tweens have a rich set of strategies for sharing information, most of which include informal information spaces (Meyers, Fisher, and Marcoux 2009, 331–336).

ELIS and Health-Related Information

Young people are using the Internet to locate information on health-related issues (Zhao 2009). Fox and Jones (2009) found that 28 percent of young people (aged 12 to 17) have used the Internet to look for health-related information. According to Gasser, Cortesi, Malik, and Lee (in press) "teenagers' desire for autonomy from authoritative figures (e.g., parents, etc.) and their preference for alternative sources of information may be contributing to the popularity of online health information" (35). Studies related to young people's tendency to search for health information are becoming more prevalent in the health sciences literature.

However, as Burek-Pierce (2007) notes, efforts to understand young people's acquisition of health-related information remain little explored by LIS researchers. The motivation for the health science studies is to develop policies for communicating and disseminating health information to youth more effectively, not, unfortunately, to understand more about why and how young people search for online health information. In her review of health science, nursing, and public health literature, Burek-Pierce outlines specific conclusions related to LIS concerns: (1) adolescents may need specialized types of information (for example information related to special populations concerns, e.g., violence in intimate relationships, or sexual relationships of disabled teens); (2) teens may possess information deficits or not understand what information is needed or available; and (3) teens experience internal and external barriers to their efforts to obtain sexual health information, for example, filters installed on computers, confidentiality, and privacy concerns (74–78).

Findings of health science research, while not focusing on specific information-seeking activities or using an information science framework, provide "valuable perspectives on young adults' needs for and efforts to find information about their developing bodies and physical relationships, . . . [the literature] raises questions about adolescents' abilities to obtain and evaluate appropriate information sources" (64).

A related psycho-socio area, young people's sexual orientation, has previously not been addressed in the everyday life information seeking research. Mehra and Braquet (2007), citing *The New Gay Teenager* (Savin-Williams 2005), note that "contemporary youngsters are coming out at a much younger age" (93). The "coming-out process" for "queer" youth is, according to Mehra and Braquet, "the intersection of multiple factors associated with the individual, other people, and context that determines the information seeking processes" (102). These factors include *thought-related* factors, such as perceptions or judgments, *behavior-related factors*, including communication, language, and social interaction skills; and *demographic factors*, including sex, age, gender, sexual orientation, race, or ethnicity (102). Their study of 21 "queer" youth from a Southern city in the United States who had experience with coming out presents a holistic approach that recognizes the cognitive, affective, and physical dimensions of everyday life information seeking of this understudied group. Using qualitative methods including in-depth interviews and informal discussions, the researchers gathered detailed information about youths' everyday life information behaviors during their experiences of coming out. The findings point out the importance of (1) types of information sources and their role in the different stages of coming out; (2) affective dimensions of information-seeking behaviors such as thoughts, feelings, and actions; and (3) ideal information support services sought during the stages. Space does not permit including all of the findings of this study so a few main highlights are summarized briefly.

1. *Sources varied with the stage of coming out.* For example, in the first stage (self-recognition as queer) sources used included message boards and chat rooms to provide them with firsthand accounts from others who had come out. Coming out stories from bookstores or websites gave more understanding about what to expect and advice on how to come out. In the second stage (disclosure to other queers), sources sought included listings of local groups or clubs, to provide a way to meet other "queers" in person. Student organizations helped them make connections on campus and raise awareness on campus. In the third stage (disclosure to family/friends), sources became less informal. Professional associations or reputable organizations were

sought to provide them with more formal and institutional support for explaining their life choice to family and friends. In the fourth stage (positive
self-identification), they sought out advocacy groups, films, and music with
"queer" themes and publications written for "queers" to learn more about
queer culture. In the final stage (integration and acceptance), they sought
self-help books, queer travel websites, queer legal websites, as well as websites with "anti-queer" attitudes to learn more about relationships and coping,
and to find gay-friendly venues to visit. Legal websites were used to find
information on legal equality issues (Mehra and Braquet 2007, 110–115).

2. *The affective dimensions of information seeking also varied with the
stage of coming out.* For example, those in the first stage reported feelings of
confusion, denial, and anxiety. Their actions included repressing their feelings. In the second stage, they reported feelings of partial acceptance of self
as "queer," and they began actively seeking local and dispersed information
and social support. In the third stage, they reported a fear of being rejected or
loss of closeness. They also began sharing knowledge of what it meant to be
queer with family and friends. In the fourth stage, they had feelings of pride,
satisfaction, or fulfillment. They sought external supportive environments
and positive relationships with other "queer" people. In the final stage, they
reported feelings of non-defensiveness about their sexual orientation and
sought out other "queer" couples for support (Mehra and Braquet 2007,
116–120).

Mehra and Braquet's study emphasizes the importance of affective variables as perhaps leading factors for *why* young people in the various stages of
coming out seek specific kinds of information and the sources they find most
useful. While their findings illustrate the need to extend the ELIS model
further to include affective variables, it also validates Agosto and Hughes-
Hassell's theoretical model of the seven selves of young people's ELIS behaviors and their emphasis on including developmental factors of young
people when studying their ELIS. This study also demonstrated the role that
different sources, both interpersonal and technological, play in young people's ELIS. Young "queer" individuals preferred a mix of interpersonal and
technological sources while in the earliest stages of coming out, and turned to
formal and technology sources in the middle and later stages.

Lu (2010) extends previous research's premise of young people's ELIS
behaviors and seeking as a way to solve problems that arise in their daily
lives to a more psycho-socio view of ELIS as a mechanism for coping. Lu's
study of fifth- and sixth-grade students' (aged 11 to 12) use of information
seeking to cope with life's everyday stressors or problems revealed that
young people seek information for problem solving but also to escape their
problems and to find a means of transitioning. Lu (2010) used semi-structured, open-ended surveys based on Sorensen's (1993) journaling questionnaire designed to elicit participants' daily worries and to find out how they

coped with the worries. Data about their reasons for seeking information (or not seeking information) to cope with daily life problems were gathered from 641 urban tweens in Taiwan. The study also examined whether or not gender and age influence tweens' information seeking. Findings showed that boys were slightly more likely to look for information (62 percent) than girls (59 percent). The sixth graders were also more likely to seek information (67 percent) than the fifth graders (50 percent) (81).

Lu also identified six factors that motivated young people to seek information: *mood changing* (to change emotional state or attitude), *problem solving* (actively seeking a solution to the problem), *escape* (to disengage or distract themselves), *helplessness* (expressions of negative emotions), *convenient access* (information was easy to find, access), and *transition* (to take a break before facing the problem). Gender and age were factors related to why tweens sought information. For example, more boys sought information because it was convenient to access, but a higher percentage of girls sought information to escape. Moreover, the findings showed that more sixth graders sought information as a way to solve problems, with fifth graders seeking information because of a sense of helplessness (81–83).

Reasons for *not* seeking information included information uselessness, personal attitudes, social constraints, preference for another distraction, preference for social support, and preference to rely on self (83). Tweens more frequently reported information uselessness as their reason for not seeking information, followed by personal attitudes and social constraints. Lu believes that this finding shows that many students have a negative perception of information and information seeking.

Lu's study extends Savolainen's ELIS model in that it also showed that young people who are seeking information for coping are not always seeking information in order to solve problems. In fact, of those that sought information (62 percent), only 16 percent said they were seeking information to solve a problem. Therefore, Lu notes, "in coping with daily-life issues, information seeking serves a much more complicated and sophisticated role than was previously understood" (85).

Pleasure Reading as ELIS

Another area of youth everyday life information research that is beginning to gain some traction is the role that pleasure reading plays in the everyday life information seeking of young people. According to Faulkner (2002) and Eyre (2003), pleasure reading can play an important role in preparing young people for adult roles in society. Howard's (2011) study of 68 Canadian youth aged 12 to 15 found that pleasure reading served three broad functions: (1) it enhanced academic performance, (2) it provided social engagement, and (3) it aided personal development. Howard also posits that teens, like adults, unconsciously use pleasure reading as a means of everyday life information seeking. Further, through pleasure reading teens fill developmental needs related to establishing mature relationships, personal values, cultural identity, aesthetic preferences, and developing a sense of social consciousness and empathy. Personal reasons reported include entertainment, escape from routine lives, relaxation, imagination enhancement, and personal reassurance.

Typologies of Information Needs

An important dimension of studying the everyday life information seeking of young people is to identify the motivating factor(s) or types of information needs that they experience. Several of the studies of young people's ELIS have resulted in typologies of information needs (Minudri 1974; Latrobe and Havener 1997; Shenton and Dixon 2003; Agosto and Hughes-Hassell 2006a, 2006b), as well as lists of the sources and channels young people use to find information for various purposes (Agosto and Hughes-Hassell 2006a, 2006b).

For example, Minudri (1974) identified five areas of information needs of teens: (1) school and curricular needs, (2) recreational needs, (3) personal development needs, (4) vocational and career information needs, and (5) accomplishment skills needs. Latrobe and Havener (1997), in their study of 18 high school honors students, identified six types of needs teens experienced in their daily activities: (1) course-related, (2) current lifestyles, (3) future plans, (4) relationships with others, (5) health, and (6) general information.

Shenton and Dixon's study of 188 young people between the ages of 4 and 18 identified thirteen main types of information needs: (1) advice, (2) response to problems, (3) personal information, (4) affective support, (5) empathetic support, (6) support for skill development, (7) school-related subject information, (8) interest-driven information, (9) consumer information, (10) self-development information, (11) preparatory information, (12) reinterpretations and supplementations of information, and (13) verificational information. All but four of the types (consumer information, self-development information, preparatory information, and verificational information) related to children (aged 4 to 8).

Upon comparison of the typologies, at this point it is evident that many of them contain overlapping categories (for example, school and curricular-related needs, recreational or interest-driven needs, personal development, relationships with others, or self-development needs). Agosto and Hughes-Hassell (2006a, 2006b) also developed a typology of urban teens' information needs topics for which teens either routinely searched for information, or chose not to search for information. Their typology included 28 information needs topics: (1) daily life routine, (2) social activities, (3) creative performance, (4) academics, (5) personal finances, (6) current events, (7) goods and services, (8) emotional health, (9) friend/peer/romantic relationships, (10) popular culture, (11) familial relationships, (12) fashion, (13) college, (14) health, (15) physical safety, (16) self-image, (17) job responsibilities, (18) social/legal norms, (19) philosophical concerns, (20) creative consumption, (21) career, (22) school culture, (23) sexual safety, (24) sexual identity, (25) religious practice, (26) civic duty, (27) heritage/cultural identity, and (28) self-actualization. The researchers applied their typology to Havighurst's developmental tasks of adolescence typology (1972) in order to develop a theoretical model to explain further the reasons the teens either searched for or chose not to search for information about their information needs. Havighurst's typology is often used as a basis for examining adolescent behaviors (e.g., Ek, Remes, and Sovio 2004; Erkut, Szalacha, and Coll 2005; McMillan and Wilhelm 2007; Pfeiffer and Pinquart 2011; Seiffge-Krenke and Gelhaar 2008). Havighurst's typology of 11 tasks comprises:

1. Adjusting to a new physical sense of self
2. Adjusting to new intellectual abilities
3. Adjusting to increased cognitive demands at school
4. Expanding verbal skills
5. Developing a personal sense of identity
6. Establishing adult vocational skills
7. Establishing emotional and psychological independence from his or her parents
8. Developing stable and productive peer relationships
9. Learning to manage his or her sexuality
10. Adopting a personal value system
11. Developing increased impulse control and behavioral maturity (Agosto and Hughes-Hassell 2006a, 1399)

Applying Havighurst's typology to the 28 topics of the teen's information needs, Agosto and Hughes-Hassell (2006a) developed a set of seven "selves" of teen development:

1. *social self:* teens' understanding of themselves and how they fit into the world
2. *emotional self:* teens' inner worlds of feelings and emotions and their reaction to the external world
3. *reflective self:* also related to teens' inner worlds, but refers to their introspection of their self-identity, beliefs, and place in the world

4. *physical self:* teens' focus on their physical presence in the world, such as personal safety, daily life routines, physical health, and job responsibilities
5. *creative self:* teens' aesthetic needs, satisfied by both the creation of creative products and acts, and by the expression of their evaluation or appreciation of another's creative work
6. *cognitive self:* teens' intellectual understanding of the physical world
7. *sexual self:* teens' understanding of sexual issues, including their own sexual identity, sexual health, and sexual practices (Agosto and Hughes-Hassell 2006a, 1399)

REVISITING THE DIGITAL YOUTH + ELIS STUDIES

Everyday life information seeking studies help us begin to form a picture of young people's everyday information lives as complex, multifaceted, and motivated by a multitude of information needs and behaviors. Young people search for information for various purposes (e.g., problem solving, coping, entertainment, self-development). Young people prefer to use informal human sources first, talking with other people such as friends and family, or others going through the same type of life changes. They also use various information and communication technologies (ICTs) to communicate with their friends and family (Agosto and Abbas 2010; Agosto, Abbas, and Naughton 2012). Secondly, they use the Internet to find information related to their various information needs, for entertainment, and to participate in social networks and online communities. What we know *little* about is whether or not they use ICTs (e.g., cell phones, smart phones) and social networking as ways to find everyday life information, or whether or not their facility with and use of ICTs, social networks, and the Internet afford them new *ways* (not just sources or channels) of conducting their everyday life information seeking. In other words, are they using ICTs, social networks, or the Internet for more than communication purposes? Also, are the new media ecologies (e.g., social network sites, fan sites, video/photo sharing sites, interest-driven online communities; Ito et al. 2010) that young people are engaging in creating different types of information needs? As many of the ELIS studies reviewed above took place before the large-scale adoption of ICTs and social networks by young people, the studies' findings include only tweens' and teens' unspecified use of the Internet as a channel for their everyday life information seeking. Young people's use of social networks and ICTs for everyday life information seeking purposes needs further exploration.

Research focused on young people's use of social networking, online community building, and new or media literacies suggests another potential social dimension to add to the ELIS picture—that of the role of *young people as experts* in online communities and social networking sites. (See chapter 6 in this book by Agosto and Abbas for a review of the themes and trends in the research on social networks and young people.) The idea of a young person as expert and the impact it may have on everyday life information seeking activities is yet to be explored. While not specifically related to ELIS behaviors of young people, researchers in communication and media studies have, however, begun to shed some light on the potential connections between a young person who is viewed as an expert in an online community and the social and educational purposes it may serve. For example, Ito et al. (2008, 2010), in a three-year multi-project study funded by the MacArthur Foundation, explored the social and cultural influences of new media practices on today's youth to determine how digital media are changing the way young people learn, play, socialize, and participate in civic life. In this comprehensive ethnographic study of 700 youth, at the University of California, Berkeley, the researchers developed a framework of "genres of participation" that helped to describe different levels of commitment of youth engagement with new media such as social networking sites, YouTube, or chat rooms. According to Ito et al. (2010), "Instead of looking to rigid categories that are defined by formal properties, genres of participation are a way of identifying, in an interpretive way, a set of social, cultural, and technological characteristics that participants recognize as defining a set of practices" (16). Ito and colleagues' genres of participation include the following:

Friendship-driven genres of participation, the dominant and mainstream practices of youth as they go about their day-to-day negotiations with friends and peers in various contexts, such as school, religious groups, school sports, and other local activity groups. Social networking sites like MySpace and Facebook are examples of online contexts for friendship-driven genres of participation.

Interest-driven genres of participation where specialized activities, interests, or niche and marginalized identities are placed first. Interest-driven practices of youth are described by young people as "the domain of the geeks, freaks, musicians, artists, and dorks, who are identified as smart, different, or creative, and who generally exist at the margins of teen social worlds" (13). Interest-driven genres of participation are driven by a young person's interests in hobbies, finding information on specific topics, and in their desire to be seen as an "expert" in their particular interest. Relationships are formed on this premise, rather than for social or interaction interests as seen in the friendship-driven genre.

Ito and colleagues also determined that young people engage with media at different levels of commitment: "(1) they 'hang out' with friends in social spaces such as Facebook and MySpace; (2) they 'mess around' or tinker with digital media, making simple videos, playing online games, or posting pictures in Flickr; and (3) they 'geek out' in online groups that facilitate exploration of their core interests" (Ito et al. 2008, 9). It is within the interest-driven genre of participation ("messing around" and "geeking out") that young people begin to see themselves as experts. "[I]nterest-driven groups also offer a way to gain recognition and reputation as well as an audience for creative work. Although participants do not always value audience feedback as the best mechanism for improving their work, most participants in interest-driven communities are nevertheless motivated by knowing that their work will be viewed by others or by being part of an appreciative community" (Ito et al. 2008, 32).

Luckin et al. (2009), while considering whether the use of social network sites and other Web 2.0 tools encourages student learning, proposed a useful taxonomy of young people's technology use styles as they create, share, collaborate, and serve as experts in online communities. The researchers categorized students' use styles into four groups. Students who acted as "Researchers" mainly read information they found online, without engaging in significant critical analysis. "Collaborators" focused on file sharing, gaming, and communicating online. "Producers" and "Publishers" used online tools for creating original content and for sharing personal experiences through social network sites.

Greenhow and Robelia (2009a, 2009b) have suggested that when using social network sites to engage in educational support, youth acquire and share information with others in their community (asking for instructions or deadlines for assignments; posting resources they found useful; sharing and brainstorming ideas; and commenting on others' works). As these studies illustrate, youth are not just consumers of information but information producers as well. They create new posts and written notes, remix existing content, edit videos and photos, and so on. As noted above, it is within the friendship-drive genre of participation that young people develop and maintain social relationships. Creating, sharing, and commenting on others' social network pages, and hence becoming part of the social online community, are essential social aspects of young people's everyday social and communicative practices, but do they also provide youth with valuable information they need to satisfy their everyday life information needs? Does participating in these new media ecologies also create new information needs for young people?

We might also ask, "What purpose does serving as an 'expert' in an online community provide for young people?" Sharing their expertise may help young people develop a sense of identity within their online community, thereby helping to fulfill several of the developmental needs or "selves" identified by Agosto and Hughes-Hassell (2006a, 2006b), such as their social, emotional, reflective, creative, and cognitive selves. But does this sharing as an expert affect their everyday life information seeking? Does it change the way young people seek information for daily needs? Interest-driven participation provides youth with not just the opportunity to find information to fulfill their information needs (to find information on a particular topic or hobby), but also provides them with a venue for sharing their work, collaborating with others, commenting on others' work, and participating in a community as an expert. The role of "young person as expert" suggests that young people's everyday life information behaviors and their use of social networks and ICTs are for more than just communication and interaction. How this aspect of young people's online behavior might fit into the ELIS models is an intriguing phenomenon that needs to be explored.

Dresang's Radical Change Theory may provide the bridge that is needed to explore the issues associated with digital youth's everyday life information seeking. Dresang and Koh (2009) suggest using Radical Change Theory as a framework for understanding more about how digital youth think and seek information; perceive themselves and others; and access information and seek community. They explain that Radical Change theory is "based on the digital age principles of interactivity, connectivity, and access. It provides a promising theoretical framework for explaining contemporary changes in information behavior and resources as well as serving as a guide for investigative studies and professional practice" (27). *Interactivity*, as characterized by Dresang's typology (1999), refers to the dynamic, nonlinear, and nonsequential learning and information behavior in the digital age. *Connectivity* is the sense of community and development of online social worlds that have emerged from young people's changing perspectives and expanded associations. *Access* is described as breaking down the longstanding information and access barriers and giving young people access to a wider diversity of formerly largely inaccessible opinions.

Building on Dresang's earlier typology and incorporating findings from new media studies such as Buckingham (2008), Gee (2007), Ito and colleagues (2008, 2010), and Jenkins (2006), Dresang and Koh extended the theory to identify three types of information behavior of digital age youth:

Type One—Changing forms of seeking information and learning (or how youth seek information and learn):

- obtaining information from a variety of sources
- multitasking
- preference for graphic and visual information
- seeking information nonlinearly and nonsequentially

• developing self-defined and controlled paths

Type Two—Changing Perspectives (or how youth perceive themselves and others):

• expressing opinions for themselves
• portraying flexible and multiple identities
• encountering information from various perspectives

Type Three—Changing Boundaries (or how do they access information and seek community):

• obtaining instant access to a wide array of information
• seeking, sharing, and creating information collaboratively
• forming new types of social networks
• participating in community engagement (Dresang and Koh 2009, 29)

Dresang and Koh's concerns echo those of the authors: "Although youth information behaviour research has shifted to focus more on the use of information and the process of information seeking in a wide variety of contexts, the research needs to reflect the developments in our knowledge of the effects of digital technology and the digital environment on youth cognition and behaviour" (31). Dresang's Radical Change Theory and the typology of digital age youth provide researchers who focus on young people's ELIS with a framework that not only incorporates library and information science principles within it but expands our thinking to incorporate findings from communication and new media studies of how youth are engaging within new media ecologies.

CONCLUDING THOUGHTS

Whether or not we see young people as Digital Natives, or as youth who are engaging with information and communication technologies and who experiment, play, learn, and grow within new information and social media ecologies, they are still young people who are grappling with the developmental issues encountered by all youth as they grow to be adults in our modern technologically dependent society. They encounter the same issues that young people have always dealt with, but now they have more sources and channels of information in which to find help with their everyday life information needs. Further, and of more importance, the ICTs, social networks, and new media ecologies they might find themselves engaged in may also present them with new everyday life information needs and with new roles to play.

While we may eschew the views of the popular media due to lack of support from research, popular media is also the first source that reports on new technology trends we need to investigate further. For example, an interesting, and perhaps troubling, new phenomenon resulting from the prevalent use of smartphones (those equipped with Internet access), is the almost addictive need to be constantly monitoring one's social network sites, Twitter accounts, or other online communities. Called "checking habits," researchers found that on average, adult study participants were compelled to check their phones 34 times a day (Cohen 2011). The study did not include young people, but as research has shown that the majority of youth that text do so daily at a very high rate, is it also highly probable that youth are prone to this "checking habit"? People are also developing the habit of daily monitoring easily accessible online information sources such as blogs and newspapers. Does smart phone use that enables these checking and monitoring activities indicate a change in everyday life information behavior? Will this emerging behavior affect how young people use ICTs for their information needs?

Research on young people's ELIS will need to explore these technologies as not just communication and interaction devices, but also as new environments that enable young people to play new roles (such as that of expert) and the accompanying everyday life information needs and behaviors that may result from these new contexts. Above all, it is important to recognize that not all young people have the same level of access to the Internet, ICTs, or social media, and that they also vary in their degree of digital comfort, facility, and use. ELIS research needs to take these realities into account as we strive to develop a fuller picture of the everyday life information behavior of young people.

REFERENCES

Abbas, June. 2010. "Children and Information Technology." In *Encyclopedia of Library and Information Sciences*, 3rd ed., 930–941. New York: Taylor and Francis.
Abbas, June, Melanie Kimball, George D'Elia, and Kay G. Bishop. 2007a. "Public Libraries, the Internet and Youth: Part 1. Internet Access and Youth's Use of the Public Library." *Public Libraries* 46 (4): 40–45.
Abbas, June, Melanie Kimball, George D'Elia, and Kay G. Bishop. 2007b. "Public Libraries, the Internet and Youth: Part 2. Youth's Opinions of the Service Characteristics of the Internet and the Public Library and Their Impact on Public Library Use." *Public Libraries* 46 (5): 64–70.
Abram, S. 2007. "Millennials: Deal with Them!" *School Library Media Activities Monthly* 24: 57–58.
Agosto, Denise E., and June Abbas. 2010. "High School Seniors' Social Network and Other ICT Use Preferences and Concerns." *Proceedings of the American Society for Information Science and Technology* 47: 1–10.
Agosto, Denise E., June Abbas, and Robin Naughton. 2012. "Relationships and Social Rules: Teens' Social Network and Other ICT Selection Practices." *Journal of the American Society for Information Science and Technology*. Accessed April 21, 2012, http://onlinelibrary.wiley.com/doi/10.1002/asi.22612/full.

Agosto, Denise E., and Sandra Hughes-Hassell. 2005. "People, Places, and Questions: An Investigation of the Everyday Life Information-Seeking Behaviors of Urban Young Adults." *Library and Information Science Research* 27: 141–163.

Agosto, Denise E., and Sandra Hughes-Hassell. 2006a. "Toward a Model of the Everyday Life Information Needs of Urban Teenagers, Part 1: Theoretical Model." *Journal of the American Society for Information Science and Technology* 57 (10): 1394–1403.

Agosto, Denise E., and Sandra Hughes-Hassell. 2006b. "Toward a Model of the Everyday Life Information Needs of Urban Teenagers, Part 2: Empirical Model." *Journal of the American Society for Information Science and Technology* 57 (11): 1418–1426.

Bennett, S., and K. Maton. 2010. "Beyond the 'Digital Natives' Debate: Towards a More Nuanced Understanding of Students' Technology Experiences." *Journal of Computer Assisted Learning* 26: 321–331.

Boyd, Danah. 2008. "Why Youth (Heart) Social Network Sites: The Role of Networked Publics in Teenage Social Life." In *Youth, Identity, and Digital Media*, D. Buckingham, ed., 119–142. The John D. and Catherine T. MacArthur Foundation Series on Digital Media and Learning. Cambridge, MA: The MIT Press.

Brown, J. S. 2000. "Growing Up Digital." *Change* 32 (2): 10–20.

Buckingham, D. 2008. "Introducing Identity." In *Youth, Identity, and Digital Media*, D. Buckingham, ed., 25–47. Cambridge, MA: MIT Press.

Burek-Pierce, Jennifer. 2007. "Research Directions for Understanding and Responding to Young Adult Sexual and Reproductive Health." In *Youth Information Seeking Behavior II: Contexts, Theories, Models, and Issues*. Mary K. Chelton and Colleen Cool, eds., 63–91. Lanham, MD: Scarecrow Press.

Cohen, Elizabeth. 2011. "Smartphone Users Have Developed 'Checking Habits.'" *CNN*, July 28, 2011.

Costello, B., R. Lenholt, and J. Stryker. 2004. "Learning Styles of the Net Generation." *The Journal of Academic Librarianship* 30: 452–460.

Dinet, J., S. Paquet, and N.G. Vinson. 2003. "An Explorative Study of Adolescent Perceptions of the Web." *Journal of Computer Assisted Learning* 19: 538–545.

Dresang, Eliza. 1999. *Radical Change: Books for Youth in the Digital Age*. New York: H. W. Wilson.

Dresang, Eliza T., and Kyungwon Koh. 2009. "Radical Change Theory, Youth Information Behavior, and School Libraries." *Library Trends* 58 (1): 26–50.

Edwards, Susan, and Barbara Poston-Anderson. 1996. "Information, Time Perspectives, and Adolescent Girls: Concerns about Education and Jobs." *Library and Information Science Research* 18: 207–223.

Ek, Ellen, Jouko Remes, and Ulla Sovio. 2004. "Social and Developmental Predictors of Optimism from Infancy to Early Adulthood." *Social Indicators Research* 69: 219–242.

Erkut, Sumru, Laura A. Szalacha, and Cynthia García Coll. 2005. "A Framework for Studying Minority Youths' Transitions to Fatherhood: The Case of Puerto Rican Adolescents." *Adolescence* 40 (160): 709–727.

Eyre, G. 2003. "Back to Basics: The Role of Reading in Preparing Young People for the Information Society." *Reference Services Review* 31 (3): 219–226.

Faulkner, J. D. 2002. *The Literacies of Popular Culture: A Study of Teenage Reading Practices*. Unpublished PhD thesis, Monash University, Australia.

Fidel, Raya, et al. 1999. "A Visit to the Information Mall: Web Searching Behavior of High School Students." *Journal of the American Society for Information Science* 50 (1): 24–37.

Fisher, Karen, Elizabeth Marcoux, Eric Meyers, and Carol F. Landry. 2007. "Tweens and Everyday Life Information Behavior: Preliminary Findings from Seattle." In *Youth Information Seeking Behavior II: Contexts, Theories, Models, and Issues*. Mary K. Chelton and Colleen Cool, eds., 1–25. Lanham, MD: Scarecrow Press.

Fox, Suzannah, and Sydney Jones. 2009. *The Social Life of Health Information*. Pew Internet and American Life Project: Washington, DC. Accessed January 2012, http://www.pewinternet.org/~/media//Files/Reports/2009/PIP_Health_2009.pdf.

Frand, J. L. 2000. "The Information-age Mindset." *EDUCAUSE Review* 35: 14–20.

Gasser, Urs, Sandra Cortesi, Momin Malik, and Ashley Lee. In press. *Youth and Digital Media: from Credibility to Information Quality*. Boston, MA: The Berkman Center for Internet and Society at Harvard University.

Gee, James. 2007. *What Video Games Have to Teach Us about Learning and Literacy*, 2nd ed. New York: Palgrave MacMillan.

Greenhow, Christine, and Beth Robelia. 2009a. "Informal Learning and Identity Formation in Online Social Networks." *Learning, Media and Technology* 34: 119–140.

Greenhow, Christine, and Beth Robelia. 2009b. "Old Communication, New Literacies: Social Network Sites as Social Learning Resources." *Journal of Computer-Mediated Communication* 14: 1130–1161.

Harris, Frances Jacobson. 2005. *I Found It on the Internet: Coming of Age Online*. Chicago: American Library Association.

Harris, Frances Jacobson. 2011. *I Found It Online: Coming of Age Online*, 2nd ed. Chicago: American Library Association.

Havighurst, R. J. 1972. *Developmental Tasks and Education*. 2nd ed. New York: Longman.

Hempel, J. 2005. "The MySpace Generation." *Business Week* 12 (December): 38–41.

Hoffman, D. L., T. P. Novak, and A. Venkatesh. 2004. "Has the Internet Become Indispensable?" *Communications of the ACM* 47 (7): 37–42.

Howard, Vivian. 2011. "The Importance of Pleasure Reading in the Lives of Young Teens: Self-identification, Self-construction and Self-awareness." *Journal of Librarianship and Information Science* 43 (1): 46–55.

Hughes-Hassell, Sandra, and Denise E. Agosto. 2007. "Modeling the Everyday Life Information Needs of Urban Teenagers." In *Youth Information Seeking Behavior II: Contexts, Theories, Models, and Issues*. Mary K. Chelton and Colleen Cool, eds., 27–61. Lanham, MD: Scarecrow Press.

Ito, Mizuko, et al. 2008. "Living and Learning with New Media: Summary of Findings from the Digital Youth Project." The John D. and Catherine T. MacArthur Foundation Series on Digital Media and Learning. Accessed January, 2012, http://digitalyouth.ischool.berkeley. edu/files/report/digitalyouth-WhitePaper.pdf.

Ito, Mizuko, et al. 2010. *Hanging Out, Messing Around, and Geeking Out: Kids Living and Learning with New Media*. Cambridge, MA: MIT Press.

Jenkins, H. 2006. *Convergence Culture: Where Old and New Media Collide*. New York: New York University Press.

Julien, Heidi. 1999. "Barriers to Adolescents' Information Seeking for Career Decision Making." *Journal of the American Society for Information Science* 50: 38–48.

Large, Andrew. 2005. "Children, Teens and the Web." In *The Annual Review of Information Science and Technology*. B. Cronin, ed., 347–392. Medford, NJ: Information Today.

Large, Andrew, and Jamshid Beheshti. 2000. "The Web as a Classroom Resource: Reactions from the Users." *Journal of the American Society for Information Science* 51: 1069–1080.

Latrobe, Kathy, and W. M. Havener. 1997. "Information Seeking Behavior of High School Honors Students: An Exploratory Study." *Journal of Youth Services in Libraries* 10: 188–200.

Lenhart, Amanda, Rich Ling, Scott Campbell, and Kristen Purcell. 2010. "Teens and Mobile Phones." Pew Internet and American Life Project: Washington, DC. Accessed January 2012, http://pewinternet.org/Reports/2010/Teens-and-Mobile-Phones.aspx.

Lenhart, Amanda, Kristen Purcell, Aaron Smith, and Kathryn Zickuhr. 2010. "Social Media and Young Adults." Pew Internet and American Life Project. Accessed January 2012, http://pewinternet.org/Reports/2010/Social-Media-and-Young-Adults.aspx.

Lenhart, Amanda, Maya Simon, and Mike Graziano. 2001. "The Internet and Education: Findings of the Pew Internet and American Life Project." Pew Internet and American Life Project: Washington, DC. Accessed January 2012, http://www.pewinternet.org/Reports/2001/The-Internet-and-Education.aspx.

Ling, Richard. 2005. "Mobile Communications vis-à-vis Teen Emancipation, Peer Group Integration and Deviance." In *The Inside Text: Social Perspectives on SMS in the Mobile Age*. Richard Harper, Leysia Palen, and Alex Taylor, eds., 175–189. London: Kluwer.

Lorenzetti, J. P. 2007. "One Student at a Time: Attracting and Supporting the Millennial Generation at Vincennes University." *Student Affairs Leader* 35: 1–2.

Lu, Ya-Ling. 2010. "Children's Information Seeking in Coping with Daily-Life Problems: An Investigation of Fifth- and Sixth-Grade Students." *Library and Information Science Research* 32: 77–88.

Luckin, Rosemary, et al. 2009. "Do Web 2.0 Tools Really Open the Door to Learning? Practices, Perceptions and Profiles of 11–16-Year-Old Students." *Learning, Media and Technology* 34: 87–104.

McMillan, Sally, and Jennifer Wilhelm. 2007. "Students' Stories: Adolescents Constructing Multiple Literacies through Nature Journaling." *Journal of Adolescent and Adult Literacy* 50: 370–377.

Mehra, Bharat, and Donna Braquet. 2007. "Process of Information Seeking during 'Queer' Youth Coming-Out Experiences." In *Youth Information Seeking Behavior II: Contexts, Theories, Models, and Issues*. Mary K. Chelton and Colleen Cool, eds., 93–131. Lanham, MD: Scarecrow Press.

Meyers, Eric, Karen Fisher, and Elizabeth Marcoux. 2007. "Studying the Everyday Information Behavior of Tweens: Notes from the Field." *Library and Information Science Research* 29: 310–331.

Meyers, Eric, Karen Fisher, and Elizabeth Marcoux. 2009. "Making Sense of an Information World: The Everyday-Life Information Behavior of Preteens." *The Library Quarterly* 79 (3): 301–341.

Minudri, R. 1974. "Library and Information Services for Young Adults and Students." In *Library and Information Service Needs of the Nation: Proceedings of a Conference on the Needs of Occupational, Ethnic, and Other Groups in the United States*. C. A. Cuadra and M. J. Bates, eds., 155–161. Washington, DC: Government Printing Office.

Oblinger, D. G. 2003. "Boomers, Gen-Xers, and Millennials: Understanding the New Students." *EDUCAUSE Review* 38 (4): 36–47.

Oblinger, D. G., and J. L. Oblinger. 2006. "Is it Age or IT? First Steps toward Understanding the Net Generation." *CSLA Journal* 29 (2): 8–16.

Palfrey, J., and U. Glasser. 2008. *Born Digital: Understanding the First Generation of Digital Natives.* New York: Basic Books.

Pfeiffer, Jens P., and Martin Pinquart. 2011. "Attainment of Developmental Tasks by Adolescents with Visual Impairments and Sighted Adolescents." *Journal of Visual Impairment and Blindness* 105: 33–44.

Poston-Anderson, Barbara, and Susan Edwards. 1993. "The Role of Information in Helping Adolescent Girls with Their Life Concerns." *School Library Media Quarterly* 22: 25–30.

Prensky, Marc. 2001. "Digital Natives, Digital Immigrants." *On the Horizon* 9: 1–5.

Rideout, V. J., U. G. Foehr, and D. F. Roberts. 2010. *Generation M²: Media in the Lives of 8- to 18-Year-Olds.* Washington, DC: Kaiser Family Foundation. Accessed January 2012, http://www.kff.org/entmedia/mh012010pkg.cfm.

Roberts, Donald F., and Ulla G. Foehr. 2008. "Trends in Media Use." *The Future of Children* 18 (10): 11–37.

Savin-Williams, Ritch. 2005. *The New Gay Teenager.* Cambridge, MA: Harvard University Press.

Savolainen, Reijo. 1995. "Everyday Life Information Seeking: Approaching Information Seeking in the Context of 'Way of Life.'" *Library and Information Science Research* 17: 259–294.

Savolainen, Reijo. 2004. "Everyday Life Information Seeking." In *Encyclopedia of Library and Information Science*. M. A. Drake, ed., pp. 1–9. New York: Marcel Dekker.

Seiffge-Krenke, Inge, and Tim Gelhaar. 2008. "Does Successful Attainment of Developmental Tasks Lead to Happiness and Success in Later Developmental Tasks: A Test of Havighurst's (1948) Theses." *Journal of Adolescence* 31: 33–52.

Selwyn, Neil. 2009. "The Digital Native: Myth and Reality."*Aslib Proceedings: New Information Perspectives* 61: 364–379.

Shenton, Andrew Kenneth, and Pat Dixon. 2003. "Just What Do They Want? What Do They Need? A Study of the Informational Needs of Children." *Children and Libraries* (Summer/Fall): 36–42.

Shenton, Andrew Kenneth, and Pat Dixon. 2005. "Information Needs. Learning More About What Kids Want, Need, and Expect from Research." *Children and Libraries* (Summer/Fall): 20–28.

Shenton, Andrew Kenneth, and Pat Dixon. 2007. "Causes of Information-Seeking Failure: Some Insights from an English Research Project." In *Youth Information Seeking Behavior II: Contexts, Theories, Models, and Issues*. Mary K. Chelton and Colleen Cool, eds., 313–364. Lanham, MD: Scarecrow Press.

Sorensen, E. S. 1993. *Children's Stress and Coping: A Family Perspective*. New York: Guilford Press.

Spink, Amanda, and Charles Cole. 2001. "Information and Poverty: Information-Seeking Channels Used by African American Low-Income Households." *Library and Information Science Research* 23: 45–65.

Thinyane, Hannah. 2010. "Are Digital Natives a World-Wide Phenomenon? An Investigation into South African First Year Students' Use and Experiences with Technology." *Computers and Education* 55 (1): 406–414.

Valenza, Joyce Kasman. 2007. "'It'd Be Really Dumb Not to Use It,' Virtual Libraries and High School Students' Information Seeking and Use—A Focus Group Investigation." In *Youth Information Seeking Behavior II: Contexts, Theories, Models, and Issues*. Mary K. Chelton and Colleen Cool, eds., 207–255. Lanham, MD: Scarecrow Press.

Van Grove, Jennifer. 2010. "Teens Experiencing Facebook Fatigue." Accessed January 2012, http://mashable.com/2010/06/30/teens-social-networks-study/. (See also http://www.scribd.com/doc/33751159/Teens-Social-Networks-Study-June-2010.)

Zhao, S. 2009. "Parental Education and Children's Online Health Information Seeking: Beyond the Digital Divide Debate." *Social Science and Medicine* 69: 1501–1505.

Chapter Five

Digital Age Libraries and Youth

Learning Labs, Literacy Leaders, Radical Resources

Eliza T. Dresang

According to the latest available statistics, 17,490 public library facilities (Manjarrez et al. 2011) and 81,900 public school libraries (National Center for Education Statistics 2011) serve youth in the United States. In comparison there are in the same time period an estimated 13,730 McDonald's outlets in the United States (Reference USA 2011). In public libraries there were 2,377,889 programs for children (64 percent of the total) attended by 61,630,017 children, and 262,196 programs (7 percent of the total) for young adults, attended by 4,414,692. Judging by numbers alone, at least in the United States, libraries continue to have a significant presence in the lives of youth.

But delving beyond these statistics, what has *changed* about the roles of libraries in children's and teens' information behavior in the Internet-dominated, media-rich participatory culture? How have libraries adapted to the needs, interests, and information seeking, use, and content creation of youth in the digitally saturated environment of the 21st century? This chapter focuses on the roles of 21st-century libraries that can be identified as research-based and that relate to the empirically established and theoretically examined information behavior of digital age youth, birth through age 18. The research reported occurred largely in the United States but has lessons applicable to potential roles for libraries wherever digital age youth and libraries connect. Underlying these changes are some assumptions about youth to keep in mind when reflecting on the roles that libraries for youth play in the 21st century.

ESSENTIAL UNDERLYING ASSUMPTIONS

In Dresang's introduction to the Radical Change Theory (1999), she listed four underlying assumptions: (1) children are capable and seeking connections; (2) the digital environment nurtures children's capabilities; (3) hand-held books offer digital-age connections; and (4) adults and youth are partners in the digital world (xxiv). Both then and now this continues to be an optimistic view of youth, not universally held. Nonetheless it is one that libraries and librarians serving youth have embraced in order to create potent participatory partnerships such as those discussed below. A cursory examination of these assumptions with an example of how they have played out in the 21st century provides the framework for the roles that libraries serving youth have played in the initial decade of the century.

Children Are Capable and Seeking Connections

Not all adults are either convinced or even aware of the manner in which the digital environment has highlighted the capabilities of youth that were often previously unnoticed or undervalued. Nonetheless the affinity of youth for various types of digital media and the many ways in which their talents have shone in using them in the past decade have increased the respect of many adults for children's capabilities. "The discourse of digital generations and digital youth posits that new media empower youth to challenge the social norms and educational agendas of their elders in unique ways" (Ito et al. 2010, 19).

The propensity of youth for "seeking connections" has been aided and abetted by the Web 2.0 environment with its social networking sites and the proliferation of mobile devices. In an Institute for Museum and Library Services–supported study of 9- to 13-year-olds' information-seeking behavior in the Saint Louis Public Library, conducted between 2001 and 2003, well before these new connective devices were readily available, a dominant theme was the tweens' preferred social, connected nature of information seeking (Dresang 2005a, 189). Without any prompts, children reported both wanting to work together on the computer and also desiring the opportunity to share the information that they had found. To its credit when presented with this research finding, the board of directors of the Saint Louis Public Library changed its policy from one child, one computer to allow the type of connected use described by the youth. Embedded in this study were two important characteristics of youth information behavior: the desire of youth to work or play together on computers and their aspiration to share what they have found or created with others. Shortly after this research took place, Web 2.0 with limitless possibilities of social networking and multitudes of sharing venues came onto the scene.[1]

The Digital Environment Nurtures Children's Capabilities

The recognition of Creating, a participatory action, as an established educational learning objective, supports this assertion that the digital environment has a positive effect on children's capabilities. In the late 1990s Lorin Anderson, a former student of educational psychologist Benjamin Bloom, revised his 1956 Taxonomy of Educational Objectives (Anderson and Krathwohl 2001). Anderson made two major changes to the original six-step hierarchy. One was to modify the words describing the levels, moving them from static nouns to active verbs, for example, Analysis became Analyzing, and Analyzing and Synthesizing were collapsed to make a place for Creating at the pinnacle of the hierarchy. Creating was defined as "Putting the elements together to form a coherent or functional whole; reorganising elements into a new pattern or structure through generating, planning or producing (Churches 2009, 61). A decade later Andrew Churches offered yet another revision, *Bloom's Digital Taxonomy* (2009). The level labels remained the same but the associated keywords and concepts incorporated a number of the creative activities including programming that had become prevalent during the previous decade. Even President Obama has stated a goal of empowering youth to become "makers and creators of things, rather than just consumers" (Springen 2011a, 38).

The graphical Scratch Programming Language is an outstanding example of how the digital world nurtures children's capabilities by providing a means for both creating and connecting. Scratch was developed by the Lifelong Kindergarten Group at the MIT Media Lab for youth aged 9 to 13 to create their own interactive stories, animations, games, music, and art, and to share them online. With the website made public in May 2007, by August 2011 there were 854,865 registered members, 248,845 project creators, 1,970,154 projects uploaded, 34,216,017 scripts, and 11,714,865 sprites (avatars). The median age of participants was 14; the majority were between 9 and 19 with the range from 5 to 70 years. Visitors to the site come from 16,798 cities around the world (Scratch Statistics 2011). Some projects are individual; others are collaborative. A few universities, including Harvard, use this youth-oriented programming language to introduce their future programmers to the concept. For those with an understanding of the digital environment, this is clearly information behavior. Even the simplest Scratch project requires the entire range of cognitive skills and at each stage the creator is likely to have to seek information to proceed. Where does he or she find it? Young *scratchers* themselves created a Scratch wiki in December 2008, which in August 2011 had 487 articles all written by youth participants, filled with information (Scratch Wiki 2011). Those seeking information about Scratch have a first stop to shop. In addition, a Scratch Resources site, again generated by youth, provides a resource library where creators can find and use pieces from other scratchers' scripts or sprites (Scratch Resources 2011). Automatic credit is given to the originators of the script or sprite, although this has caused some controversy (Monroy-Hernández et al. 2011). *Use*, the final step in the contemporary information-seeking process, has taken on a new and much more dynamic meaning with the incorporation of participatory media as a channel for creating and sharing information.

Handheld Books Offer Digital Age Connections

This assumption reminds adults of changes in print-on-paper books for youth, the only ones that were handheld when this assumption was written. Even before the advent of reading ebooks on multiple mobile devices, Radical Change Theory was proposed by Dresang to explain changes taking place in the forms and formats, perspectives, and content of books for youth (1997, 1999). The theory is based on three digital age principles: interactivity, connectivity, and access. In order to assist users with applying the theory, Dresang (1999) developed and tested indicators for each type of change. For example, indicators for changing forms and formats include graphics in new forms and formats; words and pictures reaching new levels of synergy; nonlinear organization and format; nonsequential organization and format; multiple layers of meaning; interactive formats (19); and concomitant information behaviors focused on changes in how children were thinking and learning. By 2005, Radical Change was recognized as a theory that explained and predicated the information behavior of youth as well as changes in printed resources (Dresang 2005b, 2008).

Now, of course, the distinction between print-on-paper and print-on-digital paper is very slim, and while the changes that were documented in the handheld books of the 1990s remain and have become even more radical, the digital connections between print-on-paper and digital books are even stronger and easier to recognize. Henry Jenkins (2008) writes extensively about the increasing convergence of traditional and digital media, but identifies the instigator as the consumer rather than the producer.

Adults and Youth Are Partners in the Digital World

This assumption applies to many different situations in which adults are willing to work in participatory partnerships with youth. Including youth in the design process is one such example. Druin (2002) categorizes children's roles in the design process as user, informant, tester, and design partner chronologically as they first appeared in the research literature (6). Although each project has its own needs, the collaboration with the most beneficial outcomes involves the children acting as design partners, which subsumes at least part of each of the other roles; she calls this process Cooperative Inquiry. Another extensive review of children's role in the design process focuses on a discussion of the specific type of research methodology and the extent to which children are actually involved in the design process. This participation ranges from minimal in User-Centered Design on through ever-increasing involvement in Contextual Design, Learner-Centered Design, Participatory Design, Informant Design, Bonded Design, and Cooperative Inquiry. Bonded Design provides an outstanding model for adult/child collaboration that immerses children in a potent participatory partnership (Large et al. 2007, 289).[2]

From these underlying assumptions, the discussion moves to what the roles of libraries have been in children's and youth information behavior in the past decade and how they interact with these assumptions.

LIBRARIES ARE LABS FOR LEARNING

For decades not much research focused on youth in libraries, especially not on information behavior in libraries, and libraries were not much interested in research; everyone knew that libraries were good for youth and that was that. In 1988 Dresang spoke at one of the first national gatherings of state and association leaders in children's library services, sharing research results from a mixed-method design in which she assessed change of attitude in youth exposed to different communication conditions, one of which was to allow youth to express their choice of the materials from which they would learn. The qualitative method consisted of using Brenda Dervin's micro-moment technique to assess the meaning of the information to a sample of the sixth-graders involved in the study (Dresang 1990). The reaction of the leaders in the public library children's services audience was one of disbelief and to some extent hostility that a researcher would invade the privacy of children's use of library materials—if learning took place it was the business only of the youth.[3]

That perspective has changed dramatically over the past two-plus decades. The digital age and the realization of youth capabilities in relation to new media has brought with it an increased interest in research about youth information behavior in a library environment from both scholars and library staff.

The attention that researchers are now paying to research in both school and public libraries has promoted the role of libraries as labs for learning about learning and about the information behavior of digital age youth. Two compilations of research on Youth Information Behavior were published during the first decade of the 21st century (Chelton and Cool 2004, 2007). The 2004 volume focuses on research in school library settings, largely with youth carrying out projects required of them in an instructional context, while the 2007 tome incorporates five chapters on everyday, informal information behavior of youth. No work in either book includes research in public library settings, so the presence of such studies in this review marks a move to greater diversity of setting in the study of youth information behavior. Libraries serve both as partners in research and as laboratories for field testing research conducted elsewhere.

The following library as lab experiment, one that is likely to have long-term and widespread impact, is still in its infancy, but it appears to be off to a good start. Note that all four of the assumptions mentioned above also underlie the MacArthur research.

Hanging Out, Messing Around, Geeking Out

In 2006, the MacArthur Foundation (2011) made the decision to invest 50 or more million dollars in an initiative to determine "how digital media are changing the way young people learn, play, socialize and participate in civic life." Three major questions are posed in the initiative: How are young people changing as a result of digital media? How should learning institutions change? How should learning environments change? This initiative is one of the most significant investigations involving youth to take place in the new digital world. Obviously the questions posed relate to library environments, but even more exciting is that one of the major implementations of this research is taking place in public libraries—libraries and museums across the country are about to become learning labs for this experiment. The support for the project comes jointly from MacArthur and the Institute for Museum and Library Services (IMLS). MacArthur and IMLS are behind a re-imagining of education where the emphasis is on learning, and public library youth services are at the forefront of showing how it can happen.

The research informing the Learning Labs project, a three-year, $3.3 million ethnographic study from 2005 to 2008, was conducted under the directorship of Mizuko Ito of the University of Southern California. More than 25 researchers spent three years talking with 700 youth about their use of digital media in various everyday life contexts. The results, published in commercial printed and ebook formats, but also free online, with the title *Hanging Out, Messing Around, Geeking Out* (Ito et al. 2010) are of monumental importance to libraries in defining their role in the information behavior of youth. The assumptions of this study are based on what is referred to as a new paradigm in the sociology of childhood. As Ito and colleagues explain, "we move beyond a simple socialization model in which children are passive recipients of dominant and 'adult' ideologies and norms, and instead we deploy what Corsaro calls an Interpretive Reproduction model. In this model . . . we seek to give voice to children and youth who . . . have often not been heard" (Ito et al. 2010, 23).

However, Ito and colleagues also posit that "one of the important out-comes of youth participation in many online practices is they have an opportunity to interact with adults who are outside of their usual circle of family and school-based adult relationships" (24). She "argues against the trivialization of children's media culture and sees it as a site of child-and-youth creativity and social action" (25).

The Ito and colleagues study iterates that "even youth who do not possess computers and Internet access in the home are participants in a shared culture where new social media, digital media distribution and digital media production are commonplace among peers and in their everyday school contexts" (43) paralleling Dresang's proposal that "the impact of the microchip extends beyond direct contact with digital media to influence how one gives, receives, and creates information. The digital environment is ubiquitous; it permeates everyday life" (Dresang 2005a, 179). This is a key concept that libraries have been quick to grasp—youth are "growing up digital" no matter what their access to new media is.

The terms "hanging out, messing around, and geeking out" grew out of the research and an effort to structure what the team was experiencing with youth. In contrast to many other studies, the researchers in this project came to realize that the same young person moved back and forth among various modes of engagement with media. Former studies correlated media use with demographic chracteristics such as gender, race, or socioeconomic status, or to frequency of use or type of media preference that placed the youth users in a more or less fixed position in relation to media use (Livingstone 2002; Kaiser Foundation 2005). The MacArthur group found a more flexible way to approach youth media, which took into account various modes or what they called genres of information behavior at various times. Rather than focusing on one type of media, a young person might be attending to a variety of media because of a particular interest, or a different set of media according to how he or she was interacting with friends. Gradually the terms for the most frequent modes of using media become apparent: youth move back and forth among them, finding their own comfort zones and balance. "Hanging out" has to do with getting together with friends; media is often the connecting device. "Messing around" moves toward a more serious engagement with new media. Ito and colleagues found that teens can be very focused in their searches but more often their information behavior follows an exploratory, linking pattern, resembling what Bates (2005) labeled "berry-picking" (60). Hart (2008) substantiated berrypicking as the primary mode of seeking information in a virtual high school, a very different mode of information seeking from the way students are taught to seek information, especially in school libraries. Messing around can also involve producing or creating (Ito et al. 2010, 66). The third mode or genre represents the most focused form of information behavior. "Geeking out" is "a more serious engagement with media or technology" (77). Most often these activities are undertaken in social situations. So what happens when this research is applied to libraries?

YOUmedia, opened in July 2009 in the Harold Washington Library Center of the Chicago Public Library, is the first Library Learning Lab, and a far more detailed and elaborate venue than the ones to follow. Created with expenditures of approximately $1.2 million, the center has three distinct areas: a relaxed Hang Around space for socializing after school; a Mess Around space for both individual and collaborative use of library materials such as games, books, and computers for individual interest pursuit or homework resources; and a Geek Out space for in-depth engagement with digital resources. So far, this learning lab is deemed a success by library staff and users alike (Springen 2011a).

Are the 70 or so teens that use this 5,500-square-foot space really engaged in information behavior? If meeting their interests and needs with library resources is any measure, the answer is definitely yes. Mentors and librarians encourage participation and creation. A sense of the project can be acquired through the numerous student-produced videos linked from the site such as a poetry slam based on the reading of Toni Morrison's *A Mercy* (Chicago Public Library 2011). Also instructive is a careful reading of the first-year evaluation, "YOUmedia: Re-imagining Learning, Literacy, and Libraries," conducted by the Consortium on Chicago School Research at the University of Chicago (Austin et al. 2011). One finding of the evaluation research was that the primary duty of both librarians and mentors was building relationships with teens. Until these relationships were built, despite the plethora of digital and traditional materials, teens largely did not move from "hanging out." In addition, "the process of collaboration helped teens learn how to be part of a community, while simultaneously supporting individual growth as they become educated consumers of each other's work"—keys to successful projects (34).

In the next three years, 30 additional projects in the United States will become Learning Labs. These library and museum labs will engage digital age youth in learning, socializing, and participating through the use of digital technologies that build on their interests, connect them to valuable resources and peers, and provide an opportunity for creative information behavior. While the University of Chicago Group is evaluating the flagship program in this initiative, YOUmedia, the Urban Libraries Council in partnership with the Association of Science-Technology Centers (ASTC), has been chosen to lead the implementation and evaluations of the group of other sites.

Other projects in which libraries have served as labs are not as large scale, yet they provide value information about the role of libaries in digital age youth information behavior.

YA Spaces

As the program statistics at the beginning of the chapter reveal, young adult (YA) services in and attendance at libraries is far less in numbers than that of children. In the 21st century there has been an upturn in libraries' interest in providing YA spaces. However, according to a small research project, it appears that accommodating digital age youth information behavior was not a primary outcome (Bernier 2010). One positive finding of this Bernier study was that these libraries recognized the need and desirability for YAs to participate in the planning of the design, individually and in focus groups (2009). A follow-up IMLS-funded research project, 2010–2013, is documenting in a systematic manner practices in the design of YA spaces, including the participation of youth in the design process. The investigation includes building relationships with young adults. Given the importance of relationships in encouraging YA services in the first evalution of YOUmedia, this research will provide a useful comparative perspective from another set of library learning labs.

Group versus Independent Information Seeking: Preference and Efficacy

Beyond the myriad social networking opportunities, other more formal or structured ways exist in the digital environment for children's collaborations that facilitate information exchange, and these opportunities can be either peer to peer or intergenerational. A recent study of the efficacy of groups in which students are asked to collaborate in a middle school library setting enhanced what we know about the popularity of this practice among students as well as the efficacy of this mode of information behavior (Meyers 2011). Twenty-first century information-seeking environments often require group work, so knowing the positives and negatives for students participating in them is essential. A variety of quantitative and qualitative methods, disparate means of collecting data, and a careful crossover experimental design with two multi-part experiments were used to study both processes and learning outcomes. The information-seeking situation in which the students participated was structured according to the Big6 problem-solving process (Eisenberg and Berkowitz 1990). All students worked in both three-person and individual settings. Both supporting and refuting what might be regarded as common knowledge in today's connected world, the findings indicate that "despite students' apparent preference for working in groups, this arrangement does not always provide cognitive benefits or improved learning outcomes." Moreover, Meyers was able to correlate preference as well as positive learning benefits from either social or individual work with specific steps of the Big6 information-seeking/problem-solving process. This fine-tuned analysis, with further research and model-building, may lead to a more sophisticated understanding of adult-youth partnerships. From his findings influenced by Vygotsky's research (1986), Meyers (2011) suggests a Group6 Blended Problem Model. He notes that "drawing on the rich data set . . . the model developed to find the middle path between individual and group prob-lem-solving identifies that group work involves both individual and social processes, and there are key points where the movement from individual to collaborative work can foster positive engagement, and potentially better outcomes" (252–53). Possibly this Group6 Blended Problem Solving Model will guide participants to best practices regarding adult-youth collaboration, peer-to-peer collaboration, and independent work, essential nuances in a so-cial-networked world.

Scratch in Libraries

The Scratch Programming Language was mentioned above as an example of opportunities through which digital age children demonstrate their creativity and information behavior activities. Libraries were used as learning labs to test Scratch through an IMLS-funded collaboration between the Hennepin County Library System of Minnesota, six library systems, and a science museum. This two-year lab experiment began in 2006, a year before Scratch was made widely available via its website. The final research report details how the experiment was rolled out across the nation (Phipps 2010). The first conclusion, as it was with the evaluation of YOUmedia's first year, is that the library staff are of prime importance in the success. "Based on the cases of Winchester Public Library and Lake County Library and the written reflec-tions from all of the librarians participating in the project . . . personnel are the most important factor in high quality programming" (15). A barrier that showed up in this learning lab situation was one with which the Chicago Public YOUmedia staff did not have to contend.

> Part of adapting to the 21st Century is reexamining policies created in the 20th Century. If 21st Century citizens need to be flexible and adaptable, so must the institutions on which they rely. While policies must take computer security seriously, some policies inhibit meaningful use of computers. Getting Scratch and other free creative software onto library computers has been a major challenge. (14)

The reports note that youth of many different skills and abilities use pro-grams like Scratch side by side, so this needs to be taken into account when planning programs (14); it also allows the opportunities that the children in the Saint Louis Public Library asked for to share what information they hold. In four presentations at the 2010 Scratch for Educators Conference at MIT, project personnel demonstrated how to create stories that combine LEGO robotic characters with Scratch animated characters; techniques for using Scratch as a basis for technology programming in public libraries that promotes youth as teachers and staff as partners; and a session on Design Blocks, described as a Scratch sibling (Learning Technologies Center 2011).

Capitalizing on Social Media and Mobile Devices

Three New York City public library systems have joined to explore use of students' preferred information-seeking behavior to bring homework help to students across the city (Braun 2010). Similar to the YA Spaces finding, the Project Director reported that having kids involved in the design process every step of the way is the key to making sure these tools truly work for our potential users. This project, also supported by IMLS funding, started with the establishment of a website for homework help, but interviews with 90 children and teens revealed that even among the 50 percent who had heard of it, not one had used it. Ninety percent of the kids said they wanted to get help from the web environments they already used and that apps are cool. So now it's apps for students, embedded in familiar websites such as Facebook, and a redesigned website to be used for teachers. With the type of bonded design discussed above, teens engaged with adults throughout the process. In 2011, the project was in the assessment phase and ripe for moving to mobile devices. Teens' use of mobile devices has exploded, cutting across social economic and ethnic groups (Pew Research Center 2009). In addition to this evidence of widespread use of and preference for mobile devices, developmental researchers have argued that "communicative patterns are tied to the particular developmental needs of adolescents who are engaged in negotiations over social identity and belonging" (Ito et al. 2010, 17).

Having firmly established the role of 21st-century libraries as labs for research and innovation, the next role to examine is one that may sound traditional but in many ways is not because children and research are not—that is, libraries are literacy leaders.

LIBRARIES ARE LITERACY LEADERS

Libraries have served in the role of literacy promotion since the first library for youth was established. However, the changing nature of this role is well documented through a look at the various standards and guidelines for school libraries since 1918 (Dresang and Kotrla 2010, 123). The challenge of the 21st century in relation to literacy is its breadth and depth. In the digital environment, literacy must include the ability to "read and understand text in all formats (for example, picture, video, print) and all contexts" (American Association of School Librarians 2008, 2). "Text" and "reading" are used here in the broadest sense of the words to incorporate the ability to decode and understand (as well as to create) all forms and formats of media. To put it simply, as more and more digital media have appeared and been adopted by youth as conveyors of information, the role of libraries has expanded concomitantly to incorporate assisting youth to become literate in their use. Information literacy, the ability to locate, find, use, and create information, is especially considered a responsibility of the school library. The issue of 21st-century skills has come to the forefront, and libraries are part of a coalition of educators defining and promoting them, in particular any dealing with literacy.

School Library Impact Studies

Another shift in libraries' deeper responsibility to literacy comes from an expectation that librarians will also have a role in supporting the skills children need in order to learn to read successfully and those needed to enhance vocabulary and comprehension as they grow older. This expectation has changed to some extent the role of the school library for school-age children and the role of the public library for preschool children. In the 21st century, libraries have become expected by many to be leaders, rather than ardent supporters, in shaping the literacy development of children.

This role shift for school libraries is best highlighted by a series of studies to establish the correlation between higher reading achievement and better equipped and staffed libraries. The first of these studies was conducted in 1993, but it was not until the 21st century that the additional 20 creating the School Library Impact Studies were conducted (School Library Impact Studies 2011). Fifteen of these studies correlate the state of the library with students' test scores in reading (Dresang and Kotrla 2010, 128). These studies are described in "School Libraries Work!" (National Commission on Libraries and Information Science 2008). Graduate students at Mansfield University have compiled another summary of the findings (Mansfield University 2011). Criticism of these studies has come from some scholars because of the lack of scientific sampling, the fact that one single variable, socioeconomic status, explains one- to two-thirds of the variation in the scores and because claims of causality rather than correlation have been incorrectly applied at times (Dresang and Kotrla 2010, 129). The bottom line for the role of the school libraries in the 21st century is an increased expectation that they have a demonstrable impact on student learning; particularly literacy in terms of reading, while expectations for other roles related to digital media, information literacy, and youth information behavior have increased at the same time.[4]

Every Child Ready to Read at Your Library

Is it proper to think of very young children, even babies, as information seekers? As humans with identifiable information behavior? Research conducted at the University of Washington Learning and Brain Sciences Institute (I-LABS) would say a resounding yes, even though they may not have used that terminology. In a TED talk, Patricia Kuhl, co-director of I-LABS, demonstrates the tremendous amount of information seeking that babies aged seven to nine months do in learning the sounds in their native language (Kuhl 2010). She states that we are embarking on a grand and golden age in exploring children's brain development, where we can see the development of emotions, how they learn to read, how they solve a math problem and uncover deep truths about what it means to be human. I-LABS, with the first MEG brain imaging machine focused on children, has embarked on a Developing Mind Project (Institute for Learning and Brain Sciences 2011). Since much of the learning that takes place in these early years is because of the information that the infant, then toddler, then preschooler receives, I-LABS has reached out to librarians as an appropriate partner for the outcomes of their research.

A dramatic decade-long transformation has taken place in the role of public library programs for preschool children in the 21st century due largely to two comprehensive national research reports on early literacy, the 2000 *Report of the National Reading Panel* (NRP) (National Reading Panel 2000) and the subsequent 2008 *Report of the National Early Literacy Panel* (National Early Literacy Panel 2008). This change has brought increased nationwide recognition for the role public libraries now play in preparing children to learn to read. The first version of the Every Child Ready to Read @ Your Library program (shortened to ECRR) was commissioned by the Public Library Association and the Association for Library Service to Children, divisions of the American Library Association (ALA), in partnership with the National Institute of Child Health and Human Development and Grover C. Whitehurst and Christopher Lonigan, well-known researchers in early literacy. It was a model program for parents and caregivers based on the early literacy principles found to be most closely linked to child success by the National Reading Panel (NRP) meta-analysis of scientific (experimental/control group) research. Six ALA-selected trainers held sessions for library staff, sometimes for entire states, that helped librarians and parents embed activities related to phonological awareness, vocabulary, narrative skills, print awareness, letter knowledge, and print motivation. At the time that NELP (National Early Literacy Panel) issued its meta-analysis of research on preschoolers, PLA (Public Library Association) and ALA contracted with Susan Neuman, another early learning specialist, to conduct an evaluation of ECRR and to make recommendations for ECRR2 based on her understanding of the

NELP research and the findings of the evaluation. ECRR2 became available in August 2011 and this time, in addition to the early literacy principles, it provides a great deal of guidance on those activities that give children the opportunity to seek information and practice what they learn, that is, talking, singing, reading, writing, and playing.

The evaluations of ECRR have been through the eyes of adults involved; librarians across the country were trained and grew satisfied with their ability to provide enjoyable story time programming focused on facilitating specific reading readiness skills in children. That is, until librarians, administrators and their funding agencies began to ask, "What are the real outcomes of these early literacy programs for children?" In other words, was this intensive effort making a true difference in children's skills? And, "How can we find out in informal settings using developmentally appropriate means with young children?"

To answer this question in the state of Washington, which has strong support for early learning through its one-of-a-kind cabinet-level Department of Early Learning, the Early Learning Public Library Partnership (ELPLP), founded in 2006 to assure that public libraries are "at the table" in all appropriate state literacy-related initiatives, the Foundation for Early Learning, which represents the ELPLP and many other community early learning projects, the State Library of Washington, and the University of Washington, with 32 departments or institutes focused on early learning, applied for an IMLS National Leadership Grant to try to find a way to answer these questions using libraries throughout Washington that provide early literacy story times. The early learning landscape nationally and in Washington was described in a White Paper prepared as part of a previous IMLS Planning grant (Dresang et al. 2010). In addition, members of this library-based partnership are part of the Washington Office of the Superintendent of Public Instruction Advisory Committee that has developed a birth through grade 12 literacy and learning plan in a joint leadership effort.

As a demonstration that libraries are leaders in assessing whether the early literacy programming makes a difference (a far cry from that conference 20 years ago), the Carroll County, Maryland, library initiated a project that used a valid, reliable, research-based measure, the Early Literacy Skills Assessment (ELSA), developed by HighScope in an experimental pretest-posttest design of three- and four-year-olds attending in-home daycare. The intervention was training administered by the library. Following in their footsteps the Pierce County Library System in Washington, with a grant from the Boeing Foundation, replicated the study. In both studies, the children in the intervention group scored higher on the posttest than did the children in the control group on three of four literacy principles, although not the same three (Dresang and Campana 2011). The role of librarians in information behavior of very young children is often mediated by their adult caregivers, but for the first time these studies have demonstrated that this type of intervention can make a measurable difference for children.

The digital environment has moved much of reading and information out of the physical space. What does this mean for the role of libraries in the digital present and future?

RADICALIZING RESOURCES

In February 2010, the editors of the *New York Times* felt prompted to pose the question, "Do School Libraries Need Books?" It had been a few months since James Casey, headmaster of Cushing Academy, a privileged New England school, had announced that the school's administrators had decided to give away all of the books in their school library, replacing them with ebook readers, large-screen televisions, and in place of the reference desk a café and a cappuccino machine (Abel 2009). The *Times* editors in their "Room for Debate" section had invited five guests, including Mr. Casey, to comment on this question. Mr. Casey declared the redesign, based on needs of digital-age students, a complete success.

> Our library is now the most-used space on campus, with collaborative learning areas . . . and increased reference and circulation stations for our librarians. It has become a hub where students and faculty gather, learn and explore together. By reconceptualizing our library, our teachers and students now have better access to vast digital resources for research and learning. But they need more help from librarians to navigate these resources, so we have also increased our library staff by 25 percent. (Tracy 2010)

The other respondents were not as enthusiastic about this digital radicalizing of resources. While pundits ponder the effect on libraries of an increasingly digital world, the role of libraries continues to be one to provide and protect access, albeit in ways that differ from the past. It is unlikely that libraries will "tank" in the same way that large chain bookstores have, nor does it mean that all print books will disappear overnight, but it is true that their functions are less tied to specific ways to provide and protect access than they are to the fundamental principles of doing so. The following brief study serves as a good example of the wise ways flexible librarians provide radicalized opportunities for youth information seekers.

"It'd Be Really Dumb Not to Use It"

A study Joyce Valenza conducted with two classes of students at Springfield Township High School in Pennsylvania lends insight into how the role of the digital age school library has morphed to meet the needs of digital age users.

The data collection instruments consisted of a web survey in which other students in the area also participated and in-person focus groups. The descriptive nature of the study provides insights into how librarians can virtually provide many of the services available for student in-person use of resources including online lessons, a research guide, a reference desk leading students to online reference tools, librarian-created pathfinders, and lists and categories of search tools. One student more or less summed up how all the students responded to the online services tailor-made to their needs when he said, "It'd be really dumb not to use it. Everything there's laid out for you" (Valenza 2007, 226). Students involved felt they had the kind of assistance they needed when they needed it to facilitate their information searches. Are more radicalized resources to come?

Digital Textbooks from the Library

It is a time of transition. One suspected it when the Barnes and Noble Nook servers were down for three days during the holidays (Konkoma 2010). And one knew it when Amazon.com announced in May 2011 that their sales of ebooks for the Kindle had now outsold hardback and paperback books combined (Amazon 2011). And although reports of experiments with digital textbooks at the college level have not always been bright, reports from Florida, where the legislature has invoked spending K–12 textbook monies on digital texts, are positive, and seen as a boon for school librarians—school librarians in a new role of providing radicalized resources to meet the information needs of youth (Mardis et al. 2010). The Pinellas County, Florida School District, with initiative from the District Media and Technology Coordinator, who stated she wanted her librarians to be leaders in technology and literacy at their sites, won approval from the school board in 2011 to purchase digital textbook readers for all 2,100 students at Clearwater High School; the District Media and Technology Coordinator is currently assessing the best in digital science texts. Looking to the future, school librarians see among the potential advantages of digital texts a boost for struggling readers who can use the digital voice feature to gain the information they need (Mardis and Everhart 2011). From a "big picture" point of view, school librarians may welcome a job they have long eschewed, maintaining textbooks, as they have the opportunity in doing so to supplement the texts with other digital resources without the trouble that mounds of print texts require.

What Is a Book?

This question is perhaps the most radicalizing aspect of digital access. It is likely that even a decade ago few librarians thought they would have to ask not only what a good book is, but actually what is a book? This has now become an issue as libraries struggle to maintain maximum access to books for children but are uncertain when an online book with animated figures, sound, and moving objects ceases to be a book at all. And also, librarians are faced with a cacophony of conflicting opinions about whether those that *are* deemed books promote or hinder reading. Research is only beginning to appear and is sure to report conflicting results, but in one small randomized study conducted by a reading coach in University City, Ohio, children reading Tumblebook ebooks scored 23 points ahead of those in the control group three months into the study and were able to complete the task in five months, two months ahead of the children in the control group (Guernsey 2011). According to the annual *School Library Journal* technology survey, in 2011 a majority of high school libraries had purchased ebooks (64 percent), while only 29 percent of elementary school libraries had invested in this format. And what about the young information seekers? Teens are somewhat on the fence, but many find the format cool (Springen 2011b). The major barrier now lies with neither the libraries nor the youth, but with the policies of publishers and distributors, for example, limiting ebooks to a certain number of circulations, barring them from interlibrary loan, insisting on specific types of ebook readers, or not publishing ebooks at all (Springen 2010).

Long before the proliferation of formats and styles, the International Children's Digital Library (ICDL), the first and only free digital library for children, had set as one of its goals international access for children. Libraries have it for free with none of the hassles mentioned above—and it now comes with apps for iPhone, iPod, and iPad.

Surprising to some is the fact that a digital library for youth with ebooks and amazing resources has been around since November 2002 at the University of Maryland. Its goal is to represent all cultures and languages so that no child is denied the right to read in his or her mother tongue. In 2011, the ICDL collection included 4,469 books in 55 languages with a goal to have 10,000 books in at least 100 languages. Children aged 7 to 11, part of a Cooperative Inquiry team organized by Allison Druin, work regularly on the design and accessibility of the ICDL. A series of research studies conducted with children in Germany, New Zealand, Honduras, and the United States gave children the opportunity to use the library and express their attitudes while the researchers could ascertain differences and similarities toward books, reading, technology, and culture (ICDL 2011).

But what about the role of librarians in relation to those who would block the radicalizing of resources both off and online?

Radicalizing Resources and Intellectual Freedom

One other way in which libraries' roles have adapted to the Internet-dominated, media-rich, participatory culture is in protecting children's right to access information in an arena that is even more frightening to some adult users than books are or ever were. In the past two decades children's print books have expanded to contain topics previously thought taboo (Dresang 1999). To the surprise of some, however, documented book challenges have declined during the 21st century to date, a decrease of 47 percent between 2000 and 2010 according to the website of the ALA Office of Intellectual Freedom (ALA 2011).

On the other hand, the Internet has brought a depth and breadth of material previously unavailable, forcing libraries to be mindful constantly of protecting access for youth, protecting their privacy, and at the same time remaining within the boundaries of the law. The situation is much more complex in school than in public libraries. School boards may legally remove materials because the materials are "educationally unsuitable" or "pervasively vulgar." School boards may not, however, censor materials if the removal is politically motivated and the restriction is based on disagreement with the ideas contained in the material. The only other reason school boards can restrict materials is if they are obscene, harmful to minors, or child pornography (Chmara 2010, 18–19). Filters are required on all school computers in order for schools to receive federal funding. Astute digital age librarians adjust the settings to allow the greatest access legally possible. In public libraries only one computer has to be filtered. The ALA has a number of interpretations of the Library Bill of Rights, underscoring protecting the right of youth to free speech and access. The June 2011 issue of the *Voice of Youth Advocates*, a journal for those interested in youth and their access to libraries, contains articles from librarians, authors, and others. Even with the radicalizing of both offline and online resources, stalwart librarians who believe in the rights of youth take on this challenge and make it their duty to stay informed. It is part of believing that children are capable.

DISCUSSION AND IMPLICATION

This has been a selective rather than a comprehensive picture of the research and evidence-based roles of libraries in the information behavior of youth. Within this context, some tentative conclusions about the roles of libraries related to youth information behavior in the initial decade of the 21st century follow:

- The intense Internet, media-rich participatory culture of the first decade of the 21st century has made a difference to both the roles of libraries and the information behavior of youth. The assumptions made by Dresang in 1999 have become research-based realities a decade later.
- The roles of public libraries in the information behavior of youth are more research- and evidence-based than they have been in the past, partially because researchers are addressing youth in less formal situations more often than previously and partly because libraries are convinced it is important. This is a mutually beneficial situation for researchers and libraries and youth.
- In both research and practice, adults have become more aware of the capabilities of youth and the value of substantial youth participation in planning facilities, programs, and services, and the types of partnerships that can occur. Serious participation needs to be carefully structured as in the Bonded Design and Cooperative Inquiry methods. In study after study, beneficial results have been accomplished due to the creativity of youth, for example, the development of apps for homework help in New York City and the ICDL.
- The designation of libraries as official learning labs is unfolding in the flagship YOUmedia initiative in the Chicago Public Library; the MacArthur/IMLS initiative stands to have a substantial and widespread effect on youth and their information behavior as well as highlighting libraries as learning labs.
- A research project in a school library has raised a question about whether working in groups improves products and process in a school situation. Collaborative versus individual work is much more complex and multifaceted in its effect on youth process and outcome in information seeking than it appears at first glance. But nonetheless, aspects of it remain popular with youth.
- The role of libraries as leaders in literacy has greatly expanded, with school libraries linked to student achievement and public libraries to assuring children are ready to read. Success in reading is considered part of the literacy responsibility of librarians. Programs like ECRR have fostered the enjoyment and informality in learning for children to begin to mesh with focused learning objectives.
- Librarians have recognized that there are radical changes in both print-on-paper and print-on-screen resources and that providing these is part of meeting the information needs of their users, bringing a whole new set of issues, including the biggest surprise, that it is difficult to know "what is a book?" Libraries are capitalizing on the greater youth access that these new resources bring.

- In almost all of the library studies cited, the determining factor for success was the quality of the adults/youth relationship, surpassing technology, resources, and all else. Another essential component for success is partnerships—of people and institutions.
- Libraries have shifted some policies that affect youth information behavior due to the digital environment (for example, filters are on most computers in school libraries), but astute librarians lessen the impact in every way possible in order to protect the First Amendment rights of youth. Other policies, such as blocking creative and social networking programs like Scratch, are constraining services and seem stuck in the 20th century and in need of repair.

Missing from the discussion above is a research-based, tested theoretical framework explaining youth information behavior in the digital environment through which the adequacy or inadequacy of libraries in meeting youth information needs could be examined. In future analyses such a theoretical concept will be available. For her doctoral dissertation, Kyungwon Koh (2011) lays out a unique, comprehensive theoretical framework with detailed characteristics drawn from a rigorous content analysis and synthesis of existing research, guided by the principles of Radical Change, and tested against the actual information behavior of 12 youth immersed in digital culture, some in a formal and others in an informal information seeking situation. The Interactivity, Connectivity, and Access principles of Radical Change have remained an extremely robust way to explain and predict contemporary youth information behavior and resources. The typology developed by Koh in her research provides for scholars and professionals alike what promises to be an equally robust way in which to better understand youth information behavior. As Koh explains, "the typology suggests a holistic perspective for observing youth information behavior as an interplay between various factors, including young people's (1) intrapersonal processes, (2) identity formation and value negotiation, and (3) social interactions. It also presents 14 specific characteristics, such as those related to these factors that operationalize key concepts of Radical Change Theory" (Koh 2011, vii). At the end of her article, Koh proposes a framework for studying youth information behavior, radical resources, and the outcomes for youth in obtaining 21st-century skills. Perhaps the application of her theory will be the next step in understanding digital age children's information behavior and the role of libraries in meeting their needs.

NOTES

1. For further information on social networking and children see chapter 6, "Youth and Online Social Networking: What Do We Know So Far?" in this book.

2. For further information on the bonded design model of adult child partnerships, see chapter 10, "Systems," in this book.
3. Personal experience of the author, 1988.
4. For further information on information and media literacy, see chapter 3, "Information Literacy," in this book.

REFERENCES

Abel, David. 2009. "Welcome to the Library. Say Goodbye to the Books: Cushing Academy Embraces A Digital Future." *Boston Globe*, September 4.

Amazon. 2011. "Amazon.com Now Selling More Kindle Books Than Print Books." Accessed January 2012, http://phx.corporate-ir.net/phoenix.zhtml?c=176060&p=irol-newsArticle&ID=1565581&highlight.

American Association of School Librarians. 2008. "Standards for the 21st-Century Learner." Accessed January 2012, http://www.ala.org/aasl/guidelinesandstandards/learningstandards/standards.

American Library Association. 2011. Office of Intellectual Freedom. "Number of Challenges by Year, Reason, Initiator and Institution (1990–2010)." Accessed January 2012, http://www.ala.org/advocacy/banned/frequentlychallenged/stats.

Anderson, L. W., and D. Krathwohl (Eds.). 2001. *A Taxonomy for Learning, Teaching and Assessing: A Revision of Bloom's Taxonomy of Educational Objectives.* New York: Longman.

Austin, Kimberly, Stacy Ehrlich, Cassidy Puckett, and Judi Singleton. 2011. "YOUmedia: Re-Imagining Learning, Literacy, and Libraries." Consortium on Chicago School Research at the University of Chicago Urban Education Institute.

Bates, Marcia J. 2005. "Berrypicking." In *Theories of Information Behavior*, edited by Karen E. Fisher, Sanda Erdelez, and E. F. McKechnie, 58–62. Medford, NJ: Information Today for American Society of Information Science and Technology.

Bernier, Anthony. 2009. "A Space for Myself to Go: Early Patterns in Small YA Spaces." *Public Libraries* 48 (5): 33–47.

Bernier, Anthony. 2010. "Ten Years of YA Spaces of Your Dreams: What Have We Learned?" Accessed January 2012, http://www.voya.com/2010/05/13/ten-years-of-ya-spaces-of-your-dreams-what-have-we-learned/.

Braun, Linda W. 2010. "The Big App." *School Library Journal*, 56 (12). Accessed August 10, 2011, http://www.libraryjournal.com/slj/home/887747-312/the_big_app_new_yorks.html.csp.

Burnett, Kathleen, and Eliza T. Dresang. 1999. "Rhizomorphic Reading: The Emergence of a New Aesthetic in Literature for Youth." *The Library Quarterly* 69 (4): 421–45.

Chelton, Mary K., and Colleen Cool. 2004. *Youth Information-Seeking Behavior: Theories, Models, and Issues.* Lanham, MD: Scarecrow Press.

Chelton, Mary K., and Colleen Cool. 2007. *Youth Information-Seeking Behavior II: Context, Theories, Models, and Issues.* Lanham, MD: Scarecrow Press.

Chicago Public Library. 2011. "YOUmedia Chicago." Accessed August 20, 2011, http://youmediachicago.org/featured_contents.

Chmara, Theresa. 2010. "Minors' First Amendment Rights: CIPA and School Libraries." *Knowledge Quest, 39*(1).

Churches, Andrew. 2009. "Bloom's Digital Taxonomy." Accessed January 2012, http://edorigami.wikispaces.com/.

Dresang, Eliza T. 1990. "Interviewing Using Micro-Moments and Backward Chaining." In *Evaluation Strategies and Techniques for Public Library Children's Services: Sourcebook*, edited by Jane Robbins, Holly Willett, M. J. Wiseman, and Doug Zweizig. Madison, WI: University of Wisconsin–Madison, School of Library and Information Studies.

Dresang, Eliza T. 1997. "Influence of the Digital Environment on Literature for Youth: Radical Change in the Handheld Book." *Library Trends* 45 (4): 639–63.

Dresang, Eliza T. 1999. *Radical Change: Books for Youth in a Digital Age.* New York: H.W. Wilson.

Dresang, Eliza T. 2005a. "The Information Seeking Behavior of Youth in the Digital Environment." *Library Trends* 54 (2): 178–96.

Dresang, Eliza T. 2005b. "Radical Change." In *Theories of Information Behavior: A Researcher's Guide*, edited by Karen E. Fisher, Sanda Erdelez, and E. F. McKehnie, 298–302. Medford, NJ: Information Today, Inc., for the Association of Information Science and Technology.

Dresang, Eliza T. 2008. "Radical Change Revisited: Dynamic Digital Age Books for Youth." In *Contemporary Issues in Technology and Teacher Education.* Accessed January 2012, http://www.citejournal.org/vol8/iss3/seminal/article2.cfm.

Dresang, Eliza T., Kathy Burnett, Janet Capps, and Erika Feldman. 2010. *The Early Literacy Landscape for Public Libraries and their Partners: A White Paper.* Accessed January 2012, http://cleary.ischool.uw.edu/sites/cleary.ischool.uw.edu/files/WhitePaper.SuppDoc1_0.pdf.

Dresang, Eliza T., and Kathleen Campana. 2011. "Emergent Readers Literacy Training and Assessment Program: Research Report." Tacoma, WA: Pierce County Library Foundation.

Dresang, Eliza T., and Bowie Kotrla. 2010. "School Libraries and the Transformation of Readers and Reading." In *Handbook of Research on Children's and Young Adult Literature*, edited by Shelby Wolf, Karen Coats, Patricia Enciso, and Christine A. Jenkins, 121–34.

Druin, Allison. 2002. "The Role of Children in the Design of Technology." *Behaviour and Information Technology* 21 (1): 1–25.

Eisenberg, Michael B., and R. E. Berkowitz. 1990. *Information Problem Solving: The Big Six Skills Approach to Library and Information Skills Instruction.* Norwood, NJ: Ablex Publishing.

Eisenberg, Michael, C. A. Lowe, and K. L. Spitzer. 2004. *Information Literacy: Essential Skills for the Information Age.* 2nd ed. Westport, CT: Libraries Unlimited.

Guernsey, Lisa. 2011. "Are Ebooks Any Good?" *School Library Journal* 57 (6).

Hart, Christopher Thomas. 2008. *Exploring the Information-Seeking Behavior of the Staff and Students of the Florida Virtual School: A Case Study.* The Florida State University.

ICDL Foundation. 2011. "International Children's Digital Library." Accessed August 20, 2011, http://en.childrenslibrary.org/about/mission.shtml.

Institute for Learning and Brain Sciences. 2011. "I-Labs." Accessed August 21, 2011, http://ilabs.washington.edu/.

Ito, Mizuko, et al. 2010. "Hanging out, Messing around, and GeekingOut: Kids Living and Learning with New Media." Cambridge, MA: MIT Press. Nook edition. Also Accessed August 20, 2011, http://mitpress.mit.edu/books/full_pdfs/Hanging_Out.pdf.

Jenkins, Henry. 2008. *Convergence Culture: Where Old and New Media Collide.* Rev. ed. New York: NYU Press.

Kaiser Family Foundation. 2005. "Generation M: Media in the Lives of 8–18 Year-Olds." Accessed January 2012, http://www.kff.org/entmedia/upload/Executive-Summary-Generation-M-Media-in-the-Lives-of-8-18-Year-olds.pdf.

Koh, Kyungwon. 2011. "Proposing a Theoretical Framework for Digital Age Youth Information Behavior Building Upon Radical Change Theory." Unpublished Ph.D. thesis. The Florida State University.

Konkoma, Ron. 2010. "Flood of Christmas Nooks Crashes Barnes and Noble Website." Accessed August 19, 2011, http://www.godroidgo.com/2010/12/flood-of-christmas-nooks-crashes-barnes.html.

Kuhl, Patricia. 2010. "The Linguistic Genius of Babies." Accessed August 15, 2011, http://www.ted.com/talks/patricia_kuhl_the_linguistic_genius_of_babies.html.

Large, Andrew, Beheshti Jamshid, Valerie Nesset, and Leanne Bowler. 2007. "Children's Web Portals: Can an Intergenerational Design Team Deliver the Goods?" In *Youth Information-Seeking Behavior II: Context, Theories, Models, and Issues*, edited by Mary K. Chelton and Colleen Cool, 313–64. Lanham, MD: The Scarecrow Press, Inc.

Learning Technologies Center. 2011. "2010 Scratch at MIT." Accessed August 11, 2011, http://www.smm.org/ltc/node/382.

Livingstone, Sonia. 2002. *Young People and New Media*. London, UK, and Thousand Oaks, CA: Sage Publications.

MacArthur Foundation. "MacArthur Foundation: Building the Field of Digital Media and Learning." Accessed August 20, 2011, http://digitallearning.macfound.org/site/c.enJLKQNlFiG/b.2029199/k.94AC/Latest_News.htm.

Manjarrez, C. A., K. A. Miller, T. Craig, S. Dorinski, M. Freeman, N. Isaac, P. O'Shea, P. Schilling, and J. Scotto. 2011. "Data File Documentation: Public Libraries Survey: Fiscal Year 2009 (Imls-2011-Pls-01)." Washington, DC: Institute of Museum and Library Services.

Mansfield University. School of Library and Information Technologies. 2011. "School Library Impact Studies Project." Accessed August 20, 2011, http://library.mansfield.edu/impact.asp.

Mardis, Marcia, and Nancy Everhart. 2011. "Digital Textbooks in Florida: Extending the Teacher-Librarians' Reach." *Teacher Librarian* 38 (3): 8–11.

Mardis, M. M., N. Everhart, D. Smith, J. Newsum, and S. Baker. 2010. "From Paper to Pixel: Digital Textbooks and Florida Schools." Palm Center, The Florida State University.

Meyers, Eric Matthew. 2011. "The Nature and Impact of Information Problem Solving in the Middle School Classroom." Unpublished Ph.D. thesis. University of Washington.

Monroy-Hernández, A., B. M. Hill, J. Gonzalez-Rivero, and D. Boyd. 2011. "Computers Can't Give Credit: How Automatic Attribution Falls Short in an Online Remixing Community." In *ACM Conference on Human Factors on Human Factors in Computer Systems*. Accessed August 19, 2011, http://info.scratch.mit.edu/sites/infoscratch.media.mit.edu/files/file/monroy-hernandez_et_al_chi2011.pdf.

National Center for Education Statistics. 2011. *Digest of Education Statistics 2010, Table 427. Selected statistics on public school libraries/media centers, by level of school: 1999–2000, 2003–04, and 2007–08*. Accessed August 9, 2011, http://nces.ed.gov/programs/digest/d10/tables/dt10_427.asp.

National Commission on Libraries and Information Science. "School Libraries Work!" 2008. Accessed August 10, 2011, http://listbuilder.scholastic.com/content/stores/LibraryStore/pages/images/SLW3.pdf.

National Early Literacy Panel. 2008. *Developing Early Literacy*. Accessed August 18, 2011, http://lincs.ed.gov/publications/pdf/NELPReport09.pdf.

National Reading Panel. *Summary Report*. 2000. Accessed August 10, 2011, http://www.nationalreadingpanel.org/publications/summary.htm.

Pew Research Center. 2009. "Teens and Mobile Phones over the Past Five Years: Pew Internet Looks Back." Accessed August 11, 2011, http://www.pewinternet.org/Reports/2009/14--Teens-and-Mobile-Phones-Data-Memo.aspx.

Phipps, Molly. 2010. "Meeting Learners Where They Are: A Case Study of Media Mashup Libraries' Approaches to Teaching 21st Century Literacy Skills." Accessed August 20, 2011, http://www.hclib.org/extranet/MediaMashup/casestudy_MMU_final_Jan2011.pdf.

"Reference USA." 2011. Infogroup Reference Division. Database.

School Library Impact Studies. 2011. Colorado State Library. 1993–2011. Accessed July 30, 2011, http://www.ors.org/impact.php.

Scratch. Accessed August 9, 2011, http://scratch.mit.edu/.

Scratch. "Scratch Resources." Accessed August 9, 2011, http://resources.scratchr.org.

Scratch. "Scratch Statistics." Accessed August 9, 2011, http://stats.scratch.mit.edu/community/">http://stats.scratch.mit.edu/community/.

Scratch. "Scratch Wiki." Accessed August 9, 2011, http://wiki.scratch.mit.edu/wiki/Scratch_Wiki.

Springen, Karen. 2010. "The Digital Revolution in Children's Publishing." *Publishers Weekly*, 19 July: 19–22.

Springen, Karen. 2011a. "What's Right with This Picture?" *School Library Journal* 257, 3 (March): 36–42.

Springen, Karen. 2011b. "Reaching the e-Teen." *School Library Journal* 258 (8): 21–24.

Tracy, James. 2010. "Books in All Formats." *New York Times*, February 10. Accessed August 20, 2011, http://roomfordebate.blogs.nytimes.com/2010/02/10/do-school-libraries-need-books/#james.

Valenza, Joyce Kasman. 2007. "'It'd Be Really Dumb Not to Use It': Virtual Libraries and High School Students' Information Seeking and Use : A Focus Group Investigation." In *Youth Information-Seeking Behavior II: Context, Theories, Models, and Issues*, edited by Mary K. Chelton and Colleen Cool, 207–56. Lanham, MD: Scarecrow Press.

Vygotsky, L. S. 1986. *Thought and Language*. Edited and trans. by A. Kozulin. Cambridge, MA: MIT Press.

Chapter Six

Youth and Online Social Networking

What Do We Know So Far?

Denise E. Agosto and June Abbas

Within the first decade or so of their existence, social network sites (SNS) have gained millions of users around the world, including many teens, pre-teens, and even children. Researchers are beginning to understand why and how young people use SNS, but the research is still fairly limited. In many ways, today's youth use SNS for the same purposes as past youth generations used more traditional communication and interaction media and tools, such as telephones, televisions, and paper notes. They use them to gossip; for entertainment; to discuss music, fashion, movies, and schoolwork; for socializing with friends, family, and romantic interests; and for fulfilling intellectual curiosity. Above all, SNS provide youth shared spaces for interaction and communication with known—and sometimes unknown—groups of people. This chapter will review what is known to date about why and how young people use SNS and consider directions for future research into this increasingly important aspect of youth's digital lives.

WHAT ARE SNS?

Anttiroiko and Savolainen (2011) defined SNS as "profile-based hosted services that allow people to create and maintain networks of friends and contacts based on general social interests" (89). Probably the best-known general-purpose SNS are MySpace, Facebook, and Twitter (although some people have argued that Twitter is not an SNS, but a microblogging site with fewer functions than a full-blown SNS). Each of these sites has millions of users, many of whom check their accounts daily to communicate with online "friends," to share personal news, world news, photographs, videos, and favorite Web links, and to keep up with their friends' daily activities. These are just three of the many hundreds of SNS that exist. Many smaller SNS target special interest groups, such as Care2 (for people interested in social activism and environmental issues) and VampireFreaks.com (for the discussion and exchange of all things related to vampires and vampire art).

The fundamental element of most SNS is the user profile, which typically includes basic biographical information, photograph(s), interests, and other general information about the user. The typical SNS enables subscribers to create lists of "friends," or users granted joint access to each other's full profiles and personal content. SNS bring together in one location many functions that other online services provide separately, such as blogs, short news updates, photo and video storage, link collecting, instant messaging, discussion forums, tagging, and question asking/answering. With the profile as the user's social networking home base, most SNS thus enable registered users to communicate with each other and to share and comment on each other's content, such as Web links, online news items, personal stories and updates, photographs, videos, and more. Although each site varies somewhat in design, functionality, purpose, and audience, they share the core purpose of bringing people together to communicate and engage online.

Much of the early research relating to youth and SNS focused on My-Space because of its overwhelming popularity with online youth, but this popularity has dwindled over the past few years. Facebook has since become the world's largest online social network, with more than 750 million active users as of mid-2011 (Facebook 2011). Compared to adults, U.S. teens are particularly heavy users of SNS. As of September 2009, 73 percent of online teens were SNS users, as opposed to just 47 percent of online adults (Lenhart, Ling, Campbell, and Purcell 2010, 17). In the United States, Facebook is the most popular SNS with teen users, although there does seem to be some teen movement away from Facebook toward smaller, more specialized sites (Van Grove 2010).

IDENTIFYING THE LITERATURE

Against this backdrop of heavy youth participation in SNS, a growing number of researchers interested in youth's behaviors online have begun to focus on studying SNS environments. In order to identify this body of literature, it was first necessary to select an age range with which to define "youth." Initial searching of the literature showed that the bulk of the youth and SNS studies focused on users from the ages of 12 to 18. For this reason, the literature search was limited to studies that included participants within this seven-year age range. Studies that used college students as the youngest participants were omitted from the literature search, even when 18-year-olds were studied, as the focus was on research with pre-college-aged populations.

The scope of the literature search was further limited to studies that (1) identified youth's use of one or more online social networks (such as Facebook, MySpace, or Friendster) as an area of study; (2) gathered original data directly from youth or reanalyzed existing raw data that had been gathered directly from youth; and (3) were written in English. Literature reviews, opinion essays, and other publications that did not meet these selection criteria were excluded. The resulting body of literature included 38 studies published between 2006 and 2011. They extended across a wide range of academic disciplines and domains, including communication and media studies, psychology, library and information science, education, computing, government policy studies, visual studies, and health sciences.

ANALYZING THE LITERATURE: AGES OF STUDY PARTICIPANTS

Although the analysis was limited to studies of youth in the 12 to 18 age range, there was considerable variance in the specific age ranges included in each study, with some studies including youth as young as 9, and others including those as old as 20, all under the terms "youth," "adolescents," "teens," "teenagers," "young adults," "young people," and so on. Figure 6.1 shows the number of studies for each of the age ranges used. The studies are widely dispersed across age groups, with only four age ranges (12–17, 13–16, 17–19, and 18) used in more than one study. Six of the studies did not give specific age ranges, but instead identified participant ages as "teens," "teenagers," "adolescents," "middle school students," or "high school students."

Figure 6.2 depicts the number of studies that included youth by individual age year, such as the number of studies that gathered data from 13-year-olds. It shows relatively high coverage for all seven years in the 12 to 18 target age range, with ages 14, 15, and 16 receiving the most research attention.

In the United States, the use of SNS is higher among teens than children, as many U.S.-based SNS limit membership to users aged 13 and over in response to federal regulations restricting data collection from minors. This is not to say that children under 13 do not use these sites. Quite the contrary—millions of youth from around the world have lied about their ages to get accounts. In May 2011, for example, *Consumer Reports* (2011) released a study estimating that 7.5 million Facebook users worldwide were

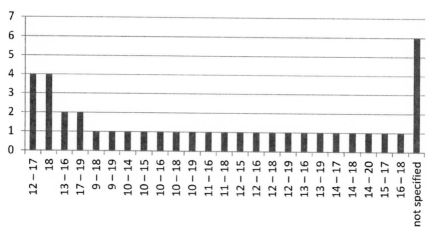

Figure 6.1.   Number of studies by participant age ranges

under 13, with over five million registered users younger than 10, despite the minimum age membership of 13, and despite Facebook's ongoing efforts to close accounts held by underage users.

Still, at least in part due to age restrictions, in the United States, older teens are more likely than younger teens to use SNS:

> As we have seen consistently over time, older online teens are more likely to report using online social networks than younger teens. While more than 4 in 5 (82 percent) of teens ages 14–17 use online social networks, just a bit more than half of online teens ages 12–13 say they use these sites. . . . Among online teens just 46 percent of 12-year-olds in the study used social network sites, while 62 percent of the 13-year-olds used them. (Lenhart, Purcell, Smith, and Zickuhr 2010, 17)

Another issue relating to the study of young people's SNS use is the question of what to call young users. Within the body of literature analyzed, researchers used many terms to identify their study populations, including "adolescents," "teens," "teenagers," "youth," "young people," and "young adults," often using multiple terms interchangeably within the same paper. Reflecting the use in the literature, these terms are used interchangeably throughout this chapter as well, even though it is recognized that there are significant developmental differences between the average 12-year-old and the average 18-year-old.

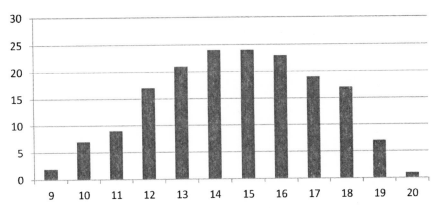

Figure 6.2. Number of studies including youth ages 9–20

ANALYZING THE LITERATURE: GEOGRAPHIC LOCATIONS

Figure 6.3 shows the distribution of studies according to the geographic location of the participants. Participants came from the United States, the UK, Australia, the Netherlands, and Canada. The five studies that did not specify geographic locations studied members of a particular social network regardless of their national origins, such as a content analysis of teen My-Space users' profiles. These studies likely included users from multiple countries, reflecting the international nature of the larger SNS.

Of the five countries shown in Figure 6.3, four are majority English-speaking. This uneven emphasis on research conducted with English-speaking youth is due mainly to the fact that the literature review was limited to studies published in English, rather than due to the majority of youth using SNS being English speakers. In actuality, social networking is popular with online youth around the world. Facebook, for example, is available in more than 70 languages, and more than 70 percent of its users come from outside the United States (Facebook 2011). Still, slightly more than half the studies analyzed here (20 studies, or 52.6 percent) were conducted with youth living in the United States.

ANALYZING THE LITERATURE: DATA COLLECTION METHODS

Coming from such a wide range of disciplines and domains, it is no surprise that the studies employed an equally wide range of data collection methods, as shown in Figure 6.4. Surveys were the most common, with 10 (26.3

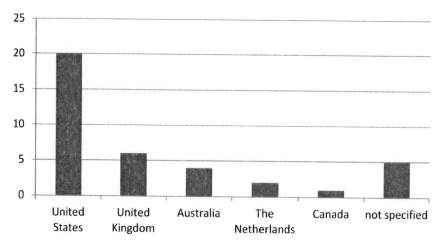

Figure 6.3.   Study participants' countries of origin

percent) of the 38 studies using surveys to gather data directly from youth. The survey distributions ranged from large-scale national surveys to small-scale local surveys conducted in classroom and university settings.

Next in frequency were focus groups used alone (six studies, or 15.8 percent) as well as content analysis of youth's SNS content, primarily profile content analysis (six studies, or 15.8 percent). In these studies, researchers analyzed SNS profiles to learn about the kinds of information youth posted online and to study their reactions to comments and responses to their online materials. Five (13.2 percent) of the studies used multiple ethnographic methods for in-depth qualitative data gathering, such as combining observations, document analysis, individual interviews, and focus groups all in one study. Four more (10.5 percent) combined surveys with focus groups. Three (7.9 percent) of the studies reanalyzed existing large-scale survey data to uncover SNS use patterns and to identify user characteristics correlated to increased SNS use. Three more studies (7.9 percent) gathered data solely via individual interviews with youth, and just one study (2.6 percent) used a controlled experiment for gathering data relating to youth's assessments of peers' SNS content. Combining studies that used focus groups exclusively with those that combined focus groups with other data collection methods yields a total of 14 studies (36.8 percent), or more than one-third of the studies, making focus groups the most popular data collection method within the body of studies analyzed.

Each of these methods or sets of methods comes with advantages and limitations. In light of the quickly evolving nature of SNS development, the time involved in designing, completing, and reporting a study can be a particular problem for SNS researchers:

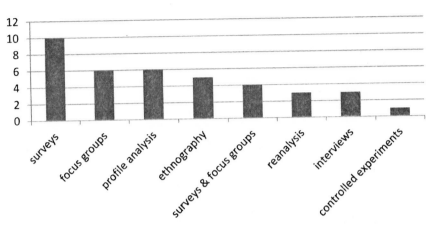

Figure 6.4.   Data collection methods

Online communication forms are in a state of flux, and many operate like a fad. By the time researchers become aware of a popular online application or site, identify the research issues, design a well thought-out study, and get IRB approval, the population of interest has moved on to the next new application. (Subrahmanyam and Greenfield 2008b, 417)

Lag time can be especially problematic for studies based on re-analysis of previously published survey data. Lag time for publication of the original survey data plus lag time for publication of the re-analysis means that at the time of publication, these studies discuss data sets that are usually two, three, or even four years old—periods that are often longer than the popularity of the platforms and applications under study. Although technologies come and go quickly, youth behaviors tend to change more slowly. For this reason, the most valuable studies over the long term tend to focus more on young people's developmentally based behaviors as SNS users, rather than focusing on their specific site choices or on fleeting use fads. Keeping youth—rather the specific SNS—as the central focus of research can thereby produce research findings of longer value to the research and practice communities, regardless of study design and data collection methods.

ANALYZING THE LITERATURE: PREVAILING THEMES

The burgeoning body of literature paints a multifaceted picture of young people's SNS practices, and of the major issues that surround their participation in social networking communities. For the most part, the kinds of activities taking place in SNS are the same kinds of activities that took place offline among previous generations of young people. The difference is not so much the *kinds* of activities that are occurring online, but the *amount, frequency*, and *semi-public nature* of these activities (Boyd 2006, 2008; Livingstone and Brake 2010). Youth are engaging with peers more frequently and more publicly than ever before, often throughout the school day and even all night via cell phone and computer access to SNS and other digital tools, platforms, and applications (Agosto and Abbas 2010).

Three categories of themes recur throughout the studies: (1) youth's motivations for using SNS, (2) potential benefits to youth who use SNS, and (3) potential harms to young SNS users. Together these themes offer a preliminary explanation of why youth use SNS and the likely outcomes of that use. Table 6.1 lists the major themes in the literature and the studies that investigated them.

Motivations for Use

Researchers have identified a number of reasons why youth choose to use SNS. These conscious motivations include social interaction and communication, relationship building and maintenance, emotional support, and convenience.

Since the initial rise of SNS, *social interaction and communication* have been driving forces behind youth participation. As Livingstone and Brake (2010) explain, "What remains constant, driving online and mobile communication, is young people's strong desire to connect with peers anywhere, anytime—to stay in touch, express themselves, and share experiences" (76).

Youth tend to use SNS more to communicate and interact with preexisting friends than for making new friends (Agosto and Abbas 2009; Boyd 2008; Clarke 2009; Luckin et al. 2009; Subrahmanyam and Greenfield 2008a; Valkenburg and Peter 2009; Williams and Merten 2008). This is generally true of both friendships and romantic relationships (Subrahmanyam and Greenfield 2008a). Young people are apt to believe that social network membership and use strengthen existing friendships as well as relationships with family members (Greenhow and Robelia 2009b). However, young people who consider themselves to be lonely do sometimes turn to these environments seeking new relationships (Bonetti, Campbell, and Gilmore 2010).

Even so, the stereotype of the socially disconnected teen spending long hours in his or her room communicating online with strangers in order to compensate for a lack of face-to-face relationships seems to be just that—a stereotype. Youth who are active offline communicators tend to be active online communicators as well. For the most part, "adolescents who are socially competent in offline settings also often use online communication technologies, such as IM, to stay in touch with these friends" (Valkenburg and Peter 2009, 3).

Table 6.1.   Major Themes in Youth and SNS Research

Motiva-tion	Social interaction/ Communication	Agosto and Abbas 2010; Agosto and Abbas, in press; Bonetti, Campbell, and Gilmore 2010; Boyd 2006; Boyd 2008; Clarke 2009; Greenhow and Robelia 2009b; Hundley and Shyles 2010; Ito et al. 2010; Luckin et al. 2009; Pierce 2009; Spires et al. 2008
	Relationship building and maintenance	Agosto and Abbas 2010; Agosto and Abbas, in press; Baker and White 2010; Bonetti, Campbell, and Gilmore 2010; Clarke 2009; Greenhow and Robelia 2009b; Hundley and Shyles 2010; Livingstone 2008; Mallan 2009; Pfeil, Arjan, and Zaphiris 2009
	Emotional support	Bonetti, Campbell, and Gilmore 2010; Clarke 2009; Greenhow and Robelia 2009b; Williams and Merten 2009
	Convenience	Agosto and Abbas, 2010; Agosto and Abbas, in press; Hundley and Shyles 2010
Benefits	Identity exploration and formation	Antheunis and Schouten 2011; Bonetti, Campbell, and Gilmore 2010; Boyd 2006; Boyd 2008; Clarke 2009; Durrant, Frohlich, Sellen, and Uzzell 2011; Greenhow and Robelia 2009a; Greenhow and Robelia 2009b; Mallan 2009; Williams and Merten 2008; Williams and Merten 2009
	Technological literacy	Agosto and Abbas 2011; Greenhow and Robelia 2009a; Greenhow and Robelia 2009b; Helsper and Eynon 2010; Ito et al. 2010; Livingstone 2008; Livingstone and Helsper 2010
	Educational support/ Formal learning	Greenhow and Robelia 2009a; Greenhow and Robelia 2009b; Luckin et al. 2009
	Positive self-esteem	Baker and White 2010; Valkenburg, Peter, and Schouten 2006
Harms	Privacy risks	Agosto and Abbas 2010; Agosto and Abbas 2011; Boyd 2008; Christofides, Muise, and Desmarais 2012; De Souza and Dick 2009; Hinduja and Patchin 2008; Livingstone 2008; Mallan 2009; Patchin and Hinduja 2010
	Security risks	Agosto and Abbas 2010; Agosto and Abbas 2011; Christofides, Muise, and Desmarais 2012; Fuller and Damico 2008; Hinduja and Patchin 2008; Ito et al. 2010; Livingstone and Helsper 2010; Mallan 2009; Moreno et al. 2009; Patchin and Hinduja 2010; Rosen, Cheever, and Carrier 2008; Sengupta and Chaudhuri 2011; Ybarra and Mitchell 2008

For today's young people, participating in SNS means taking part in a crucial component of modern society. Ito and colleagues (2010), in a three-year multi-project study, sought to gain a deeper understanding of how new media practices are embedded in the broader social and cultural practices of today's youth. The study authors concluded that "participation in online communication and gaming is becoming central to youth sociability" (Ito et al. 2010, 347) and as such, it has become an important part of young people's everyday social and communicative practices.

The next motivating factor for SNS use, *relationship building and maintenance*, is closely tied to social interaction and communication. For most teens, rather than supplanting offline relationships, social network use complements and augments existing offline relationships (Clarke 2009). In fact, a young person's set of SNS friends typically overlaps largely with friends and relatives known first in the offline world (Hundley and Shyles 2010). This overlap is increasing each year as more and more youth and adults are joining SNS communities. As Fleming and Rickwood (2004) concluded, "To date, research suggests that online relationships of some kind, whether casual or close, are formed by large numbers of teens. Reassuringly for parents, most of these relationships seem to be extensions of the young person's social circle" (51).

Although SNS serve as vehicles for relationship building and maintenance, they are not the only type of information communication technology (ICT) to play this role, or even the first choice for most daily interactions. Texting using a cell phone is teens' preferred choice of technology when communicating with friends, and cell phone calling is the second favorite choice (Lenhart, Ling, Campbell, and Purcell 2010). Teens typically view SNS as less intimate communication media, preferring them for less frequent contact with a much wider range of friends and sometimes parents, siblings, and other relatives (Agosto and Abbas 2010).

Online relationship building and maintenance can also provide *emotional support* for young users. Several studies have concluded that SNS use can contribute to youths' emotional health by helping to build strong, healthy peer relationships that can ease the emotional stress of adolescence. In their review of the literature, Valkenburg and Peter (2009) explained that "most recent studies have demonstrated that adolescents' online communication stimulates, rather than reduces, social connectedness and/or wellbeing" (2), enabling youth to discuss issues and problems with their online friends.

In addition to the general emotional support that can come from the regular use of SNS, youth sometimes turn to SNS specifically seeking emotional support in coping with difficult situations. For example, Williams and Merten (2009) studied the SNS profiles of 20 teens who had died suddenly to analyze the kinds of messages, photos, and other feedback youth had posted in the aftermath of the deaths. The study authors found that most youth used the profiles to speak directly to the deceased as a method of coping with their deaths:

> While talking to the dead as if they were an attentive audience, adolescents reminisced about past shared experiences, provided updates on their current situations, discussed the death and their bereavement process, and posted a variety of emotional commentary which, based on theory, was assessed as indication of active coping. (85)

The final motivation for SNS use is *convenience*. Young people choose to communicate and interact via SNS because they are easy to use and because most of their peers have ready access. As Boyd (2008) wrote of her work with young MySpace users, "When I ask teenagers why they joined MySpace, the answer is simple: 'Cuz that's where my friends are'" (126). SNS are a convenient way to interact with friends when face-to-face interaction is inconvenient or even impossible.

Convenience is often a motivating factor behind ICT choice in general, not just SNS use. Hundley and Shyles (2010) explained that "the devices that appear to be most appealing [to adolescents] are those perceived to make content easily accessible and shareable while being convenient and handy to use" (427). Highly technological youth are quick to express frustration when peers and family members lack access to SNS and other popular ICTs, making communication difficult and less convenient (Agosto and Abbas 2010).

Benefits of Use

Parents, educators, and even teens themselves often think of time spent using SNS as wasted (Fuller and Damico 2008). A 60 Minutes/Vanity Fair poll (October 2010) found that Americans rated social networking as their biggest waste of time, even more than TV watching and shopping (CBS, 2010). Nevertheless, most researchers working in this area have identified at least one, and often more, potential benefits for young people who use SNS. Frequently identified benefits include identity exploration and formation, increased technological literacy, educational support and formal learning, and the promotion of positive self-esteem.

Across disciplines and domains, the most commonly identified benefit of SNS use is the facilitation of *identity exploration and formation*. Much of this facilitation occurs with "the creation of online personal profiles and the formation of social networks [which] impacts directly on the expression of identity and how identity is performed and reinforced" (Greenhow and Robelia 2009a, 124). As Erikson (1968) argued more than 40 years ago, adolescence is a chief period of identity exploration, and a significant part of an adolescent's time is devoted to learning to understand and accept his or her identity. The process of identity exploration in adolescence has not changed at a fundamental level, but online adolescents have adopted new tools for engaging in the process, moving it more and more into online venues. Via SNS, youth are able to try out new identities and learn how peers and others will react to them. They use both text (words) and nontext (photos, videos, music, etc.) to experiment with different identities and social group associations (Greenhow and Robelia 2009a, 2009b). SNS's seamless integration of multiple types of information formats is ideally suited for facilitating identity exploration and for enabling youth to try out and reject many different identities and forms of personal expression.

Visual content in particular can provide a platform for identity exploration and declaration. Based on comparison of teen girls' SNS photograph collections and of their bedroom photograph displays, Durrant, Frohlich, Sellen, and Uzzell (2011) learned that "online displays were solely associated with presentations to peers *as opposed* to family; we observed that teens harnessed the Internet as a means to establish and maintain the separateness of self from family" (116). Whereas the girls' bedroom photographs tended to show them with family members, their photos online showed them with peers or alone, serving to create online identities that tied them more closely to peers than to family members.

The process of online identity exploration and building fulfills "the desire to construct a valued representation of oneself which affirms and is affirmed by one's peers" (Livingstone and Brake 2010, 76). SNS are essentially public spaces. As such, they enable teens to try on different identities and to learn how others will react to them, making identity exploration online a two-way (self and public) process. This process includes positioning and associating oneself with one's friends, especially via visual content (photographs). As Mallan's (2009) study of high school students showed,

> One aspect regarding visuals on SNS profiles that warrants attention is that many students reported putting up photographs of themselves with friends, often these dominated with no single image of the profiler alone. From the students' comments, it would seem that the profile image can itself become both the object and product of collective identity representation. (56)

Another aspect of this bi-directional identity formation involves how others perceive a young SNS user based on his or her profile, photos, comments from friends, and other online content. Antheunis and Schouten (2011) used mock profiles to study how online content affects teens' perceptions of fellow SNS users. They found that teens perceived a profile owner as more attractive when his or her online friends were attractive, and also when other teens posted positive (complimentary) messages on his or her wall. In contrast, when teens judged a person's friends as unattractive, they tended to judge the person himself or herself as unattractive. There are indications that young people understand these judgments, and they use SNS photo displays to present themselves as they wish their peers to view them, particularly to associate themselves with desirable friends and friend groups (Durrant, Frohlich, Sellen, and Uzzell 2011).

Researchers have also suggested that SNS use can be educational. Perhaps the most commonly cited educational benefit is the acquisition of *technological literacy*. Also called "technical literacy," "internet literacy," "new media literacy," and a host of similar names, the general concept suggests that to be functionally literate in modern society, today's citizens must have knowledge of basic technological issues and a command of basic technological skills. Technological literacy goes beyond merely being able to function in technological environments to being able to "access, analyze, evaluate and create online content" (Livingstone and Helper 2010, 311). It also means learning how to be a good "digital citizen" who understands social and ethical norms online (Greenhow and Robelia 2009a).

Within the literature, participation in SNS environments is often viewed as a critical component of technological literacy (e.g., Greenhow, Robelia, and Hughes 2009). Ahn (2011a) used 2007 Pew Internet and American Life data to show that technological literacy was a significant predictor of social network membership. More research is needed to understand the extent to which SNS attract youth with higher technological skills in the first place, and the extent to which SNS use itself leads to increased technological literacy. Other researchers have investigated more generally the role of SNS use in providing *educational support and formal learning* opportunities. For example, Luckin et al. (2009) considered whether the use of SNS and other Web 2.0 tools encourages student learning. They concluded that the educational benefits varied according to students' technology use styles. They assigned students' use styles to four groups. In order from lowest to highest learning benefits, students who acted as "Researchers" mainly read information they found online, without engaging in significant critical analysis. "Collaborators" focused on file sharing, gaming, and communicating online. "Producers" and "Publishers" used online tools for creating original content and for sharing personal experiences through SNS, and they reaped the most learning benefits of the four types of learners. The authors concluded that while social media can promote learning, SNS in particular might not be ideal for formal educational delivery due to students' associating them with their nonschool lives:

> Some learners viewed the online social space [of SNS] as an important *respite* from school; when asked about bringing social networking into school for learning, learners generally continued to envisage the tool being used for socialization rather than learning, unless further prompted by the researcher. (97)

Few schools to date have incorporated SNS use into the curriculum, so it is not surprising that Spires and colleagues (2008) found middle school students used SNS and other social media much more frequently outside of school than during school hours. The students in the study were particularly interested in social media for social interaction and entertainment, which they found more enjoyable than the static information searching that normally comprised their computer use while at school.

When students do choose to use SNS outside of school to support their schoolwork, the support tends to be closely tied to socialization and peer-to-peer information sharing:

> MySpace provided participants with school task-related support. This took several forms, some more direct than others, such as "chatting" online to mitigate school-related stress, asking questions about instructions or deadlines, planning study groups, broadcasting or requesting educational resources from the network (e.g., "if they know a site that would help me in my project, they'll post it up and I can go see it"), gathering project materials, brainstorming ideas, sharing written works, and exchanging feedback. (Greenhow and Robelia 2009b, 1148)

Other researchers have suggested that when using SNS to engage in educational support, youth are not just consumers of information but information producers as well. They create new posts and written notes, remix existing content, edit videos and photos, and so on. These are critical educational and literacy skills for twenty-first-century learners (Greenhow and Robelia 2009a, 2009b). Greenhow and Robelia (2009a) concluded that "students may be using MySpace outside of school to support formal content area learning, but do not necessarily recognize they are doing so" (129). Student and teacher recognition is necessary in order to begin taking fuller advantage of the possible formal educational support potential of SNS.

Lastly under benefits to SNS users, several studies have shown that SNS use can promote *positive self-esteem*, although the effects on self-esteem are not always positive. For example, Valkenburg, Peter, and Schouten (2006) used surveys to investigate the effects of peer feedback within SNS environments. They found that

> adolescents' self-esteem was affected solely by the tone of the feedback that adolescents received on their profiles: Positive feedback enhanced adolescents' self-esteem, and negative feedback decreased their self-esteem. (589)

More than three-quarters of the youth in the study received consistently positive feedback, and for those youth, SNS use provided a significant boon for self-esteem. However, about 7 percent of the participants received consistently negative feedback and suffered consequent damage to self-esteem.

Even though self-esteem does appear to be affected by SNS use, high or low self-esteem does not seem to be a predictor of whether or not youth will use SNS in the first place (Baker and White 2010). Overall, the research generally finds SNS use to be beneficial to self-esteem for most young users (Ahn, 2011b), but further investigation is needed to understand the full effects.

HARMS OF USE

Researchers have also identified potential harms from young people's SNS use, such as the possible negative effects on self-esteem described above. Most researchers recognize that there is an element of risk involved in use. Multiple studies have found that adolescents themselves are also aware that SNS use can be risky (e.g., Agosto and Abbas 2011; Hundley and Shyles 2010; Livingstone 2008; Mallan 2009). Perhaps reflecting adult attitudes and popular media representations, many youth think of SNS as the most risky digital tools (Hundley and Shyles 2010). Even younger teens, aged 10 to 14, share a widespread awareness of potential risks (Clarke 2009).

As a result of risk awareness, teens often engage in self-protection behaviors, such as friending only people known first in the offline world (Agosto and Abbas 2010; Hundley and Shyles 2010). Many youth also restrict the information that they put online, especially to prevent parents and other adults from viewing potentially objectionable material (e.g., Livingstone 2008; Subrahmanyam and Greenfield 2008a). Still other teens create accounts with partial names or even fake names to protect their identities (Agosto and Abbas, 2010; Hundley and Shyles 2010). These protective measures, however, do not ensure secure online interactions, or even a full understanding of possible risks.

Within the literature, researchers have tended to focus on two categories of risk: privacy risks and security risks. It seems that *privacy risks* are an unavoidable aspect of SNS use. Given that information sharing is the fundamental basis of most social networking activities, "privacy" in SNS is largely tied to having control over the types of personal information made available online and having control over who can access it (Livingstone 2008; Mallan 2009).

Several authors have differentiated between privacy in the online and offline worlds. Boyd (2008) suggested that SNS can be considered "networked publics." Networked publics differ from more traditional public spaces, such as parks or shopping malls, in four major ways: (1) persistence: the interactions in networked publics are recorded; (2) searchability: recorded interactions can often be accessed via search functions; (3) replicability: users can make exact copies of content that others create; and (4) invisible audiences: "unseen" or otherwise undetected audiences can witness interactions that take place in these environments. As networked publics are newer environments than traditional offline public spaces, the full implications of personal privacy in SNS are not yet understood.

Further complicating the issue of online privacy is the fact that notions of "private" and "public" often blur on the social Web. "Web 2.0 significantly reworks the distinction between public and private through its emphasis on community, friends, communication, and recognition within its cultural spaces" (Mallan 2009, 61). Many youth behaviors that were previously private, such as socializing with friends, are now taking place in public view.

Moreover, since digital technologies afford the easy replication and sharing of exact copies of personal information, privacy in SNS is more of a community responsibility than privacy in the offline world (Agosto and Abbas 2011). Although many adolescents feel that they have a good understanding of privacy risks tied to information sharing online, many are less aware of how easily their friends—and even strangers—can compromise their privacy. As Mallan (2009) explains,

> Students' comments display a sense of trust in their own ability to control any potential unwanted visitors to their sites. . . . While trust in one's own ability is one thing, another is to place trust in a person or other users who may turn out to be untrustworthy. (62)

Despite popular images of online adolescents willfully exposing their personal lives online for all to see, most researchers who have investigated youth's attitudes toward online privacy have found them to voice privacy concerns (e.g. Agosto and Abbas 2011; Christofides, Muise, and Desmarais 2012; Hinduja and Patchin 2008). It also seems likely that youth possess similar levels of interest in privacy protection as do adults:

> Although there seems to be a popular perception that adolescents care less about their privacy than adults, it seems that there are more similarities than differences across age groups in the factors that predict information sharing on Facebook. (Christofides, Muise, and Desmarais 2012, 6)

Nonetheless, there is widespread agreement within the research that adults concerned with young people's online safety must monitor the types and extent of personal information youth post in SNS. Recommended adult intervention and safety measures include "supervising adolescents online whenever possible, promoting awareness of online safety and ethical use of computers and the Internet, and investigating incidents that are potentially injurious" (Hinduja and Patchin 2008, 139). Additional measures include developing new SNS features and tools to protect youth privacy and safety, as well as focusing on educating youth about the potential dangers of and best practices for conducting SNS interactions.

Still, the popular media have persisted in representing young people as interacting in SNS without regard to personal privacy (Agosto and Abbas 2009; Hinduja and Patchin 2008; Livingstone 2008). The persistence of this inaccurate stereotype might stem partly from the fact that many youth spend more time online than many adults, and increased time online is tied to increased disclosure of personal information (Christofides, Muise, and Desmarais 2012). This suggests that the average online youth does disclose more personal information than the average online adult, but the increased disclosure is largely due to increased time spent online, not lax regard for privacy. De Souza and Dick (2009) studied additional factors that lead teens to disclose personal information on MySpace. They found three main factors: peer pressure (providing personal information to conform with peer norms), website interface design (providing personal information because a website asks for it), and signaling (providing personal information to present a desirable online identity). They also found that youth who value privacy strongly in the offline world are less likely to disclose personal information online than those who place less value on offline privacy.

Increased experience is also tied to a greater awareness of online privacy issues. Hinduja and Patchin (2008, 2010) found an increase in the number of teens who were setting their MySpace pages to private from one year to the next. In 2006, only 39.4 percent of the random youth profiles they examined were set to private, while in 2007 this number increased to 45.6 percent.

However, merely relying on SNS' privacy control settings is insufficient for protecting one's privacy online. Privacy settings are complex and often confusing, and they vary from site to site. Many adolescents have difficulty choosing the settings that best meet their desired levels of privacy (Agosto and Abbas 2011; Livingstone 2008). Further, characteristics of the SNS themselves and limitations of privacy settings encourage increased information disclosure (Livingstone and Brake 2010). When a site asks for full names, ages, physical addresses, and so on, youth are naturally inclined to provide that information, often overlooking the extent to which it will be broadcast to other site users or to the online world at large.

Security risks also received a great deal of research attention within the body of literature analyzed, perhaps spurred on by the great deal of attention security issues have received in the popular press. The media frequently portray SNS as dangerous spaces that attract "online predators and pedophiles" (Hinduja and Patchin 2008, 131). With the intention of "protect[ing] children from sexual misconduct" (White 2011), the state of Missouri has even made it illegal for teachers and students to interact via social media. In reality, the risk of encountering sexual predators and pedophiles in SNS is relatively small (Hinduja and Patchin 2008; Livingstone and Brake 2010). Based on analysis of the Growing Up with Media national survey data, Ybarra and Mitchell (2008) found that just 4 percent of U.S. youth aged 10 to 15 had experienced unwanted sexual solicitation, making SNS relatively safe in comparison with other venues where young people interact and communicate online, such as chat rooms or via instant messaging (355). The authors concluded that "the majority of youth who are online are not targeted for unwanted sexual solicitation or Internet harassment, and the majority of youth who are targeted do not report it occurring in a social networking site" (356). Rosen, Cheever, and Carrier (2008) also found a minority of teen MySpace users to have experienced sexual solicitation. For those who had, "nearly all teens either reacted appropriately to sexual solicitation by rebuffing the person, blocking him/her from their MySpace, reporting the incident to an adult, or ignoring the solicitation" (469).

Still, the popular image of young people's SNS interactions often includes encounters with dangerous adults. Some of this fear can be attributed to the newness of the technology. Throughout history the introduction of most new technologies has led to public fear, and "what is often attributed to being a fear of technology *per se* is more correctly a fear or anxiety associated with new technological modes of being in the world" (Mallan 2009, 51).

While the risks of encountering sexual predators in SNS are relatively small, researchers have documented other types of security risks that are more widespread. For example, Moreno and colleagues (2009) used focus groups to study adolescents' displaying risky offline behaviors in SNS content. Of the 32 youth (aged 11 to 18) in the study, 100 percent had seen photographs of underage youth displaying alcohol references, such as posing with alcohol. As many of the study participants interpreted these images as peers' attempts to "look cool," the authors warned that "displaying these references may lead to an expectation by peers that the adolescent will drink alcohol at a future social gathering" (422), thereby leading to an increase in risky youth behaviors in the offline world.

Just as most youth are aware that SNS use involves risks to personal privacy, most also recognize that there are security risks. For example, the teens in Agosto and Abbas's (2011) study were aware of the safety risks of posting personal and/or sensitive information online, and they were able to discuss them in depth. They discussed three categories of security risks: (1) threats to physical security, or granting potentially dangerous individuals access to their personal data; (2) threats to academic/vocational security, or enabling school and other adult officials to find potentially damning information online; and (3) threats to emotional security, or opening themselves up to cyber bullying and other emotionally damaging online practices (68).

In another study, Sengupta and Chaudhuri (2011) used Pew Internet and American Life survey data to examine whether membership in an SNS was correlated to online harassment. They found that SNS membership was not a strong predictor of online harassment. Rather, demographic and behavioral characteristics were much stronger predictors of cyber bullying (aggressive behavior by a previously known antagonist) and harassment (aggressive behavior by a previously unknown antagonist). Significant risk factors included "the amount of information [teens] disclose in the public domain, the way they use the Internet (privately or publicly), and the manner in which they interact with people online" (289). The authors stressed that guidance and education are crucial to reducing cyber bullying and online harassment.

As a whole, the research is converging to suggest that while there are indeed privacy and security risks associated with SNS use, they are not markedly higher than the risks of most everyday activities in the offline world. As Ito and colleagues (2010) concluded from their study of online youth, "We did not find many youth who were engaging in any more risky behaviors than they did in offline contexts" (Ito et al. 2010, 342). Agosto and Abbas (2011) suggested that "protecting online information privacy and security becomes a balancing act. Teens must learn to balance the need to share information with the need to make smart, safe online choices" (69).

Researchers are also coming to agree that education is key to increasing young people's online privacy and safety (e.g., Agosto and Abbas 2011; Clarke 2009; Fuller and Damico 2008; Hinduja and Patchin 2008; Sengupta and Chaudhuri 2011; Ybarra and Mitchell 2008). As Agosto and Abbas (2010) explain, "Educating students how to become smarter, safer users of ICT's is likely to be more helpful over the long term by teaching lifelong survival skills, rather than merely 'protecting' teens from potentially harmful online information, such as filtering information or restricting use" (9). Education is especially important with regard to reducing cyber bullying. It appears that youth who are bullied or are likely to be bullied offline are at significantly higher risks of online bullying and other aggressive online behaviors (Clarke 2009; Hinduja and Patchin 2008). Thus, cyber bullying intervention methods should be combined with offline bullying education and intervention methods, and "prevention efforts may have a greater impact if they focus on the psychosocial problems of youth instead of a specific Internet application" (Pujazon-Zazik and Park 2010, 82).

It is crucial for adults to recognize the full range of benefits and risks of SNS use and to work to educate youth about intelligent use of these tools. The benefits and risks of SNS are inextricably linked, and, in fact, those who use SNS more and take greater advantage of their benefits are more likely to encounter online privacy and security risks (Livingstone and Helsper 2010). In their review of the youth and SNS research, Livingstone and Brake (2010) concluded, "In all, the evidence to date suggests that, for most children, social networking affords considerable benefits in terms of communication and relationships, less proven benefits as yet regarding learning and participation, and some transfer of bullying and other social risks from offline to online domains" (80). As a result, policy makers, educators, librarians, researchers, and other adults need to approach considerations of privacy and safety with a balanced perspective informed by research in order to best develop methods for maximizing youth privacy and safety in SNS and other online environments.

CONCLUSION AND RECOMMENDATIONS FOR FUTURE RESEARCH

Most of the themes identified within the literature reflect longstanding issues of youth development that have been transferred into the SNS arena, including young people's need for social interaction and communication, relationship building and maintenance, emotional support, identity exploration, positive self-esteem, educational support, privacy, and security. Most young SNS users grapple with these issues in both online and offline venues, seamlessly integrating their two worlds on a daily basis.

As youth are increasingly intermixing their online and offline lives, they are also intermixing the use of a range of SNS and other ICTs for communicating and interacting with the members of their various social, familial, and academic groups (Livingstone and Brake, 2010; Mallan 2009). This makes it difficult to isolate youth's use of SNS for research purposes. Although the focus of this chapter has been on young people's use of SNS, most youth use multiple ICTs, often simultaneously, and SNS are just one popular choice for mediated communication and interaction. Also complicating the study of SNS use is the fact that many youth use SNS and other technologies simultaneously to multitask, such as watching TV or videos online, listening to music, working on homework, sending text messages, and engaging in SNS use all at the same time (Agosto and Abbas, 2010; Hundley and Shyles 2010).

Reflecting the integrated nature of young people's multiple ICT and other technology use, many of the studies examined here investigated young people's use of a range of devices, applications, platforms, and tools, of which SNS were just one frequent choice. Overall, the research trend seems to be toward viewing youth's mediated communication from a holistic perspective, reflecting youth's increasing integration of multiple communication media. As Agosto, Valenza, and Abbas (2011) explain,

The first thing we learned is that when we're talking about teens, it's impossible to separate social networks from other methods of mediated communication, such as texting and talking via cell phones. These teens thought more in terms of the end goal—communication—than in terms of the specific technologies they would use to reach that goal. Thus, although we had intended to focus only on social network use, we ended up studying teens' use of other ICT's as well, particularly their use of cell phones. (15)

This review of the youth and SNS literature also highlights the importance of continuing to study youth as a separate sub-group, as there appear to be differences in the ways young people and adults use SNS. Some of these differences include young people's primary communication preferences for cell phone texting and SNS use over more traditional media such as verbal phone calls (e.g., Agosto and Abbas 2010; Agosto and Abbas, in press); differences in levels of information disclosure online (Christofides, Muise, and Desmarais 2012); and differences in the amount of time spent online (Christofides, Muise, and Desmarais 2012). However, there is only limited research at this point that compares how youth and adults use SNS. Much more work is needed to fully understand the effects of age, generation, and experience on young people's social networking practices.

Gender variance in young people's SNS use is another area that is not yet well understood. It does seem that girls tend to have greater numbers of online friends (Pfeil, Arjan, and Zaphiris 2009), and that adolescent girls tend to be more active SNS communicators than their male counterparts (Bonetti, Campbell, and Gilmore 2010), especially girls who are socially anxious (Pierce 2009). Girls also report more unwanted online sexual solicitations than do boys (Ybarra and Mitchell 2008). On the whole, however, there is a lack of research literature on gender differences in SNS, and much more is needed before confident claims of differences can be made.

Still another area for further investigation is the idea of today's youth as "digital natives" (Prensky 2001) who are more comfortable and more adept than adults (so-called digital immigrants) at using technologies such as SNS. Claims that digital natives use SNS and other ICTs in fundamentally different ways than do older people are widespread, but as of yet these claims and the very concept of the digital native itself have not yet been well tested via research (Agosto and Abbas 2010; Helsper and Eynon 2010; Selwyn 2009). In one study that did test SNS use differences by age group, Pfeil, Ulrike, Arjan, and Zaphiris (2009) compared teens and adults over age 60 in their use of MySpace. They found that teens mainly used MySpace to communicate with their peers in the offline world, whereas older adults used MySpace for communication with a broader age range of friends and acquaintances from their offline lives. The teens in the study also tended to have greater numbers of online friends, perhaps reflecting greater SNS membership among teens than among older adults. Helsper and Eynon (2010) also examined Internet and SNS use by age group using large-scale survey data from the United Kingdom. They found generation (age group) to be just one of a number of significant determining factors in users' levels of SNS and Internet use in general. Other significant factors included gender, education levels, computing experience, and breadth of use. They concluded that

> it is not helpful to define digital natives and immigrants as two distinct, dichotomous generations. While there were differences in how generations engaged with the Internet, there were similarities across generalizations as well, mainly based on how much experience people have with using technologies. In addition, the findings presented here confirm that individuals' Internet use lies along a continuum of engagement instead of being a dichotomous divide between users and non-users. (515)

Despite the increasing number of researchers who are challenging the idea of the digital native, and despite a growing number of studies suggesting that age is just one characteristic tied to technology comfort and facility, much more research is needed to determine the extent to which SNS and other technology behaviors really do differ by age group, and how much of the difference in behaviors can be attributed to online experience (as opposed to chronological age). It is also important to remember that while communication via SNS and other ICTs is significant and growing among young people, face-to-face communication is still the most popular form of communication among youth peer groups (Van Cleemput 2010), as well as the first choice when possible for communication with intimate acquaintances (Agosto and Abbas, in press). The stereotype of the young person spending all of his or her free time online with little interest in social interaction in the offline world exaggerates the role of digital communication and interaction in youth's lives and misrepresents the majority of young people's online behaviors.

Above all, it is important to recognize that there is variance in the degree of digital comfort, facility, and use levels among youth, just as there is variance in behaviors among any large demographic group. As Agosto and Abbas (2010) wrote, "There is no simple picture of today's teens and ICT use, and no sound bite or slogan can provide a full picture of their attitudes toward mediated communication" (8). It is the responsibility of the research community to work toward creating a full picture of the broad range of young people's SNS attitudes and behaviors and to help bring that full picture to the attention of parents, educators, policy makers, librarians, and other adults interested in the welfare of today's youth.

REFERENCES

Agosto, Denise E., and June Abbas. 2009. "Teens and Social Networking: How Public Libraries Are Responding to the Latest Online Trend." *Public Libraries* 48: 32–37.

Agosto, Denise E., and June Abbas. 2010. "High School Seniors' Social Network and Other ICT Use Preferences and Concerns." *Proceedings of the American Society for Information Science and Technology* 47: 1–10.

Agosto, Denise E., and June Abbas. 2011. "Teens, Social Networking, and Safety and Privacy Issues." In Denise E. Agosto and June Abbas (Eds.), *Teens, Libraries, and Social Networking: What Librarians Need to Know* (59–75). Santa Barbara, CA: Libraries Unlimited.

Agosto, Denise E., and June Abbas. In press. "Relationships and Social Rules: Teens' Social Network and Other ICT Selection Practices." *Journal of the American Society for Information Science and Technology.*

Agosto, Denise E., Joyce K. Valenza, and June Abbas. 2011. "Looking Closely at Teens' Use of Social Networks: What do High School Seniors do Online?" In D. E. Agosto and J. Abbas (Eds.), *Teens, Libraries, and Social Networking: What Librarians Need to Know* (13–27). Santa Barbara, CA: Libraries Unlimited.

Ahn, June. 2011a. "Digital Divides and Social Network Sites: Which Students Participate in Social Media?" *Journal of Educational Computing Research* 45: 147–163.

Ahn, June. 2011b. "The Effect of Social Network Sites on Adolescents' Social and Academic Development: Current Theories and Controversies." *Journal of the American Society for Information Science and Technology* 62: 1435–1445.

Antheunis, Marjolijn L., and Alexander P. Schouten. 2011. "The Effects of Other-Generated and System-Generated Cues on Adolescents' Perceived Attractiveness on Social Network Sites." *Journal of Computer-Mediated Communication* 16: 391–406.

Anttiroiko, Ari-Veikko, and Reijo Savolainen. 2011. "Towards Library 2.0: The Adoption of Web 2.0 Technologies in Public Libraries." *Libri* 61: 87–99.

Baker, Rosland K., and Katherine M. White. 2010. "Predicting Adolescents' Use of Social Networking Sites from an Extended Theory of Planned Behaviour Perspective." *Computers in Human Behavior* 26: 1591–1597.

Bonetti, Luigi, Marilyn A. Campbell, and Linda Gilmore. 2010. "The Relationship of Loneliness and Social Anxiety with Children's and Adolescents' Online Communication." *Cyberpsychology, Behavior, and Social Networking* 13: 279–283.

Boyd, Danah. 2006. "Friends, Friendsters, and MySpace Top 8: Writing Community into Being on Social Network Sites." *First Monday* 11 (12), December. Accessed January 2012, http://www.danah.org/papers/FriendsFriendsterTop8.pdf.

Boyd, Danah. 2008. "Why Youth (Heart) Social Network Sites: The Role of Networked Publics in Teenage Social Life." In D. Buckingham (Ed.), *Youth, Identity, and Digital Media* (119–142). The John D. and Catherine T. MacArthur Foundation Series on Digital Media and Learning. Cambridge, MA: MIT Press.

CBS. October 31, 2010. "60 Minutes/Vanity Fair Poll: October Edition." Accessed January 2012, http://www.cbsnews.com/stories/2010/09/30/60minutes/main6915819_page6.shtml.

Christofides, Emily, Amy Muise, and Serge Desmarais. 2012. "Hey Mom, What's on Your Facebook? Comparing Facebook Disclosure and Privacy in Adolescents and Adults." *Social Psychological and Personality Science* 13 (1): 48–54.

Clarke, Barbie H. 2009. "Early Adolescents' Use of Social Networking Sites to Maintain Friendship and Explore Identity: Implications for Policy." *Policy and Internet* 1 (1). Accessed January 2012, http://www.psocommons.org/policyandinternet/vol1/iss1/art3.

Consumer Reports. 2011. "CR Survey: 7.5 Million Facebook Users Are Under the Age of 13, Violating the Site's Terms." http://www.consumerreports.org/. Accessed January 2012, http://pressroom.consumerreports.org/pressroom/2011/05/cr-survey-75-million-facebook-users-are-under-the-age-of-13-violating-the-sites-terms-.html.

De Souza, Zaineb, and Geoffrey N. Dick. 2009. "Disclosure of Information by Children in Social Networking—Not Just a Case of "You Show Me Yours and I'll Show You Mine." *International Journal of Information Management* 29: 255–261.

Durrant, Abigail, David Frohlich, Abigail Sellen, and David Uzzell. 2011. "The Secret Life of Teens: Online Versus Offline Photographic Displays at Home." *Visual Studies* 26: 113–124.

Erikson, Erik. 1968. *Identity, Youth and Crisis.* New York: Norton.

Facebook. 2011. Statistics. Accessed July 16, 2011, https://www.facebook.com/press/info.php?statistics.

Fleming, Michele, and Debra Rickwood. 2004. "Teens in Cyberspace: Do They Encounter Friend or Foe?" *Youth Studies Australia* 23: 46–52.

Fuller, Heidi A., and Amy M. Damico. 2008. "Keeping Pace with Teen Media Use: Implications and Strategies for Educators." *The Journal of Educational Research* 101: 323–330.

Greenhow, Christine, and Beth Robelia. 2009a. "Informal Learning and Identity Formation in Online Social Networks." *Learning, Media and Technology* 34: 119–140.

Greenhow, Christine, and Beth Robelia. 2009b. "Old Communication, New Literacies: Social Network Sites as Social Learning Resources." *Journal of Computer-Mediated Communication* 14: 1130–1161.

Greenhow, Christine, Beth Robelia, and Joan E. Hughes. 2009. "Learning, Teaching, and Scholarship in a Digital Age: Web 2.0 and Classroom Research: What Path Should We Take Now?" *Educational Researcher* 38: 246–259.

Helsper, Ellen J., and Rebecca Eynon. 2010. "Digital Natives: Where Is the Evidence?" *British Educational Research Journal* 36: 503–520.

Hinduja, Sameer, and Justin W. Patchin. 2008. "Personal Information of Adolescents on the Internet: A Quantitative Content Analysis of MySpace." *Journal of Adolescence* 31(1): 125–146.

Hundley, Heather L., and Leonard Shyles. 2010. "U.S. Teenagers' Perceptions and Awareness of Digital Technology: A Focus Group Approach." *New Media and Society* 12: 417–433.

Ito, Mizuko, et al. 2010. *Hanging Out, Messing Around, and Geeking Out: Kids Living and Learning with New Media*. Cambridge, MA: MIT Press.

Lenhart, Amanda, Rich Ling, Scott Campbell, and Kristen Purcell. 2010. "Teens and Mobile Phones." Pew Internet and American Life Project: Washington, DC. Accessed January 2012, http://pewinternet.org/Reports/2010/Teens-and-Mobile-Phones.aspx.

Lenhart, Amanda, Kristen Purcell, Aaron Smith, and Kathryn Zickuhr. February 3, 2010. "Social Media and Young Adults." Pew Internet and American Life Project. Accessed January 2012, http://pewinternet.org/Reports/2010/Social-Media-and-Young-Adults.aspx.

Livingstone, Sonia. 2008. "Taking Risky Opportunities in Youthful Content Creation: Teenagers' Use of Social Networking Site for Intimacy, Privacy, and Self-Expression." *New Media and Society* 10: 393–411.

Livingstone, Sonia, and David R. Brake. 2010. "On the Rapid Rise of Social Networking Sites: New Findings and Policy Implications." *Children and Society* 24: 75–83.

Livingstone, Sonia, and Ellen Helsper. 2010. "Balancing Opportunities and Risks in Teenagers' Use of the Internet: The Role of Online Skills and Internet Self-Efficacy." *New Media & amp; Society* 12: 309–329.

Luckin, Rosemary, et al. 2009. "Do Web 2.0 Tools Really Open the Door to Learning? Practices, Perceptions, and Profiles of 11–16-Year-Old Students." *Learning, Media and Technology* 34(2): 87–104.

Mallan, Kerry. 2009. "Look at Me! Look at Me! Self-Representation and Self-Exposure through Online Networks." *Digital Culture and Education* 1: 51–66.

Moreno, Megan A., et al. 2009. "Real Use or 'Real Cool': Adolescents Speak Out about Displayed Alcohol References on Social Networking Websites." *Journal of Adolescent Health* 45: 420–422.

Patchin, Justin W., and Sameer Hinduja. 2010. "Trends in Online Social Networking: Adolescent Use of MySpace over Time." *New Media and Society* 12: 197–216.

Pfeil, Ulrike, Raj Arjan, and Panayoitis Zaphiris. 2009. "Age Differences in Online Social Networking: A Study of User Profiles and the Social Capital Divide Among Teenagers and Older Users in MySpace." *Computers in Human Behavior* 25: 643–654.

Pierce, Tamyra. 2009. "Social Anxiety and Technology: Face-to-Face Communication versus Technological Communication among Teens." *Computers in Human Behavior* 25: 1367–1372.

Prensky, Marc. 2001. "Digital Natives, Digital Immigrants." *On the Horizon* 9: 1–5.

Pujazon-Zazik, Melissa, and M. Jane Park. 2010. "To Tweet, or Not to Tweet: Gender Differences and Potential Positive and Negative Health Outcomes of Adolescents' Social Internet Use." *American Journal of Men's Health* 4: 77–85.

Rosen, Larry D., Nancy A. Cheever, and L. Mark Carrier. 2008. "An Association of Parenting Style and Child Age with Parental Limit Setting and Adolescent MySpace Behavior." *Journal of Applied Developmental Psychological* 29: 459–471.

Selwyn, Neil. 2009. "The Digital Native: Myth and Reality." *Aslib Proceedings: New Information Perspectives* 61: 364–379.

Sengupta, Anirban, and Anoshua Chaudhuri. 2011. "Are Social Networking Sites a Source of Online Harassment for Teens? Evidence from Survey Data." *Children and Youth Services Review* 33: 284–290.

Spires, Hiller A., John K. Lee, Kimberly A. Turner, and Janet Johnson. 2008. "Having our Say: Middle Grade Student Perspectives on School, Technologies, and Academic Engagement." *Journal of Research on Technology in Education* 40: 497–515.

Subrahmanyam, Kaveri, and Patricia Greenfield. 2008a. "Online Communication and Adolescent Relationships." *The Future of Children* 18: 119–146.

Subrahmanyam, Kaveri, and Patricia Greenfield. 2008b. "Virtual Worlds in Development: Implications of Social Networking Sites." *Journal of Applied Developmental Psychology* 29: 417–419.

Valkenburg, Patti M., and Jochen Peter. 2009. "Social Consequences of the Internet for Adolescents: A Decade of Research." *Current Directions in Psychological Science* 18: 1–5.

Valkenburg, Patti M., Jochen Peter, and Alexander P. Schouten. 2006. "Friend Networking Sites and Their Relationship to Adolescents' Well-Being and Social Self-Esteem." *Cyberpsychology and Behavior* 9: 584–590.

Van Cleemput, Katrien. 2010. "'I'll See You on IM, Text, or Call You': A Social Network Approach of Adolescents' Use of Communication Media." *Bulletin of Science, Technology, and Society* 30: 75–85.

Van Grove, Jennifer. 2010. "Teens Experiencing Facebook Fatigue." Accessed January 2012 http://mashable.com/2010/06/30/teens-social-networks-study/. (See also http://www.scribd.com/doc/33751159/Teens-Social-Networks-Study-June-2010.)

White, Charlie. 2011. "Missouri Forbids Teachers and Students to Be Facebook Friends." *Mashable*, July 30, 2011. Accessed January 2012, http://mashable.com/2011/07/30/student-teacher-facebook/.

Williams, Amanda L., and Michael J. Merten. 2008. "A Review of Online Social Networking Profiles by Adolescents: Implications for Future Research and Intervention." *Adolescence* 24: 253–275.

Williams, Amanda L., and Michael J. Merten. 2009. "Adolescents' Online Social Networking Following the Death of a Peer." *Journal of Adolescent Research* 24: 67–90.

Ybarra, Michele L., and Kimberly J. Mitchell. 2008. "How Risky Are Social Networking Sites? A Comparison of Places Online Where Youth Sexual Solicitation and Harassment Occurs." *Pediatrics* 121: 350–357.

Chapter Seven

Gaming and Virtual Environments

Giovanni Vincenti

In today's world children are exposed to electronics and digital delivery of content from birth, truly defining them as digital natives (Prensky 2001a). This change does not only determine a radical change in a person's own life, but also how society in general functions as we are all atomic components of the same system. Social interactions have shifted from the town's square to computer-based systems, and text messaging and e-mailing often replace oral communication.

In this society where interpersonal relations are changing, adapting to new mental models, we have to ensure that we are not overwhelmed by a system that lags behind. When we think about education especially, we have to realize that lecturing and in-class exercises are not necessarily the best way to communicate notions to young students. The world of game-based learning is a significant playground that each educator should be familiar with as well as a tool present in every school's set of resources.

This chapter explores gaming and virtual environments as they are tailored around children, especially addressing their roles as "adults in training." We will focus on trends and changes that the world of education has observed over the past decade, and the technological feats that have claimed a spot for the attention of researchers and practitioners. But more importantly we will focus on the concepts that drive innovation and shape the future of interactions between educators and learners today.

DIGITAL NATIVES

One of the most common jokes in the 1990s was that if you wanted your VCR (video cassette recorder) programmed you should ask a 10-year-old. Although this statement has become outdated (these days we TIVO shows, we do not have VCRs anymore, and the age at which a child can program some electronic object is perhaps approaching five), we have to recognize its prophetic message: technology has become a staple in any youngster's life (Prensky 2000).

According to the U.S. Department of Commerce, in the late 1990s the concept of Digital Divide was significant for children, as many North American households did not have access to home computers (Attewell, Suazo-Garcia, and Battle 2003). In the early 2000s Australian children, for example, were born to households where the home computer had already reached 42 percent of the population, but by the late 2000s an Indian child was born in a country where 50 million users are connected to the Internet (Straker, Pollock, and Maslen 2009). These data should be read keeping in mind the societal contexts of each country: the United States was already one of the wealthiest nations, the distances in Australia are so significant that often social interactions are quite limited, and at last India represents perhaps one of the most socially complex structures. Once we apply these keys to the data reported above, we can imagine the revolution that technology has brought to households in recent years as the proliferation of technology is becoming more similar between wealthy countries and nations with typically more marked internal socioeconomic differences.

COMPUTERS AND EDUCATION

As children are exposed to computers more and more, one may wonder whether these tools really are helping the child's development, or are they just keeping them busy for a while? One researcher in particular decided to observe the effects of TV and computers as "assistants" to the child's growth (Fiorini 2010). In particular, the research focused on the effects that the use of home computers has on children aged four to seven. This research suggests that children who were frequently using computers showed an increased development in cognitive skills (Fiorini 2010). One may argue that the children were perhaps more curious because of an already developing set of cognitive skills, placing them already ahead of the group whose cognitive skills may not have been as developed. In either case, this study is significant because it does support the fact that computer use and cognitive skills in children are connected.

As the children continue their development, we should pay attention to the resources that are available to them. The next logical step in a child's life, after observing their development at home, involves school. The findings of Fiorini (2010) paint a very comforting picture, as long as there is no lack of resources. When we look at some simple statistics reported by the next study we can see that 66 percent of households let children utilize the Internet, and in the majority of cases (90 percent) with some type of adult supervision (Plowman, Stephen, and McPake 2010). This research highlights the importance of home resources, and strongly supports allowing children to operate technology at home with some type of parental supervision because (1) preschools may not have the necessary tools (computers) available to students, and (2) the children may not receive effective supervision while using the computers at school.

Another significant aspect of the use of computers at home, even as preparation for the first level of schooling, is highlighted by Davidson (2009). In this study the researcher focuses on the interaction of two students who are researching information about particular topics. Although the scope of these observations is quite limited by the sample size, it offers significant insight further supporting the use of computers in the home. As the children were engaged in the research, they were able to look for information from different sources, including Google and Wikipedia. The idea that they were working on multiple channels of information to acquire notions about the topics seems to develop their skills in assembling an overall picture from multiple smaller pieces, helping them prepare for the challenges they will face in school (Davidson 2009).

We can summarize these past few paragraphs by stating that the use of computers at home may offer a significant help in the development of children, and parents cannot simply rely on the resources offered by schools. Especially when focusing on this last point, we should not assume that schools are not offering much exposure to computers because there is lack of funding or a limited number of teachers. A study compared the perspectives that teachers have when it comes to the use of computers in the classroom in Japan and in the United States. Their findings reveal that Japanese teachers still believe that the interaction between children and computers is geared toward entertainment, whereas in the United States teachers are more open to letting students work with computers (Joshi et al. 2010). Findings similar to this last example were also documented when researchers analyzed ICT (information communication technology) use among Swedish children (Samuelsson 2010).

Such radical differences seem to occur mainly between different cultures. When we consider teachers and students who belong to the same culture we can see a more homogeneous group regarding the use of computing in the classroom (Jackson et al. 2008). When instead we compare different socioeconomic groups within the same culture, we may see minor differences between levels (Lebens, Graff, and Mayer 2009). Such differences can be attributed to the fact that children who belong to families of a higher status may attend better schools, which are most likely equipped with more and better computers and educational software. Children of lower-status families generally attend schools that may be providing less innovative technologies. The study, though, suggests that access to newer technology is not the only barrier that exists between these groups, as the reasons behind these differences are rooted much deeper in society (Lebens, Graff, and Mayer 2009). We can also find significant differences between sexes, where boys seem to have more access to computers than girls (Kirmani, Davis, and Kalyanpur 2009).

We should also mention that a greater use of computers also increases the possibility that children may be exposed to different kinds of risks (Livingstone and Haddon 2008):

- content risks, such as illegal content, pornography, and challenging content (suicide, violence, hate) to name a few
- contact risks, with strangers or cyber bullying
- commercial risks, for example gambling or illegal downloads
- privacy risks, where personal information can be disseminated or hacking can take place

A problem that is often mentioned in the media is the possibility of desensitization as a result of exposure to violent content (Straker, Pollock, and Maslen 2009). If, instead, we shift our focus to problems that may arise in the physical development of children who are often utilizing a computer, we can see that neck (28.15 percent), shoulder (19.33 percent), finger (10.71 percent), wrist (5.67 percent) and upper back (3.78 percent) problems are quite frequent (Lui, Szeto, and Jones 2011). For this reason we should keep simple guidelines in mind when letting children use computers (Straker, Maslen, et al. 2010):

- encourage a mix of sedentary and active tasks
- encourage reasonable postures during sedentary tasks
- encourage appropriate behavior when using and transporting notebook computers
- teach children computing skills (such as keyboard shortcuts to minimize shifting controls with the mouse)
- teach children to respond to discomfort

These guidelines are not only good advice, but they may change a child's physical development drastically as the use of computers becomes a routine in their daily lives. Some of these items can also be built into the system, for example, through a richer user interface (reminding users about keyboard shortcuts), or through the use of special joysticks that are controlled by the movement of the arm (Nintendo 2011).

GAME-BASED LEARNING (AKA SERIOUS GAMES)

The phenomenon of early acquaintance with technology has a series of benefits, but it also poses a significant number of threats. Ask teachers how the student body has changed, and they will offer many anecdotes from their own experience supporting this observation. The fact is that students have changed drastically as a result of early attachment to technology, thus effectively creating a serious problem for the education system (Prensky 2001a). Such a problem arises from the discrepancy between a system that was designed decades ago and rapidly changing generations where computers are easier to interpret than books. This fact can be explained through the brain's malleability (Prensky 2001b), which has adapted itself to a non-linear learning pattern and can be slowed by an education system that is based on a linear approach (Moore 1997).

For these reasons, it is necessary to alter traditional educational approaches with new and innovative paradigms, including gaming. Some novice teachers may argue that it may be impossible to teach someone with a short attention span and such a non-linear way of thinking. But games do engage young players, effectively capturing their attention without releasing it for a moment (Prensky 2001b). Learning through some type of game is perhaps one of the most natural aspects of life. In many documentaries we can observe young animals playing with peers while at the same time developing their predatory or defensive skills. As these behaviors do not only belong to less intelligent animals, we can transfer the same concept to humans: we can learn while playing. Prensky (2000) outlines 12 aspects of games that engage players. They:

- are a form of fun, which generally evokes a sense of enjoyment and pleasure
- are a form of play, which typically results in involvement in the activity
- have rules, which constitute structure
- have goals, which result in motivation
- are interactive, involving the player into some type of action
- have outcomes and feedback, which may result in learning
- are adaptive, giving some flow to the experience

- have win states, resulting in ego gratification
- have conflict/competition/challenge/opposition, which sparks the player's interest and involvement into the situation
- have problem solving, stimulating the player's creativity
- have interaction, which often involves social groups
- have presentation and story, giving the player emotions

Ideally these characteristics should resonate with the learning preferences of digital natives (Derryberry 2007):

- receiving information quickly from multiple multimedia sources
- parallel processing and multitasking
- processing pictures, sounds, and video before text
- random access to hyperlinked multimedia information
- interacting/networking simultaneously with many others
- learning "just-in-time"
- instant gratification and instant rewards
- learning that is relevant, instantly useful, and fun

The use of games is particularly significant when we wish to include an educational computer-based component to integrate material learned in formal schooling settings, as gaming is the preferred activity of children, especially in the age range of four to seven, while using the computer (McKenney and Voogt 2010). Such activity seems to increase self-esteem (Miller and Robertson 2010) and motivation toward learning (Shih, Chuang, and Liu 2010), although this last finding is not consistent in all studies (Whitton 2007).

COTS OR CUSTOM-MADE?

Although we cannot expect that any computer game designed with learning in mind will be successful in achieving its goals, we can expect that the intersection of gaming and education may produce significant results. One of the most common decisions when trying to solve a particular real-life problem through computing is the decision between creating a custom product and choosing software that is already available on the market, typically referred to as Commercial Off-the-Shelf (COTS). The same approach can be carried out by teachers who wish to complement a particular series of class materials with game-based learning. Educators can try to identify games that are already available commercially and that somewhat fit the material in question, such as reviewing history through the game Civilization (Meier

2010). In the majority of cases, if the software was not designed with classroom use in mind, students will not gain much benefit (Miller and Robertson 2010).

In order to increase the chances of success, we should either identify software solutions (games) that are designed for educational purposes or create custom software that will satisfy our needs. If we wish to follow the first route, we can find a wide array of games already for sale. We should remember that often researchers enjoy sharing their creations with others, so the choice of a serious game should not be limited to stores, but we can also look at academic research to identify successful games. By contacting the authors we may have access to those very resources, either paying a fee or perhaps agreeing to let the researchers collect data about the software's usage. Later in this chapter we will review some games, giving a short but eclectic list of what has already been done.

When instead we wish to address a particular educational need by creating our own software solution, we have to take into account a significant number of aspects. Just like in any software project, the development process typically includes five main phases: planning, analysis, design, implementation, and maintenance (Dennis, Wixom, and Roth 2008). Although these five steps are not necessarily of the same length in time, their sequence is usually set.

Perhaps the first decision we need to make relates to the type of learning we wish to incorporate: formal, contextual, or informal (Protopsaltis et al. 2011). A formal type of learning generally is connected with planned learning activities, for example, in a classroom or in a video game designed to let children learn the alphabet. Contextual learning is achieved when someone learns while performing activities that are not necessarily designed for learning, such as when we play flight simulating games that lead to the concepts of drag and lift, essential for flight. Informal learning refers to those environments where learning is non-intentional, and an example would be going to a restaurant of another culture and learning new terms simply because the menu is written in a different language.

The foundation of education is based on learning theories. When we are working with serious games we should not forget these ideas, which add structure to the entire project. In particular, we will briefly focus on behaviorism, cognitivism, and constructivism. Research suggests that different characteristics accompany the chosen learning theory (Zaibon and Shiratuddin 2010):

Behaviorism

- State objectives and break them down into steps.
- Provide hints or cues that guide players to desired behavior.

- Use consequences to reinforce the desired behavior.
- Provide good feedback and response to the players.

Cognitivism

- Organize new game information.
- Link new game information to existing knowledge.
- Use techniques to guide and support learners' attention, encoding, and retrieval processes.
- Provide good screen design, interface, and navigation.
- Supply a variety of game resources for choices and game options.
- Provide adventurous storylines and game play.

Constructivism

- Pose good problems that are realistically complex and personally meaningful.
- Create group learning activities.
- Model and guide the knowledge construction process.
- Offer different types of game levels, game play, and challenges.

Anyone who is facing the daunting task of preparing an application for today's market generally faces this next challenge, which should also be considered when designing serious games: what type of mobility should this application have? Typically we should consider platforms such as desktops, laptops, smartphones, tablets, or a mix of them (Laine et al. 2010). In order to reach ubiquitous learning, we have to consider the use of highly mobile technologies that are particularly aware of the context they are in (for example, the student's geographical location). If, instead, we are not particularly worried about the need for mobility or context awareness, we can resort to more bulky computing solutions such as games designed for desktop computers. The researchers should also analyze many other aspects such as the ease of use of the platform itself, the reliability of the underlying network, and the coordination between the language utilized by the application as opposed to the one supported by the devices to name a few (Laine et al. 2010). A thorough discussion of all these aspects goes beyond the scope of this chapter and is closely related to the most popular technologies available at the time of development.

Once we have established what type of learning we would like to achieve (typically formal or contextual), our learning theory of choice, and the level of mobility, we can proceed with the essential elements of any game. Some items were mentioned earlier, but in order to further reinforce the importance, we will also cite the findings of another research group (csikszentmihalyi 1996). This second research highlights eight components as essential to the success of a game:

- clearly defined goals
- concentration on the task at hand
- merging of action and awareness
- an altered sense of time
- clear and responsive feedback
- balanced level of challenge and difficulty
- a sense of control over the task at hand
- a challenging task requiring skill to execute

Any process of creation can be difficult, especially one that aims at entertaining while really satisfying the hidden purpose of teaching something to the user. For this reason we need to be aware of three main factors (Derryberry 2007). Creating serious games is often a team effort; although we may be talented in multiple areas, there are many technological aspects that often have to merge in order to create a single yet multi-leveled solution (different programming languages, computer platforms, communications standards). You will need experts from the fields of education as well as game design. Gaming experts and education experts may have very different approaches to the workflow, and managing the process may prove to be quite challenging.

Perhaps one of the most significant examples of why we need experts from multiple fields is the fact that the educational content should not appear to be "bolted on" to the game, but instead it should be deep within the game's structure (Isbister, Flanagan, and Hash 2010). Imagine playing a go-kart game that aims at teaching geography. It would be rather disruptive and probably not so educational if the children were shown maps of different countries while they stopped for refueling. The software would probably have much more pedagogical success if the path the children had to take was carefully chosen from a real map of Europe, for example, and then they had to navigate correctly onto the appropriate ramps and roadways to reach a particular country.

The typical classroom requires that a teacher should proactively change the pace of activities in response to how the students are performing. When we choose to teach through games, we sometimes take away the dynamicity of a teacher's experience in favor of a system that is sometimes completely hard-coded when it comes to the sequence of events. Given the plasticity that a custom-made software system may have, we should consider building in a "supervising" facility that allows us to gauge the students' performance and perhaps change the course of the game to create a more meaningful experience (Marty and Carron 2011).

The process of developing serious games is often complex and requires several iterations of trial and error. Protopsaltis et al. (2011) summarize some of the key elements we should be particularly careful about when creating our own game-based learning solution:

- matching users' expectations
- matching trainers' expectations
- finding a balance between learning and fun/engagement
- finding a form suited for self-learning but also for introduction in a training program while guaranteeing freedom of use
- giving enough guidance without taking the challenge away and without interfering with the narrative and the game play
- how to give meaningful feedback
- how to make it a meaningful experience
- how to involve the emotional side of the learner
- how to consider gender-dependent aspects
- being close to context (no bias in the content to introduce narrative aspects)
- graphical appeal

Even if you are not planning on designing your own games, you should review carefully the material discussed in this section, as it can give you a valuable metric for evaluating the potential effectiveness of serious games. If instead you are planning on making a career out of what you have read so far, you can find formal education programs that live in the intersection between education and game design, such as the Serious Game Design Master's Program at Michigan State University (Michigan State University, n.d.).

EXAMPLES OF SERIOUS GAMES

The area of game-based learning has registered a significant surge in interest from the world of research starting around 2003, with a peak of publications between 2008 and 2009 (Chang 2010). Although more recent data is not available, it is possible to find a significant amount of new research being published, especially in online databases of education and sociology. In this section we will briefly review some projects as well as COTS solutions for serious games.

Perhaps one of the most widely advertised COTS products within the category of game-based learning is Nintendo's "Brain Training" software, Brain Age (Nintendo, n.d.). This system allows the user to play games in order to develop or maintain mental elasticity. In one study (Miller and Robertson 2010), the researchers compared the performance of one group of children that was exposed to this game and another that worked with the Brain Gym program (Brain Gym International, n.d.).The children in this study were 10 to 11 years of age. Although in both groups the researchers found an improvement in self-esteem, the group that used the Nintendo-based system performed significantly better in the math curriculum. Interestingly, another research study (Khasawneh and Al-Awidi 2008) shows that the types of serious games that are played most often by Jordanian children are about languages and math, which is an encouraging fact for the development of children with hopefully greater language and mathematical skills.

When we think about serious games we may be biased in the idea of what the application actually looks like. We shouldn't think about dragons or wizards battling for the conquest of earth, but instead a simple drawing program may suffice. In the next study (Course and Chen 2010) we can see the effect of introducing tablets in early childhood education (three to six years of age). The group showed a high interest in drawing and a quick adaptation to the tablet system. This study highlights the importance of the teachers as a guide through the technology.

In the next example, the researchers (Knol and De Vries 2011) studied a game that focused on sustainability and energy conservation, EnerCities (EnerCities, n.d.). The game allows the player to build a self-sustaining large city starting from a small village. Parameters that affect the style of life include energy conservation and CO_2. Although this was just a preliminary study, the researchers found that the game was very interesting to students and raised their awareness about the focus topics. The students were enrolled in secondary school and belonged to several European Union countries. EnerCities is a project funded by the Intelligent Energy project of the European Union (European Union 2011).

Games can also play a role in one's culture (Chen et al. 2010). The game FORmosaHope was created to study the effects of students' perception of culture. Game play involves a first role, where the user explores a village freely. In the second, the player visits different stands within the village, each representing a city in Taiwan. Here the students will learn about different features of the cities. FORmosaHope also includes 11 sub-games that the students can use to accomplish different tasks. Overall, the students reported a greater sense of pride in their own culture and more knowledge about Taiwan. In this study the users were 11 to 12 years old.

In this next study (Mazzone, Read, and Beale 2008), the researchers wanted to create a game that would let disaffected students learn how to relate to others. In this case the students were between 13 and 16 years of age. The game consisted of the player studying the facial expression of a character displayed on the screen, and correctly choosing the emotion expressed by the character. The key finding of this research group is that students seemed to be engaged the most by the process of creating the game in conjunction with the development team.

Even studying a subject as boring as computing can be more entertaining and effective through serious games. Although the target population of this next project (Papastergiou 2009) is slightly older (high school students), we can still appreciate how a two-dimensional maze containing bits and pieces of information about a computer's memory and its operations can be effective in covering a part of the nation's required computer science (CS) curriculum. Another study focusing on CS aimed at first-grade children shows that the game can be effective if there is significant supervision from the teacher (Grieshaber 2010).

Although these are just a few examples of how serious games can span different subjects and age ranges, we can easily find myriad examples by browsing the Internet. It is also important to realize that serious games are not just for learning notions, but also motor skills. Programs such as flight simulators are utilized constantly by the aviation industry to train pilots (X-Plane 2011), custom-built simulators can train machine operators (CAT 2011), and driving games can teach teenagers how to drive (3D-Fahrschule 2011) or educate them on the influence of alcohol on drivers (DriveSquare 2011).

MULTI-USER VIRTUAL ENVIRONMENTS (MUVES)

The idea of virtual environments comes from the three-dimensional representation of what is generally conceived as two-dimensional content, with the addition of a reference of neighboring resources in relation to one's position. When we surf the web we typically access a web browser that looks for a particular text address (URL), translates it into an IP address, then fetches any documents associated with the target we are looking for. Except for the "Forward" and "Back" button, there exists no linearity in the way we approach the navigation of the Web. The nature itself of the Web does not lend itself to the concept of proximity. We cannot identify other people who are connected to the same site, unless the site itself gives us such information. Likewise, we have no idea what other websites are hosted on a particular computer. When we wish to switch websites, we either follow links or type addresses in the address bar. If the second site we visit is hosted on the same hardware as the first, we would not be able to easily tell.

This concept is very different from real life, where we cannot jump from one store to another if we cannot find what we are looking for. We physically need to walk out of one store, cover the distance that exists between the two stores, and then physically enter the second store. Virtual environments aim at replicating the very same concept: the user is able to visualize the idea of proximity with resources and other users by simply looking at the three-dimensional representation of the world one is in.

Virtual environments then present several advantages over traditional navigation methods: (1) users have a much wider and immediate perspective of the amount of resources available at one location; (2) users are able to easily perceive others who are also present within the same location, and interact directly with them; (3) the objects that are represented in virtual worlds feature a wide variety of built-in and custom behaviors, which are often consistent through different locations, thus not requiring users to learn a new system of interactions every time they visit a new site. The main drawback of virtual environments lies in the belief that many hold about these technologies: they are just games, thus they are probably not useful. There are two main pitfalls in these arguments: (1) games can be educational; (2) virtual environments simply use the same representation techniques as most games, but their content is often extremely different from what their cousins, designed only for entertainment purposes, feature.

One of the most significant barriers that multi-user virtual environments face is acceptance as an innovative technology rather than some computer game. They look too much like games, even though they are just very pliable and versatile environments. Convincing users that such technology is not simply entertaining but also highly educational and stimulating is often a project in itself. We can imagine what kinds of objections may arise when entire school systems have to be convinced to spend part of their already tight budget on teaching material that is delivered through MUVEs. This very topic was the focus of attention by Laughlin (2010), who identifies these possible objections:

- video and computer games are inherently frivolous
- video and computer games have caused a surge in violence in the United States
- games and MUVEs are inherently anti-social and addictive
- games and MUVEs only appeal to males
- MUVEs are an inefficient educational tool
- being online puts you at risk
- the technology requirements are too high
- MUVEs promote mental laziness

Although at least some of these points may appear valid at a first and very superficial glance, Laughlin (2010) thoroughly analyzes each item and gives significant examples that rebut these statements. We have already analyzed some literature that supports the use of games as learning tools, which should address the concerns that MUVEs are too similar to games, thus debunking the myth that they cannot be educational (Duruz 2010). Through some examples that we will give next, we hope to also address the remaining items and show that MUVEs are not only entertaining, but also a great means to learning and education.

MUVES AND EDUCATION

The intersection between multi-user virtual environments and education has been gaining significant momentum in recent years. In particular, we are witnessing a significant shift in the application of pedagogical approaches to embrace the new technological frontier offered by MUVEs (Vincenti and Braman 2010), and as a result we are registering an increased number of practical implementations that are reaching classrooms and students (Vincenti and Braman 2011).

Perhaps the most well-known virtual environment that allows for multi-user interaction is Linden Labs' Second Life (Linden Research, Inc. 2011). This service requires the user to download an application to the computer, install it, and then use it to navigate through its world. This application allows for the creation of and interaction with extremely realistic virtual environments that can replicate physics as well as complex structures. The main backbone of the system originally allowed for a physical separation between adults and children in order to minimize the possibility of pedophiles approaching young users. Recently the "Teen Grid," as it was known, has ceased to exist, turning the entire Second Life platform over to a more adult audience. Given this fact, we will focus on projects that have been realized in the main area.

It is important to understand that the focal part of our discussion is not the medium through which content is delivered, but the content itself. Once we have identified projects that would work for us, we can replicate them in other worlds. Some of the other virtual worlds dedicated to children are Habbo (Sulake Corporation Oy 2011), Club Penguin (Disney Online Studios Canada Inc. 2011), Secret Builder (Renaissance 2.0 Media 2011), Whyville (Numedeon, Inc. 2011), and Pet Society (Playfish 2011). Other worlds that are dedicated to an older audience include ActiveWorlds (ActiveWorlds Inc. 2011), Open Wonderland (Open Wonderland Foundation 2011), and Twinity (Metaversum 2011).

When working in virtual worlds, we can leverage on even more ways for children to interact with the environment. This creates a significant increase in the educational potential that a particular world (or environment) may serve. Research suggests that MUVEs offer six features that are essential for education (Lim 2009):

- learning by exploring
- learning by collaborating
- learning by being
- learning by building
- learning by championing
- learning by expressing

These six features ensure that, in one way or another, all types of learners are included (DeMers 2011). Perhaps the most significant barrier to entry, though, is the fact that each virtual world requires some basic skills that can only be acquired by experimenting with the controls and learning how the overall system operates. Things become even more complex once we choose to create our own custom material for the courses. The most important step consists in utilizing a virtual world that we know, which is based on technology (programming language, for example) that we are familiar with, and that offers the potential that we require for adding our own material (Capanni and Doolan 2011). Another significant problem that often quickly arises in group work when using virtual worlds, and any type of technology in general, consists of the varying levels of ability that each user shows in using the technology itself (Crosby-Nagy and Carfora 2010). This problem can be easily overcome through some initial sessions dedicated to ensuring that each student is able to carry out the functions necessary for the educational activities.

One of the focal aspects of our everyday use of Internet-based technologies exists in the asynchronous type of communications. The idea that we have to respond to e-mail messages immediately as they are received is often contemplated but never necessary. We also do not have to ensure that we visit a particular web page within a certain time range, because web pages are (nearly) always available and they are not like stores that have business hours. MUVEs are slightly different though, as they live in a grey area that contains both asynchronous as well as synchronous characteristics (Dimitropoulos and Manitsaris 2010). If we wish to access content such as objects or buildings, then they are available to us asynchronously: the creator does not need to be connected for us to utilize their creations. If, instead, we intend to interact with others either for a simple exchange of messages or to work on a project, then there exists a need for synchronicity: we cannot send e-mails that will be read at a later time; we need to interact with them directly, thus all parties have to be connected at the same time.

Limited usage of this type of technology is a significant barrier to educational content through multi-user virtual environments. A survey shows that users typically prefer using computers to access instant messaging and social networking, which are typically asynchronous activities that are easily available through simple web browsers. We can see that fewer users access virtual environments mainly for gaming purposes (Wood 2010). When we are used to accessing particular services that are available through a widely known web browser, then we are likely to be less intimidated by exploring new material. If, instead, the delivery method is also unknown to us, there is more resistance. In this case, the view that most people hold about virtual environments (as gaming environments) creates the perfect storm opposing the potentially wide and effective use of these technologies.

VIRTUAL ENVIRONMENTS IN THE CLASSROOM

Experiences such as crossing the street cannot be easily replicated in two-dimensional environments and still give a sense of immersion to the user. For this reason, researchers have developed a three-dimensional virtual environment where children could practice crossing the street (Schwebel, Gaines, and Severson 2008). Such an environment closely replicated a real environment that was also utilized for this research. The study included 102 children aged seven to nine along with 74 adult participants. The results indicate that the children were able to transfer to the real environment the experience acquired in the virtual one, showing that such an approach can be successful, for example, in health education classes. Similar results were achieved in another study where researchers used virtual environments to teach children aged 10 to 12 about the road-crossing behavior of cyclists (Babu et al. 2011).

Perhaps some of the most interesting applications of virtual environments to educational contexts are found when they intersect with the sciences. In this first example the researchers modeled the Mediterranean Sea, so that students of natural sciences and ecology could interact directly with this environment (Wrzesien, Perez Lopez, and Alcaniz Raya 2009). Perhaps a more interesting approach can be found when we represent chemistry through this type of technology, as we are finding a relatively simple way of representing three-dimensionally, and nearly tangibly, material that otherwise would remain abstract (Nunez Redo et al. 2010).

Virtual environments can also be quite effective when teaching geography. In this next study (Tuzun et al. 2009), the researchers created a game that required students to complete tasks within a mix of two-dimensional and three-dimensional environments. The main platform utilized in this case was Quest Atlantis (Indiana University 2011), a pliable environment that is easily customized to the needs of educators. The students collaborated to collect artifacts while navigating through different continents. The overall findings of this study report that the students' performance on tests was higher, and they were more motivated to study since they had such an interesting game. The children who participated in this study were fourth and fifth graders.

Virtual environments are also promising for the education of children with different types of disabilities. The plasticity of virtual environments allows autistic children to feel more in control, especially when they are able to manipulate the environment (Pares et al. 2005). More recent research, also focusing on autistic children, looked into communication between these students, with an emphasis on empathy (Cheng et al. 2010).

A NOTE ABOUT MIXED REALITY

A necessary addition to the topics discussed in this chapter leads us to the work of Milgram, Takemura, Utsumi, and Kishino (1994), who formalized the ideal gap between real life and what exists within a computing system: the Reality-Virtuality Continuum (Figure 7.1). The Reality-Virtuality Continuum represents an ideal bridge between life in the physical world (where we have a physical presence, interact directly with others, and communicate face to face) and the virtual world (which requires a constant mediation by the computer system).

As in most aspects of life, we should not simply stop and analyze the extremes; we should pay particular attention to the shades of grey. The work by Milgram and his colleagues (1994) is particularly significant because it covers the entire span from real life to virtual environments. Although in this chapter we dedicate quite some time to the latter, it is important to understand that the future lies in the gradient that exists between these extremes.

We can identify several applications of mixed—or augmented—reality when we browse app stores for our smartphones or tablets, but they are generally geared toward adults, and they are typically not designed with education in mind. We would like to report one significant application of augmented reality (AR) in an education context for children. Researchers have created an AR module for the Scratch environment (MIT 2011) and introduced it to children aged 9 to 11 for a pilot study (Radu and MacIntyre 2009). After watching tutorial videos, the students were able to operate the Scratch platform easily and create their own AR-enhanced program. The findings of this study seem promising regarding the success of AR-aware education.

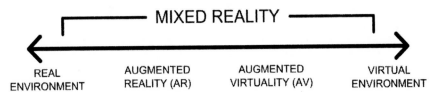

Figure 7.1.   Reality-virtuality continuum (Milgram et al. 1994)

A QUICK LOOK AT APPS

As technology evolves, we are seeing a significant shift in the typical hardware available to consumers. Today's trends seem to push portable computing solutions that are powerful yet energy efficient. This nearly contradictive concept enables anyone with a smartphone or some other type of portable computer (such as tablets) to have considerable access to resources.

As the main limiting factor is the screen's size, when designing a fully inclusive system, we must account for small as well as large displays. The overall hardware still presents significant differences, which may not necessarily be easy to account for if designing for a particular manufacturer. But projects such as Google's Android allow developers to spread their work over multiple hardware solutions, granted that they are all based on the Android operating system. This idea was originally brought forth in practice by Sun's Java (which is now the property of Oracle), suggesting a "compile once, run everywhere" concept to spreading stand-alone applications. As Android is significantly based on Java technologies, the multi-platform aspect of the original philosophy was retained and elevated to a much more powerful level than the original Java Mobile Edition.

What is perhaps the market's leader in portable computing is represented by Apple's projects: iPhone and iPad. These two solutions are proprietary, which means that their inner workings are sealed from the public's view. This take is diametrically opposite to Android's, which allows anyone to download and customize their solution. Apple's choice is supported by the market share that they still retain, even after their competitors have been working hard to catch up. The iPad was projected to conquer 61 percent of the market by the end of 2011, as reported in an article published shortly before this chapter (Camm-Jones 2011). Less predominant is the success of the iPhone, which still manages to be first on the market but reporting a less overwhelming lead (Reisinger 2011).

No matter which platform we choose, we have access to a wide array of applications that are tailored to our needs. The idea of "apps," or applications, has become popular with games such as Angry Birds (Rovio Mobile 2010) and utilities like iBooks (Apple 2011). Although we have always worked with applications or computer programs designed to carry out particular tasks, "Apps" have gained a significant popularity since portable computing has reached such high peaks. When browsing for new applications, we can find many examples of programs designed for education. These apps range from geography (Cho 2011), math (Palaware 2011), and science (Encyclopaedia Britannica, Inc. 2011), to languages (EuroTalk 2011).

CONCLUSIONS

This chapter represents a simple overview of gaming and virtual environments designed for children and education. The researchers and practitioners that work daily at improving existing solutions or creating new ones face the challenge of not only advancing the state of the art, but also the genuine and hopefully constructive criticism of children who simply cannot realize how much time and effort have been spent in creating something for them to use. This chapter attempts to highlight this tireless dedication and illustrate the complexity involved in creating entertaining yet educational systems.

REFERENCES

3D-Fahrschule. 2011. 3D Simulator. http://www.3dfahrschule.de/uk_index.htm (accessed August 12, 2011).

ActiveWorlds Inc. ActiveWorlds. 2011. http://www.activeworlds.com/ (accessed August 12, 2011).

Apple. iBooks. 2011. http://www.apple.com/ipad/built-in-apps/ibooks.html (accessed August 7, 2011).

Attewell, Paul, Belkis Suazo-Garcia, and Juan Battle. 2003. "Computers and Young Children: Social Benefit or Social Problem?" *Social Forces* 82 (1): 277–296.

Babu, Sabarish, et al. 2011. "An Immersive Virtual Peer for Studying Social Influences on Child Cyclists' Road-Crossing Behavior." *IEEE Transactions on Visualization and Computer Graphics* 17, 1 (January): 14–25.

Brain Gym International. *Brain Gym.* http://www.braingym.org/ (accessed August 12, 2011).

Camm-Jones, Ben. 2011. "iPad Expected to Grab 61% of 2011 Tablet Market." *PCWorld.* August 6. http://www.pcworld.com/article/237376/ipad_expected_to_grab_61_of_2011_tablet_market.html (accessed August 7, 2011).

Capanni, Niccolo, and Daniel Doolan. 2011. "Mapping Current Teaching and Learning Practices to Multi-User Virtual Environments." In *Multi-User Virtual Environments for the Classroom: Practical Approaches to Teaching in Virtual Worlds*, by Giovanni Vincenti and James Braman, 17–30. Hershey, PA: IGI Global.

CAT. Heavy Equipment Simulator. 2011. http://www.cat.com/simulators (accessed August 12, 2011).

Chang, Ben. 2010. "Pilot Study of Past Decade Game-Based Learning Journal Papers Survey from the Technology Prespective." *2010 10th IEEE International Conference on Advanced Learning Technologies*, 748–749.

Chen, Hsiang-Ping, Chi-Jui Lien, Len Annetta, and Yu-Ling Lu. 2010. "The Influence of an Educational Computer Game on Children's Cultural Identities." *Educational Technology and Society* 13 (1): 94–105.

Cheng, Yufang, Hsuan-Chi Chiang, Jun Ye, and Li-Hung Cheng. 2010. "Enhancing Empathy Instruction Using a Collaborative Virtual Learning Environment for Children with Autistic Spectrum Conditions." *Computers and Education* 55: 1449–1458.

Cho, Seung-Bin. "History: Maps of World." 2011. http://itunes.apple.com/us/app/history-maps-of-world/id303282377?mt=8 (accessed August 12, 2011).

Course, Leslie, and Dora Chen. 2010. "A Tablet Computer for Young Children? Exploring Its Viability for Early Childhood Education." *Journal of Research on Technology in Education* 43 (1): 75–98.

Crosby-Nagy, Michelle, and John Carfora. 2010. "ICT Applications in U.S. higher education." In *Teaching through Multi-User Virtual Environments: Applying Dynamic Elements to the Modern Classroom*, by Giovanni Vincenti and James Braman, 47–58. Hershey, PA: IGI Global.

Csikszentmihalyi, Mihaly. 1996. *Creativity: Flow and the Psychology of Discovery and Invention.* New York: Harper Perennial.

Davidson, Christina. 2009. "Young Children's Engagement with Digital Texts and Literacies in the Home: Pressing Matters for the Teaching of English in the Early Years of Schooling." *English Teaching: Practice and Critique* 8 (3): 36–54.

DeMers, Michael. 2011. "Linking MUVE Education and Best Educational Practices." In *Multi-User-Virtual Environments for the Classroom: Practical Approaches to Teaching in Virtual Worlds*, by Giovanni Vincenti and James Braman, 1–16. Hershey, PA: IGI Global.

Dennis, Alan, Barbara Haley Wixom, and Roberta Roth. 2008. *Systems Analysis and Design, 4th Edition.* Hoboken, NJ: Wiley.

Derryberry, Anne. 2007. "Serious Games: Online Games for Learning." Adobe.com. September. http://www.adobe.com/resources/elearning/pdfs/serious_games_wp.pdf (accessed August 10, 2011).

Dimitropoulos, Kosmas, and Athanasios Manitsaris. 2010. "Designing Web-Based Educational Virtual Reality Environments." In *Teaching through Multi-User Virtual Environments: Applying Dynamic Elements to the Modern Classroom*, by Giovanni Vincenti and James Braman, 157–178. Hershey, PA: IGI Global.

Disney Online Studios Canada Inc. *Club Penguin.* 2011. http://clubpenguin.com/ (accessed August 12, 2011).

DriveSquare. Impaired Driving Simulator. 2011. http://www.drivesquare.com/prevention/ (accessed August 12, 2011).

Duruz, Timothy. 2010. "The Techno-Pedagogical Context of Distance Learning: Conceptual Roots." In *Teaching through Multi-User Virtual Environments: Applying Dynamic Elements to the Modern Classroom*, by Giovanni Vincenti and James Braman, 27–46. Hershey, PA: IGI Global.

Encyclopaedia Britannica, Inc. 2011. Britannica Kids: Volcanoes. http://itunes.apple.com/us/app/britannica-kids-volcanoes/id388309543?mt=8&ign-mpt=uo%3D4 (accessed August 12, 2011).

EnerCities. http://www.enercities.eu/ (accessed August 12, 2011).

European Union. 2011. Intelligent Energy Europe. August 12, 2011. http://ec.europa.eu/energy/intelligent/ (accessed August 12, 2011).

EuroTalk. 2011. uTalk HD Chinese (Mandarin). http://itunes.apple.com/WebObjects/MZStore.woa/wa/viewSoftware?id=318293048&mt=8&ign-mpt=uo%3D4 (accessed August 12, 2011).

Fiorini, Mario. 2010. "The Effect of Home Computer Use on Children's Cognitive and Non-Cognitive Skills." *Economics of Education Review* 29: 55–72.

Grieshaber, Susan. 2010. "Beyond Discovery: A Case Study of Teacher Interaction, Young Children and Computer Tasks." *Cambridge Journal of Education* 40 (1): 69–85.

Indiana University. *Quest Atlantis.* 2011. http://atlantis.crlt.indiana.edu/ (accessed August 12, 2011).

Isbister, Katherine, Mary Flanagan, and Chelsea Hash. 2010. "Designing Games for Learning: Insights from Conversations with Designers." *Proceedings of CHI 2010*: 2041–2044.

Jackson, Linda, et al. 2008. "Culture, Gender and Information Technology Use: A Comparison of Chinese and U.S. Children." *Computers in Human Behavior* 24 (6): 2817–2829.

Joshi, Arti, Alex Pan, Masaru Murakami, and Shankar Narayanan. 2010. "Role of Computers in Educating Young Children: U.S. and Japanese Teachers' Perspectives." *Computers in the Schools* 27: 5–19.

Khasawneh, Omar, and Hamed Al-Awidi. 2008. "The Effect of Home Computer Use on Jordanian Children: A Parental Perspective." *Journal of Educational Computing Research* 39 (3): 267–284.

Kirmani, Mubina Hassanali, Marcia Davis, and Maya Kalyanpur. 2009. "Young Children Surfing: Gender Differences in Computer Use." *Dimensions of Early Childhood* 37 (2): 16–22.

Knol, Erik, and Peter De Vries. 2011. "EnerCities, a Serious Game to Stimulate Sustainability and Energy Conservation: Preliminary Results." *eLearning Papers* 25 (July).

Laine, Teemu, Carolina Islas Sedano, Mike Joy, and Erkki Sutinen. 2010. "Critical Factors for Technology Integration in Game-Based Pervasive Learning Spaces." *IEEE Transactions on Learning Technologies* 3 (4): 294–306.

Laughlin, Daniel. "Overcoming Objections to MUVEs in Education." 2010. In *Teaching through Multi-User Virtual Environments: Applying Dynamic Elements to the Modern Classroom*, by Giovanni Vincenti and James Braman, 1–14. Hershey, PA: IGI Global.

Lebens, Morena, Martin Graff, and Peter Mayer. 2009. "Access, Attitudes and the Digital Divide: Children's Attitudes towards Computers in a Technology-Rich Environment." *Educational Media International* 46 (3): 255–266.

Lim, Kenneth. 2009. "The Six Learnings of Second Life." *Journal of Virtual Worlds Research* 2: 1.

Linden Research, Inc. 2011. Second Life. http://secondlife.com/ (accessed August 12, 2011).

Livingstone, Sonia, and Leslie Haddon. 2008. "Risky Experiences for Children Online: Charting European Research on Children and the Internet." *Children and Society* 22: 314–323.

Lui, Donald, Grace Szeto, and Alice Jones. 2011. "The Pattern of Electronic Game Use and Related Bodily Discomfort in Hong Kong Primary School Children." *Computers and Education* 57: 1665–1674.

Marty, Jean-Charles, and Thibault Carron. 2011. "Observation of Collaborative Activities in a Game-Based Learning Platform." *IEEE Transactions on Learning Technologies* 4(1): 98–110.

Mazzone, Emanuela, Janet Read, and Russell Beale. 2008. "Design with and for Disaffected Teenagers." *Proceedings of NordiCHI 2008*: 290–297.

McKenney, Susan, and Joke Voogt. 2010. "Technology and Young Children: How 4–7 Year Olds Perceive Their Own Use of Computers." *Computers in Human Behavior* 26: 656–664.

Meier, Sid. "Civilization." 2010. http://www.civilization.com/ (accessed August 12, 2011).

Metaversum. "Twinity." 2011. http://www.twinity.com/ (accessed August 12, 2011).

Michigan State University. *Serious Game Design.* http://seriousgames.msu.edu/ (accessed August 1, 2011).

Milgram, Paul, Haruo Takemura, Akira Utsumi, and Fumio Kishino. 1994. "Augmented Reality: A Class of Displays on the Reality-Virtuality Continuum." *Telemanipulator and Telepresence Technologies* 2351: 282–292.

Miller, David, and Dereck Robertson. 2010. "Using a Games Console in the Primary Classroom: Effects of 'Brain Training' Programme on Computation and Self-Esteem." *British Journal of Educational Technology* 41 (2): 242–255.

MIT. Scratch. 2011. http://scratch.mit.edu/ (accessed August 12, 2011).

Moore, Peter. 1997. "Inferential Focus Briefing." New York: Inferential Focus, Inc. September 30.

Nintendo. Brain Age. http://brainage.com/ (accessed August 12, 2011).

———. Wii Controllers. 2011. http://www.nintendo.com/wii/console/controllers (accessed August 9, 2011).

Numedeon, Inc. Whyville. 2011. http://www.whyville.net/ (accessed August 12, 2011).

Nunez Redo, Manuela, Arturo Quintana Torres, Ricardo Quiros, Inma Nunez Redo, Juan Carda Castello, and Emilio Camahort. 2010. "New Augmented Reality Applications: Inorganic Chemistry Education." In *Teaching through Multi-User Virtual Environments: Applying Dynamic Elements to the Modern Classroom*, by Giovanni Vincenti and James Braman, 365–386. Hershey, PA: IGI Global.

Open Wonderland Foundation. 2011. Open Wonderland. http://openwonderland.org/ (accessed August 12, 2011).

Palaware. MathBoard. 2011. http://itunes.apple.com/us/app/mathboard/id373909837?mt=8&ign-mpt=uo%3D4 (accessed August 12, 2011).

Papastergiou, Marina. 2009. "Digital Game-Based Learning in High School Computer Science Education: Impact on Educational Effectiveness and Student Motivation." *Computers and Education* 12: 1–12.

Pares, Narcis, Paul Masri, Gerard van Wolfered, and Chris Creed. 2005. "Achieving Dialogue with Children with Severe Autism in an Adaptive Multisensory Interaction: The 'MEDIATE' Project." *IEEE Transactions on Visualization and Computer Graphics* 11, 6 (November/December): 734–743.

Playfish. Pet Society. 2011. http://www.petsociety.com/ (accessed August 12, 2011).

Plowman, Lydia, Christine Stephen, and Joanna McPake. 2010. "Supporting Young Children's Learning with Technology and Home and in Preschool." *Research Papers in Education* 25 (1): 93–113.

Prensky, Marc. 2000. *Digital Game-Based Learning*. New York: McGraw Hill.

Prensky, Marc. 2001a. "Digital Natives, Digital Immigrants, Part I" *On the Horizon* 9 (5 and 6): 1–6.

Prensky, Marc. 2001b. "Digital Natives, Digital Immigrants, Part II: Do They Really Think Differently?" *On the Horizon* 9 (6): 1–6.

Protopsaltis, Aristidis, Lucia Pannese, Dimitra Pappa, and Sonia Hetzner. 2011. "Serious Games and Formal and Informal Learning." *eLearning Papers* 25 (July).

Radu, Iulian, and Blair MacIntyre. 2009. "Augmented-Reality Scratch: A Children's Authoring Environment for Augmented-Reality Experiences." *Proceedings of IDC 2009*: 210–213.

Reisinger, Don. 2011. "Apple iPhone Tops Smartphone Charts in 2nd Quarter." *cnet News.* August 5. http://news.cnet.com/8301-13506_3-20088561-17/apple-iphone-tops-smartphone-charts-in-2nd-quarter/(accessed August 7, 2011).

Renaissance 2.0 Media. 2011. Secret Builder. http://secretbuilders.com/ (accessed August 12, 2011).

Rovio Mobile. 2010. Angry Birds. http://www.rovio.com/index.php?page=angry-birds (accessed August 7, 2011).

Samuelsson, Ulli. 2010. "ICT Use among 13-Year-Old Swedish Children." *Learning, Media and Technology* 35 (1): 15–30.

Schwebel, David, Joanna Gaines, and Joan Severson. 2008. "Validation of Virtual Reality as a Tool to Understand and Prevent Child Pedestrian Injury." *Accident Analysis and Prevention* 40: 1394–1400.

Shih, Ju-Ling, Chien-Wen Chuang, and Eric Zhi-Feng Liu. 2010. "A Preliminary Outcome-Oriented Review of Game-Based Learning Research." *2010 IEEE International Conference on Digital Game and Intelligent Toy Enhanced Learning*: 228–230.

Straker, Leon, Barbara Maslen, Robin Burgess-Limerick, Peter Johnson, and Jack Dennerlein. 2010. "Evidence-Based Guidelines for the Wise Use of Computers by Children: Physical Development Guidelines." *Ergonomics* 53 (4): 458–477.

Straker, Leon, Clare Pollock, and Barbara Maslen. 2009. "Principles for the Wise Use of Computers by Children." *Ergonomics* 52 (11): 1386–1401.

Sulake Corporation Oy. 2011. *Habbo Hotel.* http://www.habbo.com/ (accessed August 12, 2011).

Tuzun, Hakan, Meryem Yilmaz-Soylu, Turkan Karakus, Yavuz Inal, and Gonca Kizilkaya. 2009. "The Effects of Computer Games on Primary School Students' Achievement and Motivation in Geography Learning." *Computers and Education* 52: 68–77.

Vincenti, Giovanni, and James Braman. 2010. *Teaching through Multi-User Virtual Environments: Applying Dynamic Elements to the Modern Classroom.* Hershey, PA: IGI Global.

Vincenti, Giovanni, and James Braman. 2011. *Multi-User Virtual Environments for the Classroom: Practical Approaches to Teaching in Virtual Worlds.* Hershey, PA: IGI Global.

Whitton, Nicola. 2007. "Motivation and Computer Game-Based Learning." *Proceedings of the ascilite Conference*: 1063–1067.

Wood, Denise. 2010. "The Benefits and Unanticipated Challenges in the Use of 3D Virtual Learning Environments in the Undergraduate Media Arts Curriculum." In *Teaching through Multi-User Virtual Environments: Applying Dynamic Elements to the Modern Classroom,* by Giovanni Vincenti and James Braman, 236–257. Hershey, PA: IGI Global.

Wrzesien, Maja, David Perez Lopez, and Mariano Alcaniz Raya. 2009. "E-Junior: A Serious Virtual World for Natural Science and Ecology Learning." *Proceedings of the International Conference on Advances in Computer Entertainment Technology*: 319–322.

X-Plane. X-Plane. 2011. http://www.x-plane.com/ (accessed August 12, 2011).

Zaibon, Syamsul Bahrin, and Norshuhada Shiratuddin. 2010. "Adapting Learning Theories in Mobile Game-Based Learning Development." *Proceedings of the 2010 IEEE International Conference on Digital Game and Intelligent Toy Enhanced Learning*: 124–128.

Chapter Eight

Everyday Life Information in Support of Enhanced Quality of Life for Young Adults with Intellectual Disabilities

Dana Hanson-Baldauf

At age 14, Eric stood a head taller than most of his eighth- grade classmates. He was an unusual-looking boy with a high flat forehead and long and narrow face, anchored by two large and protruding ears. His crystal blue eyes rarely made eye contact with others, but left little unnoticed. Eric's voice was deep and gruff and when he spoke, his head nodded almost rhythmically to his words. With words came spittle, trickling out of his mouth, down the side of his chin and wiped with the shrug of his shoulder. Moving between classes, it was not unusual to hear Eric shouting, "Outta da way!" while charging with arms outstretched and fists shaking fiercely through the crowded and locker-lined hallways. Although the students parted, they typically paid little attention. This was nothing new. They had gone to school with Eric since kindergarten, sat across from him at lunch, partnered with him in gym class. They knew Eric and more than that, they liked Eric. He was a keenly observant individual who easily endeared himself by taking genuine interest in those around him and offering odd compliments ("I like your eyebrows, Lisa!"). In class, Eric often rocked back and forth in his chair with his hands tightly fisted and positioned at his mouth. His knuckles were painfully red, both raw and calloused by years of biting, a nervous habit developed over the years in response to an often noisy and over-stimulating world.

Eric was born with Fragile X, a chromosomal abnormality and one of the most common inherited causes of intellectual disability (ID). Fragile X presents itself in a variety of ways, affecting individuals in areas of cognition, behavior, sensory intake, motor development, and speech and language. As an eighth grader, Eric received support through his middle school special

167

education program and spent two of seven class periods in a self-contained classroom. In this class, instruction focused on individual goals with emphases on the development of independent life skills and strengthening functional reading and math. For the remaining five periods, Eric was mainstreamed with his same-age peers in classes including language arts, science, physical education, social studies, and an elective of his choosing. He was often shadowed by a teaching assistant and his assignments were modified to accommodate for his individual learning needs. Although Eric's academic skills were significantly behind his peers, his teachers accepted him with warmth and respect. He was hard working, eager to please, and had a way of bringing out the best in his classmates. Attentive and curious, Eric was particularly known for engaging his teachers in conversation, asking streams of unabashed questions ("Ms. Hanson, Where dya get those cool shoes? How much they cost, Ms. Hanson? Why ya got such big feet, Ms. Hanson? "). Eric loved to be "in the know" and his expressed need for information was displayed with great sincerity and a smile—a beautifully crooked, day-brightening, and perfect smile.

Francis Bacon's saying "knowledge itself is power" speaks directly to the influence of information in our daily lives and the great advantage of one's ability to access, make sense of, and use it to construct meaningful outcomes. This might include developing a new skill, finding employment, supporting a healthy lifestyle, gaining a deeper sense of self and spirituality, expanding a personal interest or knowledge area, or simply satisfying curiosities. Eric often sought and used information to connect and engage with others. In turn, he was well liked by his peers and gained a level of acceptance not typically experienced by many with ID.

The significance of everyday life information for enhanced quality of life is highlighted in the Developmental Disabilities Assistance Act and Bill of Rights, as disseminated by the Administration on Developmental Disabilities in 2000. Number 16 states the following:

The goals of the Nation properly include a goal of providing individuals with developmental disabilities with the information, skills, opportunities, and support to
A. make informed choices and decisions about their lives;
B. live in homes and communities in which such individuals can exercise their full rights and responsibilities as citizens;
C. pursue meaningful and productive lives;
D. contribute to their families, communities, and States, and the Nation;
E. have interdependent friendships and relationships with other persons;
F. live free of abuse, neglect, financial and sexual exploitation, and violations of their legal and human rights; and

G. achieve full integration and inclusion in society, in an individualized manner, consistent with the unique strengths, resources, priorities, concerns, abilities, and capabilities of each individual.

This important legislation ensures the provision of funding for State, public, non-profit agencies that promote and foster opportunities for independence, productivity, and self-determination for persons with developmental disabilities. Despite recognition of information as an important aspect of improved life quality, until recently little consideration has been given to issues of access for persons with cognitive challenges.

In 2010, the United States Department of Justice issued an advanced notice of proposed rulemaking to gather public input into possible revisions of the Americans with Disabilities Act, specifically title II and III. These statutes broadly prohibit discrimination on the basis of disability by State and local government entities and in places of public accommodation, though they do not specifically address digital environments of public accommodations. The Internet has dramatically changed our way of life by increasing access to goods and services, education, health care information, and each other. However, these benefits remain unobtainable for many persons with ID and other disabilities who are unable to gain access as a result of the sizable challenges they face, not only as a result of their disability but also because of society's response to their disability. Recent studies on typical teen experiences and their transitions into adulthood depict a dismal and unwelcoming future for our youth with ID. These findings also point to broad and significant areas of unmet information need. The dearth of cognitively accessible information has become a recurrent theme in the literature, cited as a detrimental factor in life quality (Stewart et al. 2009; Yalon-Chamovitz 2009; Karreman, Van der Geest, and Buursik 2007; Salmi 2007; Tarleton and Ward 2005; Britz 2004; Edyburn 2002).

Although persons with ID have long been recognized as an underserved population by the library and information science (LIS) community (Casey 1971; Mendel 1995; Jaeger, Bertot, and Franklin 2010), little effort has been made to rectify this neglect. In conducting a search of the LIS literature, one can find few studies examining the information experiences and needs of individuals with ID. Practitioner literature fares only slightly better in terms of the number of articles on the topic of services and resources for this patron group. Further, Jaeger, Bertot, and Franklin (2010) found few preparatory programs for future LIS professionals that adequately address diversity in relation to individuals with ID and other disabilities within their curriculum (179).

The LIS community is in the position to empower individuals with ID and positively influence lives. However to do so, research and practice must be informed and reflective—grounded in the everyday reality of these individu-

als and with thoughtful contemplation of one's own assumption and biases of
not only individuals with ID, but also that which we call and consider "information." Initiatives conducted in a vacuum (however admirable and well-
meaning) will be disjointed, less relevant, and have minimal impact if absent
these essential considerations.

The intent of this chapter is to begin to lay a foundation from which LIS
service and research might emerge in support of our young people with ID.
The first section of the chapter presents an introduction to ID: definition,
history, and quality of life. This includes a landscape view of typical adult
life outcomes. The second section of the chapter focuses specifically on teens
with ID, their common adolescent experiences, and the role of everyday life
information. An emerging profile of information need is presented along
with a discussion of some of the most oft cited information access issues
encountered. The chapter concludes with a call for action to the LIS community.

INTELLECTUAL DISABILITY

Definition

The American Association on Intellectual and Developmental Disabilities
(2010) defines intellectual disability as "characterized by significant limitations both in intellectual functioning and in adaptive behavior as expressed in
conceptual, social, and practical adaptive skills. This disability originates
before age 18" (1). *Intellectual functioning* encompasses learning and rate of
learning, attention, memory, abstract thinking, transferability of knowledge
and skills, understanding complex ideas, problem solving, planning, and reasoning (31–42). *Adaptive behavior* refers to skills necessary to function and
adapt in everyday life. These include

> *conceptual skills:* language and literacy, money, time, and numbers;
> *social skills:* interpersonal skills, social responsibility, self-esteem, social
> problem solving, following rules and obeying laws, personal safety; and
> *practical skills:* self-care, health, community mobility, occupational
> skills, self-direction, use of money, use of the telephone, schedules and rou-
> tine. (43–55)

Five assumptions accompany the identification of ID:

1. Limitations in present functioning must be considered within the context of community environments typical of the individual's age peers
   and culture.
2. Valid assessment considers cultural and linguistic diversity as well as
   differences in communication, sensory, motor, and behavioral factors.

3. Within any individual, limitations often coexist with strengths.
4. An important purpose of describing limitations is to develop a profile of needed supports.
5. With appropriate personalized supports over a sustained period, the life functioning of the person with ID generally will improve. (1)

Formerly referred to as mental retardation, intellectual disability is a developmental disability and can result from genetic, physical, or non-physical origins.[1] In the United States, 40 to 50 percent of individuals diagnosed with ID have no identifiable origin (FAQ on Intellectual Disability 2011).

In function, the term *intellectual disability* serves as a communication tool to describe a common set of characteristics, challenges, and needs experienced by a small segment of the population (3 percent) for purposes of support, services, education, advocacy, funding, and research. However, individuals inextricably coupled with this label, many times without want or say,[2] are highly heterogeneous. Although they may experience common difficulties, these challenges are manifested in diverse ways and experienced by persons unique in personality, interest, history, and need.

Rarely acknowledged in textbook definitions, though readily shared by friends and loved ones, are positive attributes displayed by many individuals with ID: authenticity, honesty, generosity, forgiveness, positive spontaneity, trust, and the unique ability to bring out gentleness, patience, and tolerance in others.[3] J. David Smith (2009) writes of the "powerful humanizing influence" individuals with ID have on others and the benefit to society by virtue of their inclusion. He states,

> When I reflect on the importance of these children and adults and their qualities, I find I must say something that I have often lacked the courage to say directly and publicly: A disability can be a valuable human attribute. (4)

History

The history of ID is not kind.[4] It is a past marked by centuries of marginalization, neglect, gross mistreatment from a society largely informed by superstition, fear, and ignorance. Although the dawn of modern medicine brought about a more sophisticated understanding of disability, this understanding authoritatively perpetuated the notion of individuals with ID as defective and in need of medical intervention. Up until the latter half of the 20th century, treatment included shock therapy, lobotomies, pharmaceutical drugging, and sterilization. Institutionalization was also a common prescription. Overcrowded and understaffed, these facilities served as human warehouses. Residents lived in deplorable conditions, regularly deprived of adequate clothing, food, and any semblance of compassion. Physical and sexual abuse was rampant. All the while, families were kept oblivious to the horrific circumstances experienced by their loved ones inside. In the 1966 book titled *Christmas in Purgatory*, Burton Platt and Fred Kaplan helped to bring public attention to the everyday life of individuals inside these institutions. The introduction starts, "There is a hell on earth, and in America there is a special inferno. We were visitors there during Christmas, 1965" (v).

The public responded with revulsion and outrage. Their fury fueled the flames of a burgeoning disabilities rights movement and led to a major overhaul of systems and services and the creation of U.S. public policies and landmark legislation in protection of the rights of all persons with disabilities.

Quality of Life

Referred to as "the degree to which a person enjoys the important possibilities of his or her life" (Raphael et al. 1999, 201), the concept of quality of life (QOL) has evolved over the past few decades into an important field of study for understanding, measuring, and influencing the overall well-being of individuals with ID. From this work, eight core domains and key indicators have emerged as principal factors influencing life quality for all individuals, with or without ID (see Table 8.1).

In 2006, the United Nations General Assembly issued the Convention on the Rights of Persons with Disabilities in support of the promotion, protection, and assurance of human rights and fundamental freedoms of individuals with disabilities. It outlined essential sociopolitical conditions necessary for life quality, including

Table 8.1. Quality-of-Life Conceptual and Measurement Framework (Schalock et al. 2011, 19)

Emotional well-being	Contentment, self-concept, lack of stress
Interpersonal relations	Interactions, relationships, supports
Material well-being	Financial status, employment, housing
Personal development	Education, personal competence, performance
Physical well-being	Health and health care, activities of daily living, leisure
Self-determination	Autonomy/personal control, goals and personal values, choices
Social inclusion	Community integration and participation, community roles, social supports
Rights	Human (respect, dignity, equality) and legal (citizenship, access, due process)

- access to the physical environment, transportation, information and communication technologies and systems, and to all public facilities and services;
- freedom of expression and opinion, and access to information;
- inclusive education;
- access to quality and affordable health care;
- freedom from exploitation, violence and abuse;
- equal recognition before the law and equal access to justice;
- the right to live independently and with privacy;
- non-discrimination against persons in all matters relating to marriage, family, parenthood, and relationships;
- non-discrimination in the work place and employment practices;
- adequate standard of living and social protection;
- community participation and personal mobility;
- participation in political and public life; and
- participation in cultural life, recreation, leisure and sport.

While this decree presented an impressive show of global support, the conditions asserted have yet to be realized by many with disabilities. In September 2011, the assembly reconvened with Deputy Secretary-General Asha-Rose Migiro (2011) providing the opening address,

> Even today, almost five years after the adoption of the Convention, too many persons with disabilities do not even know this historic instrument exists. Far too many are denied the rights it is supposed to guarantee. As long as they are denied those rights, we cannot rest. . . . You and I and millions of others know, that when we respect the inherent dignity of persons with disabilities, we enrich our human family.

Undeniably, the interplay between society and disability is complicated. While one cannot deny the inherent challenges individuals face as a result of their cognitive and physical limitations, history has also shown the disabling impact of society. Although these events have led to a more compassionate and holistic understanding of disability, remnants of this cruel and neglectful past remain. Individuals with ID continue to be denied the most basic human rights, regularly encounter blatant and veiled forms of discrimination, and are largely excluded in their own communities. The following presents a landscape of shared challenges and inequities still experienced by many with ID.

Employment

Over 70 percent of adults with ID are unemployed (AAIDD 2010, 157). Although Title I of the American's Disability Act prohibits employment discrimination, individuals with ID have an exceedingly difficult time obtaining employment in the general workforce. Of those employed, most are relegated to the most undesirable positions, earn minimum wage, are entitled to few benefits, and have minimal opportunities for advanced skill development or promotion (Butterworth et al. 2008). Multiple studies have found that most individuals with ID possess a strong desire to be competitively employed in integrated work settings and when given the opportunity and support, can contribute in diverse and meaningful ways (Certo et al. 2008; Migliore et al. 2007; Brown, Shiraga, and Kessler 2006). Unfortunately, these opportunities are rarely afforded and the large majority of individuals with ID spend their days in federally funded segregated sheltered workshops.[5] Although promoted as a transitional path to cultivate work skills for future competitive employment, a recent study by the National Disabilities Rights Network (2011) found individuals engaged in menial and repetitive tasks in isolating environments. The report states,

> Most are paid only a fraction of the minimum wage while many company owners make six-figure salaries. Many people profit off of their labor. All, except the worker. For many people with disabilities, their dream of leaving their "job training program" will never come true. (3)

Comparison studies of participants and non-participants of sheltered workshop programs found that individuals transitioning from workshops into the general workforce are generally less skilled, require more support, work fewer hours, and earn lower wages than those who have not participated in sheltered workshop programs (Cimera 2011; Cimera et al. 2011).

Poverty

Not surprisingly, adults with ID generally live 20 percent below the poverty threshold, typically earning only one-third the median household income (Stancliffe and Lankin 2007, 429). Though eligible for governmental support, individuals encounter a bureaucracy that is both confusing and intimidating and their supplemental income makes little impact in raising one's income level over the poverty line (Certo et al. 2008, 93). If it is determined that there is a need, these programs can draw individuals into a vicious cycle of poverty by creating disincentives to work. Although in a study by Migliore et al. (2007), individuals with ID expressed a strong desire to work (14), many feel forced to reject opportunities for increased pay out of fear they will be penalized with a reduction or loss of government support (Certo et al. 2008, 93). Given the great difficulty many experience obtaining and keeping employment, the stability and assurance of a monthly government check is often a much safer bet when forced to choose. In recognition of this dilemma, the U.S. Social Security Administration has made efforts to eliminate these disincentives to work, yet they are not well publicized to those who would benefit most (Certo et al. 2008, 93).

Housing

In 1999, the Supreme Court ruled that individuals with disabilities have the right to live in "the most integrating settings appropriate" and that the unnecessary placement of individuals with disabilities in institutional type settings "perpetuates the unwarranted assumptions that persons so isolated are incapable or unworthy of participating in community life" (The Olmstead Decision). Given the level of need and available options, living situations vary. Many individuals with ID live in group home settings with three to four roommates and full- or part-time staff. Others live in apartments either independently or with a roommate and receive daily or weekly support. Oftentimes, individuals continue to live at home with their aging parents. The waiting lists for supported living placements can be lengthy and the quality of services and staff vary widely among providers. For individuals able and wanting to live more independently, affordable housing is nearly impossible to find. A recent report by the Technical Assistance Collaborative, Inc., and the Consortium for Citizens with Disabilities Housing Task Force noted, "there is not one state or community in the nation where a person with a disability receiving SSI payments can afford to rent a modest—not luxurious—one-bedroom or efficiency housing unit" (Cooper et al. 2009, 1). Although the Department of Housing and Urban Development offers financial subsidies under Section Eight voucher programs, the application process and system are overly complex and waiting lists are long (AAIDD 2010, 158).

Health

On average, adults with ID tend to have poorer physical and mental health than those without ID. They experience higher rates of obesity, poorer vision, late-stage cancer diagnoses, depression, anxiety, high levels of stress, increased rates of epilepsy, and other complex health conditions, and have more frequent and extended hospital stays than those without ID (Krahn et al. 2010). They often have difficulty communicating their healthcare concerns to medical professionals and following through with prescribed treatment. Incomplete or absent medical histories are not uncommon among this population (Spitalnik and White-Scott 2001, 203–220). Health-related services also tend to be more reactionary than preventative, particularly in areas of sexual health. The social stigma attached to sex and misperceptions of persons with ID as child-like, even asexual, prevent individuals from getting the information they need to make informed, healthy decisions, to learn appropriate socio-sexual behaviors, and be proactive in their sexual health. This denial of information greatly increases vulnerability to abuse, exploitation, unintended pregnancies, and sexually transmitted diseases (Gougeon 2009, 283).

Social Support Networks

In general, individuals with ID tend to have small social support networks and few stable friendships. Instead, many rely on family members and care providers for social engagement and emotional support. This population reports higher degrees of loneliness, social isolation, and depression than those without ID (Smiley 2005). Typical opportunities for social engagement and a sense of connectedness commonly afforded most individuals through work and educational environments, spiritual communities, and other types of community gatherings are less available for persons with ID, who have difficulty accessing transportation and are otherwise physically segregated from the general population (Verdonschot et al. 2009; Vogel et al. 2006; Cummins and Lau 2003). Although efforts toward community integration are increasing, studies show that physical presence in an environment does not guarantee social acceptance, inclusion, or reduced stigma (Lippold and Burns 2009).

Online social networks have been a positive outlet for increased connection among many isolated individuals; however, those with ID are less likely to benefit from these support systems given the related costs of having the technology and the skills necessary to connect and engage. Compared to persons without ID, individuals with ID are less likely to own even a basic cell phone. While cost is one prohibiting factor, the highly monitored environments in which individuals with ID typically live can create a perception of less need, unnecessarily enabling increased dependence (Bryen et al. 2007).

Crime

Individuals with ID are at an elevated risk of becoming victims of crime, particularly sexually based crimes (Sobsey and Doe 1991).[6] Perpetrators specifically target this population with assumptions that they are easily manipulated, will not or cannot escape, and that assaults will go unnoticed and unreported. Usually, assailants are known to their victims. Repeat and ongoing victimization is not uncommon (National Sheriff's Association 2008, 14). The high invisibility and isolation experienced by individuals with ID increases their vulnerability, and unfortunately, some may not recognize their abuse and mistreatment as abnormal. The legal system, including police, lawyers, judges, and courts, have overwhelmingly been ineffective in supporting, gathering evidence, and prosecuting perpetrators. Additionally, cognitively accessible legal resources are rarely available. Commonly, cases are dropped because victims with ID are perceived as unreliable informers (Sorenson 2003).

Community Mobility

Individuals with ID often have few opportunities for independence in their communities and are dependent on others for their transportation needs. However, a study by Bryen et al. (2007) found that with appropriate instruction, practice, and cell phone access, many individuals—even with more severe degrees of ID—can be independently mobile in their communities. Unfortunately, way-finding studies[7] highlight the inaccessibility of common navigational constructs, including public signage, maps, schedules, labels, and landmarks due to a high reliance on print to convey meaning (Martinez, Mattson, Hough, and Abeson 2010; Fischer and Sullivan 2002). Although much attention has been paid to the mobility needs of individuals with physical and sensory disabilities (cut curbs, ramps, Braille signage, audio crosswalk signals), the mobility needs of individuals with cognitive disabilities have been largely ignored.

These barriers to mobility exacerbate many of the other challenges, making it difficult to find and keep a job, obtain medical care and legal support, engage in civic events and responsibilities, participate in spiritual communities, and socialize with friends and families (Verdonschot et al. 2009; Conley and Taylor 2003). Moreover, these challenges contribute to the invisibility of individuals with ID in their communities, increasing their vulnerability and leaving many of their life circumstances unknown and needs dangerously unmet.

INTELLECTUAL DISABILITY AND THE TEEN YEARS

The teen years are a time of profound change. Normatively, this is a period classically characterized by identity construction. Inwardly, teens are contemplating questions of "Who am I?" and "Where do I belong?" and outwardly they may be experimenting in look, behavior, and relations. Curiosities and interest in intimacy, sexuality, and sex increase during this time as peer relations become more intense and family dependency wanes. Experimentation, testing rules and limits, and questioning of authority are common teen behaviors. Although frustrating to parents, these behaviors contribute to the development of self and feelings of self-efficacy. Despite tendencies to prioritize present concerns over future considerations, no doubt teens are consciously and unconsciously making definitive movements toward adulthood. Havighurst (1949) describes this transition as the developmental tasks of adolescence.

Few studies have examined the developmental trajectories of teens with ID, though little evidence is available to suggest wide dissimilarity from teens without ID (Hauser-Cram, Krauss, and Kersch 2009, 589). However, notable points of departure from the normal adolescent experiences do exist and it would be remiss to diminish the impact an ID has on making sense of developmental changes and in negotiating the complexities of adolescent life.

The School Experience

Students with ID experience high segregation in the school setting, particularly by the time they reach high school. As general curriculum demands heighten, instructional emphasis turns pointedly toward the strengthening of independent living and work skills for post-school life. A shortage of special education teachers, as reported by the U.S. Department of Education in 2011, and high turnover rates (Boe and Cook 2006, 443) have major implications on the continuity and quality of instruction for students with ID. Student absenteeism rates tend to increase during secondary schooling (Newman et al. 2009) and approximately 29 percent of teens with ID drop out before graduation (Polloway et al. 2010, 62).[8] Commonly cited reasons for dropping out include poor relations with teachers and peers, overall dislike for school, stigmatization from segregation, and irrelevant education and transition goals and vocational experiences (Snell 2011; Wagner et al. 2006, 7).

Transition Planning

Issues of transition from secondary schooling to post-school life have received considerable attention in recent years in an effort to address poor post-school outcomes for many with ID. The following barriers have been identified as major obstacles impeding successful transitions into adulthood:

- inadequate transition planning—too little and too late (Griffin, McMillan, and Hodapp, 2010);
- limited options for post-secondary education and employment (Conley and Taylor 2003);
- lack of accessible information related to post-secondary options, services, and supports (Griffin, McMillan, and Hodapp, 2010; Stewart et al. 2009);
- overly complex public support systems, fragmented supports and services, and long waiting lists (Martinez 2009; Beresford 2004);
- governmental disincentives to work (Martinez 2009; Certo et al. 2008; Conley and Taylor 2003); and
- lack of public awareness/understanding about individuals with ID (Kersh 2011).

The Individuals with Disabilities Education Improvement Act (IDEA) of 2004 mandates that public schools begin transition planning for all students with disabilities by the age of 14, with transition program implementation by the age of 16. Although intended to be a person-centered process tied to the strengths, preferences, and interests of the student, Powers and colleagues (2005) found that many young people with ID play a minimal role in their post-school planning and are often prescribed goals unrelated to their personal preference or interests (53). A National Longitudinal Transition Survey 2 (NLTS-2) of over 11,000 students with disabilities revealed that students with ID are typically steered toward sheltered workshop programs over other post-school options (Grigal, Hart, and Migliore 2011, 11). The same study also found that that workshop related transition goals are the primary predictor of future unemployment (13).

With passage of the Higher Education Opportunity Act of 2008, opportunities are expanding for students with ID to continue their education beyond secondary schooling. Think College, an initiative of the Institute for Community Inclusion at the University of Massachusetts, provides a growing database of available programs located at trade schools and community colleges, four-year colleges, and universities across the United States. Migliore and Butterworth (2009) found that students who completed post-secondary education programs were more likely to secure competitive employment and earned over 70 percent more than those who did not continue their education (1). Unfortunately, parents and transition-aged students are unaware that these programs may be an option. In a 2010 study by Griffin, McMillan, and Hodapp, 73 percent of parents surveyed indicated that they did not receive information nor were provided adequate guidance in pursuing these programs (342).

Peer Relations

Peer relations are an influential part of the teen years and contribute to the strengthening of appropriate social behaviors necessary for adult life. Friendships, in particular, help to develop competencies in areas of reciprocity, conflict resolution, trust, and loyalty, and create a sense of belonging and acceptance during a time of heightened insecurities and social stratification (Bukowski 2001). However, many teens with ID have difficulty recognizing complex social cues and negotiating many of the subtle nuances involved in developing and maintaining friendships. They typically have fewer friends than their peers without ID (Hauser-Cram, Krauss, and Kersch 2009). Additionally, teens with ID often experience a high degree of social stigma and alienation related to their disability and special education status in school. Rates of harassment and bullying are high for teens with ID, particularly for those with differences that are more visible.

In an effort to fit in, teens with ID (particularly those who have higher IQs)[9] will sometimes attempt to mask their challenges by exaggerating their abilities or rejecting critical supports if they perceive these supports may draw negative attention to them (Snell et al. 2009, 225). These actions can backfire in detrimental and devastating ways. Their often strong desire to please and their naïveté can make them easy targets for exploitation.

Sense of Self

Psychological well-being incorporates a sense of belonging, feelings of competence, personal fulfillment, and the belief that one's life has value and purpose. Studies on children and youth with disabilities show a strong correlation between psychological well-being and one's perceived level of social inclusion. Meaningful and positive interactions with peers contribute to an enhanced self-esteem and personal agency (Arvidsson, Granlund, and Thyberg 2008; Wehmeyer and Gamer 2003). Further, the ways young people with disabilities perceive themselves and their lived experience have a direct impact on learning and life outcomes (Simeonsson et al. 2001; Skinner and Belmont 1993).

Teens with ID report higher degrees of depression, worry, and anxiety than their peers without ID (Forte, Jahoda, and Dagnan 2011). On self-assessments of self-worth, teens with ID who have higher IQs tend to score themselves lower than their peers without ID *and* lower than teens with more severe degrees of ID. It has been suggested that these lower ratings are due to a heightened awareness of their peer hierarchy system and their perceived place in it (Cooney et al. 2006). However it would be wrong to assume that those with lower IQs are oblivious to their social circumstances. Numerous studies have shown that individuals with both mild and moderate degrees of ID are acutely aware of their devaluation and lack of acceptance in society (Jahoda et al. 2010; Cooney et al. 2006).

Self-Determination

Many young people with ID have few opportunities for personal control and tend to exhibit a diminished sense of self-determination (Stancliffe and Lankin 2007, 429–448). Self-determined behavior is defined as "acting as the primary causal agent in one's life and making choices and decisions regarding one's quality of life free from undue external influence or interference" (Wehmeyer et al. 2003, 177). It encompasses feelings of self-worth and personal agency and skill sets of decision making, problem solving, goal setting, risk taking, safety, self-instruction, self-advocacy, and self-awareness. The development of self-determined behavior hinges on meaningful opportunities for choice and personal control, more than IQ score (Wehmeyer et al. 2003). Studies on post-school outcomes of youth with ID found that teens with higher self-determination assessments were more likely to be employed, earn higher wages with benefits, and live outside the family home than teens with lower self-determination scores.

TEENS WITH ID AND EVERYDAY LIFE INFORMATION

Despite marked differences in how young people with ID experience and perceive their adolescent lives compared with their peers without ID, it is the shared nature of being human to explore, ask questions, seek answers, and construct and share meaning in our everyday lives. These processes of information discovery and engagement have received growing attention in the LIS field as a critical area of research. Savolainen (2008) defines everyday information practice as

> a set of socially and culturally established ways to identify, seek, use, and share the information available in various sources such as television, newspapers, and the Internet. These practices are often habitual and can be identified both in job-related and non-work contexts. (2–3)

Everyday life information (ELI) studies of young people have examined the experiences of adolescent girls, tweens, honor students, gay and lesbian youth, urban youth (Hughes-Hassell and Agosto 2007), and typical college students.

Everyday Life Information

Hughes-Hassell and Agosto's (2007) theoretical model of the everyday life information-seeking (ELIS) needs of urban teenagers highlights the developmental significance of teen ELIS behavior in support of their transforming and multifaceted lives. The researchers posit teen ELIS as a process of "self-exploration and world exploration that helps them to understand the world and their positions in it as well as helping them to understand themselves now and to understand who they aspire to be in the future" (53). Similarly, Ross Todd (2000) describes this process as one of "*inward forming*" or *information*, stating, "adolescents need to be able to engage with their information world, construct their own understanding and meaning, and use their knowledge in making lifestyle decisions" (165).

Not much is known about the everyday information experiences of teens with ID; however, recent research related to young people with autism by O'Leary (2011) suggests an emerging interest. Bilal examined the mediated information experiences of children with autism and found parents serving as information-seeking proxies in support of their children's need for information. Her findings draw attention to the need for increased, customized instruction to support technology skill development and Internet use by children with autism. O'Leary conducted a case study of a young man with Asperger's syndrome, exploring his information practice within the context of a hobby. She determined his interactions with information were a means to support identity construction and social connection. Preliminary dissertation findings by Hanson-Baldauf (2011) on the ELI needs, practices, and challenges of young adults with ID point to broad and critical areas of everyday life and future information needs in support of enhanced quality of life. The young adults in Hanson-Baldauf's study primarily sought information in support of their most immediate needs, curiosities, and interests relating to peer and family relationships, hobbies, interests and curiosities, and daily routines and activities. This concrete frame of reference is a common characteristic of many with ID, likewise, typical of the average teen—orientation in the here and now. Parents and teachers in the study placed emphasis on present and future everyday life information needs, prioritizing information that supported the development of independent life skills, self-care, employment, and personal safety.

As surmised by these three studies and the current research on common life experiences of young adults and adults with ID, Figure 8.1 presents an emerging model of ELI needs in support of enhanced everyday and future life quality. Given the diversity of this population, the presented typology reflects only a sampling of need type and does not imply applicability to all young people with ID.

Although the model identifies the multiple QOL domains of ELI need, the center sphere represents the potential ripple effect that attention to one area can have on other areas. For instance, information supporting personal development may impact feelings of self-esteem that may, in turn, promote emotional well-being.

Everyday Life Information and Issues of Access

Indisputably, uninhibited access to information supports overall well-being and is critical for decision making, problem solving, and world- and self-discovery. Furthermore, the right to information in comprehensible form is understood as a fundamental human right. The United Nations Universal Declaration of Human Rights (1948) states that all individuals have the right to "seek, receive and impart information and ideas through any media and regardless of frontiers" (Article 19). Both the International Federation of Library Associations and Institutions and the American Library Association assert the principles of intellectual freedom that include free and equal access

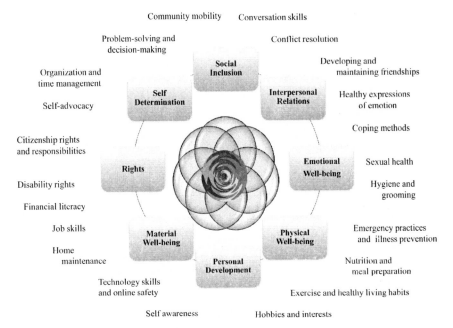

Figure 8.1. An emerging model

to information for all individuals, without discrimination and regardless of medium. The World Wide Web Consortium emphasizes a "Web for All" philosophy, stating

> The social value of the Web is that it enables human communication, commerce, and opportunities to share knowledge. One of W3C's primary goals is to make these benefits available to all people, whatever their hardware, software, network infrastructure, native language, culture, geographical location, or physical or mental ability.

Though these tenets explicitly convey a message of inclusivity, the prerequisites and conditions necessary for meaningful information engagement continue to exclude individuals with ID. Despite limited research, much can be inferred about their everyday life information needs when presented with the confounding and crushing matrix of challenges they experience. While some of these challenges are simply the reality of living with a cognitive impairment, many more are a direct result of how we, as a society, further disable ourselves with our unaccommodating structures and systems, our misperceptions and assumptions, our failure of attention and neglect, even our well-intentioned yet over-protective treatment. While not easily parsed, the following areas have been highlighted as issues of access for many with ID.

Exclusivity of Information in Print Form

Print is perhaps one of the most obvious and imposing barriers to information for many individuals with ID who struggle with literacy. We live in a world dominantly navigable by the written word and highly reliant on its use to convey meaning. In 2006, it was estimated that only 5 percent of the world's English-language publishing products were available in alternative non-text formats. Traditional librarianship and collections, both physical and digital, principally revolve around these textual representations of knowledge. Not surprisingly, Holmes (2008) found that individuals with developmental dis- abilities (DD) were less likely to use the library than the general public, concluding "the reasons for this discrepancy could be numerous, but one very basic reason could be that people with DD or those who care for them do not view the library as a viable resource" (538). The near exclusivity of information in print form is insufficient and places an inequitable onus on users with ID to meet the often unobtainable prerequisite of literacy. This failure to adequately understand and accommodate the cognitive accessibility needs of individuals with ID is discriminatory and contradicts universal and professional tenets of intellectual freedom and access for all.

Complexity of Content

Regardless of medium, complexity of content can also diminish meaningful information engagement by demanding higher levels of attention and com- prehension than individuals are capable. One common approach used to ad- dress issues of complexity is the cognitive scaling or rescaling of information (Edyburn 2002). This refers to the creation or modification of information in summative easy-to-understand content, for example Hi-Lo books. Yalon- Chamovitz (2009) expresses caution, however, noting that these processes of simplification are not intuitive and content creators have a tendency to infan- tilize materials in their use of language or pictures (396). For many teens with ID, these types of materials can have a stigmatizing effect and are sometimes shunned (Morgan and Moni 2008, 93).

Information Gatekeeping

Individuals with ID regularly experience the withholding of information. Circumstantially, access is prohibited as a result of our institutionalized structures and systems that fail to include, accommodate, and anticipate their participation in everyday life. As an example, teens with ID spend large portions of their days in self-contained special education classrooms apart from their same-aged peers. As a result of their exclusion, many are denied important information contained in the general curriculum content, such as information about democracy and their rights, and responsibilities as citizens.

Their segregation limits opportunities for information acquired through the invisible curriculum of school environments, as well. This includes information relating to teen culture, values, norms, and appropriate social behavior. On the same note, adults with ID are also regularly denied information as a result of their exclusion from the general workforce, including specialized vocational skills and work-related behavior. This denial of information is potential-limiting, significantly impacting their economic stability and overall well-being.

The purposeful withholding of information is also an experience shared by many with ID. This may include information about one's disability and rights (Hauser-Cram, Krauss, and Kersch 2009, 597; Davies and Jenkins 1997), information about sexual health, appropriate sexual behavior, and sexuality (Gougeon 2009), information about critical health issues such as cancer or information about death (Sormanti and Ballan, 2011; Tuffrey-Wijne et al. 2006). It may occur out of well-intentioned over-protectiveness, an avoidance of an uncomfortable conversation, perceptions of need, or feelings that individuals are incapable of understanding the complexities of certain topics (Sormanti and Ballan, 2011, 181; Hauser-Cram, Krauss, and Kersch 2009, 597; Tuffrey-Wijne et al. 2006, 114; Davies and Jenkins 1997). While it may be necessary to adjust informational content in order to assure the meaningful transfer of information, completely denying information out of a false perception of adults with ID as childlike can leave individuals vulnerable with harmful consequences. Further, it disregards the wisdom and maturity many individuals have acquired simply by years lived and experiences encountered.

Technology Access and Accessibility

In recent years, information and communication technologies (ICT) have dramatically transformed modern society. Particularly popular among young adults, a 2010 Pew Internet and American Life study found that approximately 75 percent of teens have their own cell phones, 79 percent have an iPod or other type of mp3 player, 93 percent of teens engage in online activities, and 73 percent have a social network presence. Similarly, Hanson-Baldauf (2011) found these technologies enjoyed by the young research participants with ID in her study. Despite a wide range of literacy competence, all participants regularly initiated engagement in online environments—as information seekers, consumers, and providers. Examples of use included e-mail and social network systems, gaming, downloading and listening to music, uploading and looking at photographs, and watching video clips. Interactive and multimedia websites seem most popular.

Other studies investigating ICT use by individuals with ID show promising possibilities for increasing access to information, promoting skill development, and facilitating new opportunities for personal control and independence (Kagohara 2011). Increasingly, many of these popular tools are replacing once bulky and obtrusive assistive technology equipment. One example, Proloquo, an augmentative communication device, is now available as an app (Proloquo2Go) for use with Apple's iPhone, iPad, and iTouch technologies. Sleek and customizable, these tools allow individuals with disabilities to fit in—or at minimum not stand out—among their peers (Pattison and Stedmon 2006, 269; Plos and Buisine 2006, 1230). Other appealing features of these tools include multimedia and communication capabilities, extended memory support, built-in GPS systems, portability, and high tolerance for error in use. Addressing the significant influence these tools can have in the lives of individuals with ID, Marks and Milne (2008) state, "tools such as iPods are not neutral, objective devices." Rather, they are tools that can transform the lives and learning of students with severe intellectual disabilities. As Callister and Burbules (n.d.) observe, "The use of a tool does more than accomplish some purpose; it creates new purposes, new needs, and new expectations. It allows for new possibilities and new ways of doing things, which in turn suggest new things to be done" (169).

Despite the benefits, a number of barriers prohibit their use. Cost, interface complexity, and physical manipulation are three of the most frequently cited barriers (Bryen et al. 2007; Carey et al. 2005). Lack of opportunity and perception of need have also been noted (Marks and Milne 2008; Bryen et al. 2007). For example, in a study examining cell phone use by individuals with ID, Bryen and colleagues (2007) commented that non-use may stem from "the rather sheltered environments in which many of the respondents live and work (for example, unemployment or sheltered employment, living arrangements with little opportunity to engage in community activities)" (6). They go on to say, "these environments may provide limited opportunity and support for technology use in general and cell phone use in particular. They might foster unnecessary dependence on others as opposed to use of enabling assistive and generic technologies to promote independence." Marks and Milne also suggest that many teachers less adept with technology fail to recognize the potential of these tools and are less inclined to integrate them into teaching and learning opportunities (168).

Professional Disconnect

Historically, there has been little overlap between the LIS and ID fields of knowledge and practice. Individuals with ID have been underserved and minimally acknowledged in the LIS literature; similarly, librarians, libraries, and terms including *information* and *information literacy* are infrequently found in descriptions of resources, instruction, services, and support for individuals with ID. Norlin (1995) speculated that the neglect of patrons with ID may be a result of misperceptions by the LIS community of their information needs and capabilities. Also, unfamiliarity or discomfort with individuals who are different may negatively influence some in the LIS field, inhibiting service and outreach (182). Another explanation, perhaps, is the "out of sight, out of mind" invisibility of many individuals with ID who may be physically unable to get to the library or feel it serves no purpose for them. As for ID professionals, the high illiteracy rate of many with ID combined with biases of information as something deliverable through print and traditional assumptions of librarianship may limit their consideration of library services and collections as appropriate resources for individuals with ID.

Perceptions of Information and Access

Emerging concepts of metaliteracy and transliteracy[10] acknowledge the multifaceted aspect of information (Thomas et al. 2007). Defined as "the ability to read, write and interact across a range of platforms, tools, and media from signing and orality through handwriting, print, TV, radio and film, to digital social networks," these terms reflect a renewed recognition that (1) information is not something strictly limited to the printed word and (2) the ways we become informed are innumerable. As Brookes (1979) once shared, "the seemingly empty space around us is seething with potential information" (132).

With this in mind, information access is more than simply having access to the written word, technology, and traditional information resources. It is also about access to and full participation in everyday and digital environments in which information is embedded in experiences and interactions with others. What does this mean for individuals who experience such high degrees of segregation on a daily basis, even to the point that they sometimes become invisible? And how do the ways individuals with ID perceive themselves as a result of the exclusion, discrimination, and stigma they experience, which affects their confidence and motivation to seek the information they need to improve their lives?

CONCLUSION

As evident from this discussion, the life challenges and information needs experienced by young people with ID are significant and issues of access and equity, complicated. However, when such a disparity in life quality exists, continued inaction is not an acceptable option. More research is needed. The possibilities for exploration are many and have powerful and long-range implications for our youth with ID. Library and information service and outreach must be proactive, starting early and ongoing. Emphasis on information skills and technology are critical, as are collaborations with school special education staff and the families. Spend time getting to know these young people, their interests and preferences, and their hopes and goals for the future. Though library collections may lack the appropriate in-hand physical resources to sufficiently address their diverse information needs, David Lankes, professor at Syracuse University's School of Information Studies and one of the most vocal advocates for libraries, reminds us that contemporary librarianship is not about the books, materials, or technology. They are tools only. We are in the knowledge business—not simply providing information but making sure that people can act and therefore change the world around them.

Contemporary librarianship is about being an information intermediary and facilitating the creation of knowledge in our youth and adults with ID. It is about recognizing and advantaging information in its multiple and diverse forms and expanding information horizons through traditional, digital, and human resources. It is about inclusion and information embedded in meaningful experiences and interactions. It is about belonging, acceptance, feelings of safety, respect, and support. It is about fostering self-determination and empowering young people with the skills, resources, and beliefs so that they may change their own worlds, create their own meaningful outcomes, and live lives of quality.

NOTES

1. A few examples of genetic-related ID include Fragile X, Down syndrome, phenylketonuria (PKU), and Prader-Willi syndrome. ID can also result from fetal alcohol syndrome and drug exposure, environmental toxins, traumatic brain injury, severe poverty and malnutrition, under-stimulation, and neglect.

2. Multiple studies show the rejection of labels by persons with various disabilities. The reasons cited include denial of disability, protection of self-esteem, associated stigma, uncertainty of label meaning, and irrelevance.

3. Wolf Wolfensberger was one of the first to publically highlight these positive attributes in his 1988 article, "Common Assets of Mentally Retarded People that are Commonly Not Acknowledged."

4. For a thorough history of disability, refer to Braddock, 2002.

5. Social Security Online (https://secure.ssa.gov/apps10/poms.nsf/lnx/0302101270!opendocument) defines a sheltered workshop as "a private non-profit or State or local government institution which provides individuals who have physical and/or mental impairments with services designed to prepare them for gainful work in the general economy. These services may include (but are not limited to) physical rehabilitation, training in basic work and life skills (how to apply for a job, attendance, personal grooming, handling money, etc.), training on specific job skills, and/or providing actual work experience in the workshop."

6. Sobsey and Doe (1991) estimated that approximately 90 percent of individuals with ID will experience some form of sexual abuse in the course of their lives.

7. Wayfinding refers to the ways individuals orient themselves and navigate unfamiliar surroundings.

8. The U.S. national dropout rate of teens is approximately 8 percent.

9. This categorization constitutes approximately 80 to 90 percent of all individuals with ID, with IQs ranging roughly between 70 and 75.
10. These terms are often used interchangeably.

REFERENCES

American Association on Intellectual and Developmental Disabilities. 2010. *Intellectual Disability: Definition, Classification, and Systems of Supports*, edited by American Association on Intellectual and Developmental Disabilities. Washington, DC: American Association on Intellectual and Developmental Disabilities.

Arvidsson, Patrik, Mats Granlund, and Mikael Thyberg. 2008. "Factors Related to Self-Rated Participation in Adolescents and Adults with Mild Intellectual Disability—A Systematic Literature Review." *Journal of Applied Research in Intellectual Disabilities* 21 (3): 277–291.

Beresford, B. 2004. "On the Road to Nowhere? Young Disabled People and Transition." *Child: Care, Health and Development* 30 (6): 581–587.

Bilal, D. 2010. "The Mediated Information Needs of Children on the Autism Spectrum Disorder (ASD)." *Workshop in Accessible Search Systems, SIGIR '10, July 23, 2010*. 42–49. Geneva, Switzerland: ACM.

Blatt, Burton. 1966. *Christmas in Purgatory; a Photographic Essay on Mental Retardation*, edited by Fred M. Kaplan. Scituate Harbor, MA.

Boe, Erling E., and Lynne H. Cook. 2006. "The Chronic and Increasing Shortage of Fully Certified Teachers in Special and General Education." *Exceptional Children* 72 (4): 443–460.

Booth, T., and W. Booth. 1996. Sounds of Silence: Narrative Research with Inarticulate Subjects. *Disability and Society* 11 (1): 55–69.

Braddock, David L. 2002. *Disability at the Dawn of the 21st Century and the State of the States*. Washington, DC: American Association on Mental Retardation.

Britz, Johannes J. 2004. "To Know Or Not to Know: A Moral Reflection on Information Poverty." *Journal of Information Science* 30 (3): 192–204.

Brookes, B. C. 1979. "Theoretical Informatics in Stage II Mechanization of IR Processes." In *International Federation for Documentation, Theoretical Problems of Informatics: New Trends in Informatics and Its Terminology*. FID 568. 10–18. Moscow: VINITI.

Brown, L., B. Shiraga, and K. Kessler. 2006. "The Quest for Ordinary Lives: The Integrated Post-School Vocational Functioning of Fifty Workers with Significant Disabilities." *Research and Practice for Persons with Severe Disabilities* 31: 93–121.

Bryen, Diane Nelson, Allison Carey, Mark Friedman, and Steven J. Taylor. 2007. "Cell Phone Use by Adults with Intellectual Disabilities." *Intellectual and Developmental Disabilities* 45 (1): 1–2.

Bukowski, William M. 2001. "Friendship and the Worlds of Childhood." *New Directions for Child and Adolescent Development* (91): 93–106.

Butterworth, J., Aaron Smith, Alberto Migliore, and J. Winsor. 2008. *State Data: The National Report on Employment Services and Outcomes*. Boston: University of Massachusetts Institute for Community Inclusion.

Callister, Thomas A., Jr., and Nicholas C. Burbules. "Be Careful What You Ask For: Paradoxes About the 'Digital Divide.'" AESA paper, University of Illinois.

Carey, Allison C., Mark G. Friedman, Diane Nelson Bryen, and Steven J. Taylor. 2005. "Use of Electronic Technologies by People with Intellectual Disabilities." *Mental Retardation* 43 (5): 322–333.

Casey, Genevieve M. 1971. "Library Service to the Handicapped and Institutionalized." *Library Trends* 20 (2): 350–366.

Certo, N. J., R. G. Luecking, S. Murphy, L. Brown, S. Courey, and D. Belanger. 2008. "Seamless Transition and Long-Term Support for Individuals with Severe Intellectual Disabilities." *Research and Practice for Persons with Severe Disabilities* 3 (3): 85–90.

Cimera, Robert E. 2011. "Does Being in Sheltered Workshops Improve the Employment Outcomes of Supported Employees with Intellectual Disabilities?" *Journal of Vocational Rehabilitation* 35 (1): 21–27.

Cimera, Robert E., P. Wehman, Michael West, and Sloane Burgess. 2011. "Do Sheltered Workshops Enhance Employment Outcomes for Adults with Autism Spectrum Disorder?" *Autism.* doi:10.1177/1362361311408129.

Conley, R. W., and Steven J. Taylor. 2003. "Supported Employment in Maryland: Successes and Issues." *Mental Retardation* 41 (4): 237–249.

Cooney, G., A. Jahoda, A. Gumley, and F. Knott. 2006. "Young People with Intellectual Disabilities Attending Mainstream and Segregated Schooling: Perceived Stigma, Social Comparison and Future Aspirations." *Journal of Intellectual Disability Research* 50 (6): 432–444.

Cooper, Emily, Ann O'Hara, and Andrew Zovistoski. 2009. *Priced Out in 2008—The Housing Crisis for People with Disabilities.* Technical Assistance Collaborative, Inc.; Consortium for Citizens with Disabilities, Housing Task Force.

Cummins, Robert A., and Anna L. D. Lau. 2003. "Community Integration or Community Exposure? A Review and Discussion in Relation to People with an Intellectual Disability." *Journal of Applied Research in Intellectual Disabilities* 16 (2): 145–157.

Davies, Charlotte Aull, and Richard Jenkins. 1997. "'She has Different Fits to Me': How People with Learning Difficulties See Themselves." *Disability and Society* 12 (1): 95–109.

Department of Education. "Teacher Shortage Areas," accessed September 21, 2011, http://www2.ed.gov/about/offices/list/ope/pol/tsa.html.

Deputy Secretary-General Asha-Rose Migiro. 2011. "Give Disabilities Issues Attention they Deserve Beyond Conference Room, Urges Deputy Secretary-General as Conference of Parties Begins Session." New York: United Nations, Department of Public Information.

"Developmental Disabilities Assistance and Bill of Rights Act of 2000," Administration on Developmental Disabilities. Accessed September 22, 2011, http://74.125.47.132/search?q= cache:otTvXOk7li8J:www.acf.hhs.gov/programs/add/ddact/DDACT2.html+U.S,.+ developmental+disabilities+act+and+bill+of+rights+2000&cd=1&hl=en&ct=clnk&gl=us& client=firefox-a.

Edyburn, Dave L. 2002. "Cognitive Rescaling Strategies: Interventions That Alter the Cognitive Accessibility of Text." *Closing the Gap* 21 (1): 10–11, 21.

Erikson, Erik H. 1968. *Identity, Youth, and Crisis,* edited by Susanna Leona Chase. New York: Norton.

"FAQ on Intellectual Disability," American Association on Intellectual and Developmental Disabilities. Accessed September 21, 2011, http://www.aamr.org/content_104.cfm.

Fischer, Gerhard, and James Sullivan. 2002. "Human-Centered Public Transportation Systems for Persons with Cognitive Disabilities: Challenges and Insights for Participatory Design." In *Proceedings of the Participatory Design Conference,* June 2002, Malmo University, Sweden, edited by T. Sweden, J. Gregory, and I. Wagner. Palo Alto, CA, 194–198.

Forte, Marisa, Andrew Jahoda, and Dave Dagnan. 2011. "An Anxious Time? Exploring the Nature of Worries Experienced by Young People with a Mild to Moderate Intellectual Disability as They Make the Transition to Adulthood."*British Journal of Clinical Psychology* 50 (4): 398–411.

Gougeon, Nathalie A. 2009. "Sexuality Education for Students with Intellectual Disabilities, a Critical Pedagogical Approach: Outing the Ignored Curriculum." *Sex Education* 9 (3): 277–291.

Griffin, Megan M., Elise D. McMillan, and Robert M. Hodapp. 2010. "Family Perspectives on Postsecondary Education for Students with Intellectual Disabilities." *Education and Training in Autism and Developmental Disabilities* 45 (3): 339–346.

Grigal, Meg, Debra Hart, and Alberto Migliore. 2011. "Comparing the Transition Planning, Postsecondary Education, and Employment Outcomes of Students with Intellectual and Other Disabilities." *Career Development for Exceptional Individuals* 34 (4). doi:10.1177/ 0885728811399091.

Hanson-Baldauf, Dana. 2011. "Juried Posters from YALSA's Research Poster Session at ALA Annual 2011: Exploring the Everyday Life Information Needs, Practices, and Challenges of Young Adults with Intellectual Disabilities." *The Journal of Research on Libraries and Young Adults.* Accessed on October 29, 2011, at http://www.yalsa.ala.org/jrlya/2011/08/juried-posters/.

Hauser-Cram, Penny, Marty Wyngaarden Krauss, and Joanne Kersh. 2009. "Adolescents with Developmental Disabilities and Their Families." In *Handbook of Adolescent Psychology*, edited by Richard M. Lerner and Laurence Steinberg. 3rd ed. Vol. 1, 589–617. Hoboken, NJ: John Wiley and Sons, Inc.

Havighurst, Robert J. 1949. *Developmental Tasks and Education*, edited by University of Chicago Committee on Human Development. Chicago: University of Chicago Press.

Holmes, Jennifer L. 2008. Patrons with Developmental Disabilities: A Needs Assessment Survey." *New Library World* 109 (11/12): 533–545.

Hughes-Hassell, Sandra, and Denise E. Agosto. 2007. "Modeling the Everyday Life Information Needs of Urban Teenagers." In *Youth Information-Seeking Behavior II: Context, Theories, Models, and Issues*, edited by Mary K. Chelton and Colleen Cool, 27–61. Lanham, MD: Scarecrow Press, Inc.

Jaeger, Paul T., John Carlo Bertot, and Renee E. Franklin. 2010. "Diversity, Inclusion, and Underrepresented Populations in LIS Research." *The Library Quarterly* 80 (2): 175–181.

Jahoda, A., A. Wilson, K. Stalker, and A. Cairney. 2010. "Living with Stigma and the Self-Perceptions of People with Mild Intellectual Disabilities." *Journal of Social Issues* 66 (3): 521–534.

Kagohara, D. M. "Three Students with Developmental Disabilities Learn to Operate an iPod to Access Age-Appropriate Entertainment Videos." *Journal of Behavioral Education* 20 (1): 33–43.

Karreman, Joyce, Thea van der Geest, and Esmee Buursink. 2007. "Accessible Website Content Guidelines for Users with Intellectual Disabilities." *Journal of Applied Research in Intellectual Disabilities* 20 (6): 510–518.

Kersh, Joanne. 2011. "Attitudes about People with Disabilities." In *International Review of Research in Developmental Disabilities*, edited by Robert M. Hodapp, 199–231.

Krahn, Gloria, Michael H. Fox, Vincent A. Campbell, Ismaila Ramon, and George Jesien. 2010. "Developing a Health Surveillance System for People with Intellectual Disabilities in the United States." *Journal of Policy and Practice in Intellectual Disabilities* 7 (3): 155–166.

Lankes, David. "The Grand Challenges of Librarianship," Virtual Dave. Accessed October 3, 2011, http://quartz.syr.edu/rdlankes/blog/?p=1183.

Lenhart, Amanda, Kristen Purcell, Aaron Smith, and Kathryn Zickuhr. 2010. *Social Media and Mobile Internet Use among Teens and Young Adults*. Washington, DC: Pew Internet and American Life Project. Accessed December 29, 2011, http://pewinternet.org/Reports/2010/Social-Media-and-Young-Adults.aspx.

Lippold, T., and J. Burns. 2009. "Social Support and Intellectual Disabilities: A Comparison between Social Networks of Adults with Intellectual Disability and Those with Physical Disability." *Journal of Intellectual Disability Research* 53 (5): 463–473.

Lloyd, Vicki, A. Gatherer, and S. Kalsy. 2006. "Conducting Qualitative Interview Research with People with Expressive Language Difficulties." *Qualitative Health Research* 16 (10): 1386–1404.

Marks, Genee, and Jay Milne. 2008. "IPod, Therefore I Can: Enhancing the Learning of Children with Intellectual Disabilities through Emerging Technologies." Accessed September 22, 2011, http://sixestate.com/wp-content/uploads/2010/08/marks086.pdf.

Martinez, Donna C. 2009. *Parents Involvement in Transition Planning for Their Young Adult Children with Intellectual Disabilities*. Washington, DC: ProQuest Information and Learning Company (UMI No. 3331458).

Martinez, Donna Claire, Jeremy Mattson, Jill Hough, and Alan Abeson. 2010. *Assessing Existing and Needed Community Transportation for People with Disabilities in North Dakota*. Fargo, ND: Small Urban and Rural Transit Center within the Upper Great Plains Transportation Institute at North Dakota State University.

Mendel, Jill. 1995. "Library Services for Persons with Disabilities." In *Library Users and Reference Services*, edited by Jo Bell Whitlatch, 105–122. New York: Haworth.

Migliore, Alberto, and J. Butterworth. 2009. "Postsecondary Education and Employment Outcomes for Youth with Intellectual Disabilities," *DataNote Series*, DataNote XXI. Boston, MA: Institute for Community Inclusion.

Migliore, A., D. Mank, T. Grossi, and P. Rogan. 2007. "Integrated Employment or Sheltered Workshops: Preferences of Adults with Intellectual Disabilities, their Families, and Staff." *Journal of Vocational Rehabilitation* 26 (1): 5–19.

Morgan, Michelle F., and Karen B. Moni. 2008. "Meeting the Challenge of Limited Literacy Resources for Adolescents and Adults with Intellectual Disabilities." *British Journal of Special Education* 35 (2): 92–101.

National Disability Rights Network. 2011. *Segregated and Exploited: A Call to Action! The Failure of Disability Service System to Provide Quality Work*. National Disability Rights Network.

National Sheriff's Association. 2008. *First Response to Victims of Crime*. Office for Victims of Crime, U.S. Department of Justice.

Newman, Lynn, Mary Wagner, Renee Cameto, and Anne-Marie Knokey. 2009. *The Post-High School Outcomes of Youth with Disabilities Up to 4 Years after High School: A Report from the National Longitudinal Transition Study—2.*

Norlin, D. 1995. Helping adults with mental retardation satisfy their information needs. In L. L. Walling and M. M. Irwin (Eds.), *Information Services for People with Developmental Disabilities: The Library Manager's Handbook*, 181–1995. Westport, CT: Greenwood Press.

O'Leary, K. 2011. "Information Seeking in the Context of a Hobby: A Case Study of a Young Adult with Asperger's Syndrome." *Journal of Research on Libraries and Young Adults*. Accessed March 2012, http://www.yalsa.ala.org/jrlya/2011/02/information-seeking-in-the-context-of-a-hobby-a-case-study-of-a-young-adult-with-asperger%E2%80%99s-syndrome/.

"The Olmstead Decision: Fact Sheet, January 2000," United States Administration on Developmental Disabilities. Accessed December 29, 2011, http://www.acf.hhs.gov/programs/add/otherpublications/olmstead.html.

Pattison, M., and A. Stedmon. 2006. "Inclusive Design and Human Factors: Designing Mobile Phones for Older Users." *Psychology Journal* 4 (3): 267–284.

Plos, O., and S. Buisine. 2006. "Universal Design for Mobile Phones: A Case Study." *CHI*: 1229–1234.

Polloway, Edward A., Jacqueline Lubin, J. David Smith, and James R. Patton. 2010. "Mild Intellectual Disabilities: Legacies and Trends in Concepts and Educational Practices." *Education and Training in Autism and Developmental Disabilities* 45 (1): 54–68.

Powers, Kristin M., Eleanor Gil-Kashiwabara, Sarah J. Geenen, Laurie E. Powers, Julie Balandran, and Catherine Palmer. Spring 2005. "Mandates and Effective Transition Planning Practices Reflected in IEPs." *Career Development for Exceptional Individuals* 28 (1): 47–59.

Raphael, Dennis, Brenda Steinmetz, Rebecca Renwick, Irving Rootman, Ivan Brown, Hersh Sehdev, Sherry Phillips, and Trevor Smith. 1999. "The Community Quality of Life Project: A Health Promotion Approach to Understanding Communities." *Health Promotion International* 14 (3): 197–210.

Salmi, P. 2007. "Wayfinding Design: Hidden Barriers to Universal Access." *Implications* 5 (8): 1–6.

Savolainen, R. 2008. *Everyday Information Practices: A Social Phenomenological Perspective*. Lanham, MD: Scarecrow Press.

Schalock, Robert L., Kenneth D. Keith, Miguel Ángel Verdugo, and Laura E. Gomez. 2011. "Quality of Life Model Development and Use in the Field of Intellectual Disability." In *Enhancing the Quality of Life of People with Intellectual Disabilities [Electronic Resource]: From Theory to Practice*, edited by Ralph Kober, 17–32. Dordrecht: Springer Science+Business Media B.V.

Simeonsson, Rune J., Dawn Carlson, Gail S. Huntington, Janey Sturtz McMillen, and J. L. Brent. 2001. "Students with Disabilities: A National Survey of Participation in School Activities." *Disability and Rehabilitation* 23 (2): 49–63.

Skinner, Ellen A., and Michael J. Belmont. 1993. "Motivation in the Classroom: Reciprocal Effects of Teacher Behavior and Student Engagement across the School Year." *Journal of Educational Psychology* 85 (4): 571–581.

Smiley, Elita. 2005. "Epidemiology of Mental Health Problems in Adults with Learning Disabilities: An Update." *Advances in Psychiatric Treatment* 11 (3): 214–222.

Smith, J. David. 2009. "Power and Epiphany: Reflections on the Personal and Cultural Meanings of Developmental Disabilities in the 21st Century." In *Research-Based Practices in Developmental Disabilities*, edited by Howard P. Parette and George R. Peterson-Karlan. 2nd Edition, 43–56. Austin, TX: Pro-Ed.

Snell, Martha E. "Martha Snell Interview Transcript." American Association on Intellectual and Developmental Disabilities. Accessed September 22, 2011, http://www.aamr.org/snell-transcript.cfm.

Snell, Martha E., Ruth Luckasson, with W. S. Borthwick-Duffy, V. Bradley, W. H. Buntinx, D. L. Coulter, E. P. Craig, et al. 2009. "Characteristics and Needs of People with Intellectual Disability Who have Higher IQs." *Intellectual and Developmental Disabilities* 47 (3): 220–233.

Sobsey, D., and Tanis Doe. 1991. "Patterns of Sexual Abuse and Assault." *Sexuality and Disability* 9 (3): 249–259.

Sorensen, D. 2003. "Invisible Victims." *TASH Connections* 29: 31, 33–35.

Sormanti, Mary, and Michelle S. Ballan. 2011. "Strengthening Grief Support of Children with Developmental Disabilities." *School Psychology International* 32 (2): 179–193.

Spitalnik, D., and S. White-Scott. 2001. "Access to Health Services: Improving the Availability and Quality of Health Services for People with Mild Cognitive Limitations." In *The Forgotten Generation: The Status and Challenges of Adults with Mild Cognitive Limitations*, edited by A. J. Tymchuk, K. C. Lakin, and R. Luckasson. Baltimore, MD: Brookes.

Stalker, Kirsten. 1998. "Some Ethical and Methodological Issues in Research with People with Learning Difficulties." *Disability and Society* 13 (1): 5–19.

Stancliffe, R. J., and K. C. Lankin. 2007. "Independent Living." In *Handbook of Developmental Disabilities*, edited by S. L. Odom, R. H. Horner, M. E. Snell, and J. Blacher, 429–448. New York: Guilford Press.

Stewart, Debra, Matt Freeman, Mary Law, Helen Healy, Jan Burke-Gaffney, Mary Forhan, Nancy Young, and Susan Guenther. 2009. "Transition to Adulthood for Youth with Disabilities: Evidence from the Literature | International Encyclopedia of Rehabilitation." Accessed August 30, 2011, http://cirrie.buffalo.edu/encyclopedia/en/article/110/.

Tarleton, B., and L. Ward. 2005. "Changes and Choices: Finding Out What Information Young People with Learning Disabilities, Their Parents and Supporters Need at Transition." *British Journal of Learning Disabilities* 33 (2): 70–76.

Thomas, Sue, Chris Joseph, Jess Laccetti, Bruce Mason, Simon Mills, Simon Perril, and Kate Pullinger. 2007. "Transliteracy: Crossing Divides." *First Monday* 12 (12).

Todd, Ross J. 2000. "A Theory of Information Literacy: In-Formation and Outward Looking." In *Information Literacy around the World: Advances in Programs and Research*, edited by Christine Bruce and Philip Candy, 163–175. Wagga Wagga, N.S.W.: Centre for Information Studies, Charles Sturt University.

Tuffrey-Wijne, Irene, Jane Bernal, Amelia Jones, Gary Butler, and Sheila Hollins. 2006. "People with Intellectual Disabilities and Their Need for Cancer Information." *European Journal of Oncology Nursing* 10 (2): 106–116.

United Nations. 2008. *Convention on the Rights of Persons with Disabilities.* Accessed September 22, 2011, http://www.un.org/disabilities/convention/conventionfull.shtml.

United Nations. 1948. *The Universal Declaration of Human Rights.* Accessed September 22, 2011, http://www.un.org/en/documents/udhr/.

Verdonschot, M. M. L., L. P. De Witte, E. Reichrath, W. H. E. Buntinx, and L. M. G. Curfs. 2009. "Community Participation of People with an Intellectual Disability: A Review of Empirical Findings." *Journal of Intellectual Disability Research* 53 (4): 303–318.

Vogel, Jeannine, Edward A. Polloway, J. David Smith, and Steven J. Taylor. 2006. "Inclusion of People with Mental Retardation and Other Developmental Disabilities in Communities of Faith." *Mental Retardation* 44 (2): 100–111.

Wagner, Mary, Lynn Newman, Renee Cameto, Phyllis Levine, and Nicolle Garza. 2006. *An Overview of Findings from Wave 2 of the National Longitudinal Transition Study-2*. National Center for Special Education Research.

Wehmeyer, Michael L., B. Abery, D. E. Mithaug, and Roger J. Stancliffe. 2003. *Theory in Self-Determination: Foundations for Educational Practice*, edited by Michael L. Wehmeyer. Springfield, IL: Charles C. Thomas.

Wehmeyer, Michael L., and Nancy W. Gamer. 2003. "The Impact of Personal Characteristics of People with Intellectual and Developmental Disability on Self-Determination and Autonomous Functioning." *Journal of Applied Research in Intellectual Disabilities* 16 (4): 255–265.

Yalon-Chamovitz, Shira. 2009. "Invisible Access Needs of People with Intellectual Disabilities: A Conceptual Model of Practice." *Intellectual and Developmental Disabilities* 47 (5): 395–400.

Chapter Nine

Defining the Line on Cyber-Bullying

How Youth Encounter and Distribute Demeaning Information

Shaheen Shariff

The digital age has facilitated easy access to information for children and teens, while creating new challenges for parents, educators, and society. Among these are cyber-bullying and cyber-lurking, which may be defined as the use of ICT (information and communication technologies) for a deliberate and hostile act intended to harm others. This chapter highlights perceived dangers and clarifies the legal risks that help to "define the line" between cyber-bullying and digital citizenship when children and teens search for, encounter, view, modify, and distribute demeaning or false information about peers, teachers, and other authority figures on digital media.

My objective in this chapter is to highlight the consequences of harmful online information, or misinformation that is searched and accessed in ways that lead to and exacerbate cyber-bullying, often engaging much wider audiences that sustain the pain and dehumanization of those targeted. To that end, this chapter introduces readers to legal risks and emerging legal standards that help to clarify the blurred lines at which information accessed online can lead to cyber-bullying that makes youth vulnerable to legal liability. Later in this chapter I provide case studies as examples to illustrate the legal frameworks and standards that are beginning to take shape as our educational and judicial systems grapple with more cases of cyber-bullying. I discuss empirical research and case studies within relevant legal frameworks to explain the legal risks to guide and alert stakeholders (parents, educators, librarians, policy makers, and youth) to the online boundaries that are beginning to surface, even though at first glance they appear elusive. Before entering that discussion, it is important to describe cyber-bullying as it is considered within the context of this book.

WHAT IS CYBER-BULLYING?

Bullying in any form is a serious matter, whether it occurs in the physical context or online. Bullying behaviors are deeply rooted in societal attitudes of discrimination such as sexism, homophobia, racism, and ableism. Bullying is informed by ignorance, intolerance, and disrespect. Historically, it has resulted in exclusion, isolation, lost reputations, loss of self-esteem, physical and emotional harm, and in too many tragic cases, death from beatings or suicide (Patchin and Hinduja 2006, 2010; Hinduja and Patchin 2008). Regrettably, adults are often the worst role models of bullying. Examples are everywhere—in global politics, institutions, health care, education, families, and police forces. Sadly, it is often (but not always), the most vulnerable members of society such as seniors, children, the disabled, and those from lower socioeconomic or underrepresented communities who are targeted. Moreover, global societies are increasingly obsessed with money, perfection, celebrity idolization, conformity, and voyeurism. Our research (Shariff 2009) discloses a disturbing trend among young adults and youth that suggests at least 60 percent are less sensitive to, or sometimes cannot distinguish the difference between, harmless jokes or teasing, and harmful threats, privacy harm, comments, rumors, and persistent harassment. These online behaviors can cross the line to defamation and libel, sexual or homophobic harassment, criminal threats, and in the case of "sexting" (posting of intimate and sexual videos or photographs online), charges of possession and distribution of child pornography, because that is the only way law enforcement can reduce the spread.

Information encounters that result in cyber-bullying. In the last decade cyber-bullying has been defined in numerous ways but rarely in the context of information studies. Accordingly, it is important to explain what types of information can be searched for, accessed and reviewed, saved, and subsequently spread. It is also interesting to learn, from a gender perspective, how and why teenage girls post and access more personal information online, sometimes subjecting their information to greater risk of being misinterpreted and distributed without their consent. Increasingly, cases of cyber-bullying involving youth and young adults ("digital natives") start off as information posted on social media such as YouTube or Facebook. This information can take the form of a derogatory joke, rumors, gossip, insults, modified photographs, identity theft of Facebook pages with made-up content by the imposter, or videos showing a beating or even rape, posted on

YouTube. In addition to social media sites, this genre of information is also easily searched and retrieved using search engines like Google. Therefore, once the word gets around that scintillating information has been posted, the more controversial and offensive it is, the faster it spreads like a virus.

Types of digital media. The types of digital media used include mobile technologies such as iPhones, Blackberries, and iPads; social networking sites such as Facebook and YouTube (*inter alia*); bulletin boards; rating programs; e-mails, Skype, and digital camera capabilities; avatars and the full range of information systems that are currently available and continue to evolve resulting in the rapid sharing of information within seconds.

Cyber-bullying, bystanders, and cyber-lurker/voyeurs. Cyber-bullying is an extension of traditional bullying and spills back and forth between real and virtual environments. For example, a group of students may plan to beat up a victim on the school playground, film the beating, and post it online. This becomes new and valuable information to those who want it publicized. News about this new online information spreads virally. The more extreme the beating or rape, the more it is retrieved, viewed, saved, distributed, and reviewed. Interestingly, this supports Salmivalli and colleagues' European studies in 2001. Salmivalli's team looked at group voyeuristic behavior as it occurs in traditional bullying. They found that 30 percent of bystanders support perpetrators and that bystander participation increases as the bullying persists (see also Coloroso 2003; National Center for Education Statistics 2008). Salmivalli's and Coloroso's findings hold true in 2011, but the group effects are magnified extensively in cyberspace.

The difference online is that there can be an infinite number of voyeurs or bystanders. Racist, sexist, or homophobic statements and compromising sexual photographs can be altered and sent to limitless audiences. Chu (2005) explains that incidents of online bullying are like cockroaches: for every incident that is reported, many others go unrecorded because they are difficult to track. What is most disturbing about this is that the person targeted is re-victimized every time someone new views it! This has serious implications for focused research and attention to the variety of ways in which offensive and demeaning information is retrieved, viewed, used, saved, and distributed. Filters and bans are ineffective because the offensive information can be spread through so many online venues. Moreover, freedom of expression is still the most valued constitutional right in North America. Corporate intermediaries are still considered "distributors" rather than "publishers" at law, reducing their responsibility to remove offensive information. Consequently, efforts to remove such information can be time consuming and expensive, with numerous bureaucratic and legal barriers that increase the anguish of those victimized.

Prevalence and reluctance to be identified. It is not surprising then to learn that teenagers in particular self-isolate because they are too afraid to report cyber-bullying for fear of further ramifications. As my own study of 800 grade 6 and 7 students from the Montreal region found in 2006, 50 percent of teenagers will not report cyber-bullying for fear that

• their perpetrators will accuse them of "ratting" and the bullying will increase;
• the adults (especially teachers) they report to will not do anything about it; and
• their parents will withdraw their online privileges to keep them safe but this will result in even further isolation.

We also observed (Shariff and Churchill 2009) that 70 percent of 11- to 15-year-olds reported being bullied or cyber-bullied often or occasionally, and 43 percent confessed to "pretending to be someone else" online to engage in bullying. Seventy-two percent of females reported being cyber-bullied compared to 28 percent of males, the former noting that they would only report cyber-bullying if they could do it anonymously (see also Hoff and Mitchell 2009).

Dehumanizing to justify the harm. In many cases of bullying, the sense of isolation increases. Perpetrators demonstrate a lack of remorse and denial that the harm they inflict has long-lasting consequences. People targeted for abuse are often dehumanized and blamed for something they did, allowing perpetrators to convince themselves and others that their targets *deserve* the teasing, insults, and even physical beatings. Sibelle Artz (2004) found this to be prevalent among girls who engage in physical bullying. Over the last decade, with the proliferation of digital communication, this phenomenon has taken on another dimension that is more subtle and difficult to address.

New dimensions of justification—just "joking." Our research finds that digital natives and some adults do not recognize the line between entertainment that is funny for its own sake and entertainment that can significantly harm others and cross legal boundaries. With the rapid advent and evolution of digital media that enable texting, video, and camera capabilities in mobile phones and increased popularity of social media such as Facebook, Twitter, and YouTube, bullying has taken on new dimensions. Digital media enable perpetrators to hide behind screen names, IP addresses, and fake Facebook and Twitter profiles, creating a false sense of anonymity. Photographs can be modified and posted online with accompanying insults and a range of offensive forms of expression that are geared to demean, defame, and embarrass their victims. In 2010 a young adult named David Abitbol posted threats against his former teachers and photographs of himself with guns that he claimed he slept with. He was arrested when the guns were actually found in his home, but his parents insisted he would never harm anyone and that he was "just joking." We have noted increasingly voyeuristic tendencies that lean toward entertainment at the expense and humiliation of others (Heckman, 2010).

Consider these Canadian examples of on- and offline voyeuristic and planned cyber-bullying incidents at the serious expense of female victims:

- The swarming, beating, and videotaping of a teenage girl in Nanaimo, British Columbia, in April 2011, was pre-planned with the purpose of filming and posting it online. It was sent to a well-known Canadian rapper, Jason McDonald, who put music and words to it and posted it on his Facebook page to advertise his music. It was also posted on YouTube. As a result, the beating of the girl involved appeared repeatedly, re-victimizing her every time the video was watched as "entertainment." Although the video was taken down it could quite easily by then have been saved on numerous computers and re-viewed (http://www2.canada.com/nanaimodailynews/news/story.html?id=8500d5d3-0d4a-4005.acff-fcab7ec480c0, accessed April, 26, 2011).

- In September 2010, a 16-year-old girl in Maple Ridge, British Columbia, attended a rave at a farm one Saturday night. She was drugged and gang raped by 10 youths. A 16-year-old bystander digitally recorded the rape, and instead of sending it to the police or someone in authority, he posted the video on YouTube (http://www.theglobeandmail.com/news/national/.../article1710072, accessed September 27, 2010). The video spread virally. The only way that Maple Ridge police were able to reduce the spread was to issue a message that anyone downloading the video would be charged with distribution of child pornography. Conversations on Facebook added to the victim's pain by stating that she "asked for it" and was enjoying it (because she was heavily drugged, the video made it look as though she consented to the violation).

In both cases more attention was paid by the news media to the online postings than the actual physical harm and injuries that the girls sustained.

Gendered hierarchies in cyberspace. Although both genders engage in cyber-bullying, there are differences. Cyber-bullying involves substantial sexual harassment, and as we found in 2006, 72 percent of the females we interviewed admitted to being cyber-bullied as compared to 28 percent of males. Barak (2005) identifies online sexual harassment as including offensive sexual messages or remarks, gender humiliating comments, offensive nicknames and online identities, unwanted pornographic content and pop-up windows, uninvited communication of sexual desires or intentions, and sexual coercion. Adolescents are influenced by hormones and by socialization. They also face intersecting and interlocking systemic barriers based on age, race, sexual orientation, and abilities/disabilities. While females are more likely targets of cyber-violence because of their location in the hierarchies of power, adolescent girls are also active instigators of cyber-bullying. Chu (2005) reported that out of 3,700 American adolescents, 7 percent of the girls confessed to online bullying compared to 10 percent of the boys. A recent website developed by my affiliate colleagues Colette Vogel and Erica Johnstone at the Center for Internet and Society at Stanford University Law School titled *Without My Consent* advises girls and women who are violated and harassed online to seek legal remedies (see http://www. withoutmyconsent.org/and related *New York Times* report http://www. nytimes.com/2011/04/24/magazine/mag-24lede-t.html?_r=3&ref= technology. See also L. Y. Edwards 2005).

IMPACT AND RELUCTANCE TO BE IDENTIFIED

Harm from bullying in physical settings is tangible and easily identified as "real" violence. But threats or harassment in cyberspace, and their impact, are less tangible and therefore more difficult to establish as actually harmful. There is no escape for victims, who feel trapped knowing that an infinite audience can view their humiliation and identify them as the brunt of their jokes. For the two victims described earlier, both identities were known by their classmates. This subjected them to ridicule and re-victimization every time the video was saved, distributed, and viewed. They were compromised if they returned to their regular schools because they had to face their peers knowing that most classmates would have seen the videos. Gossip and jokes about the incident would proliferate, making it very difficult for anyone to focus on learning. Relocating and changing schools makes no difference because wherever they go it is possible that they will be identified as the girls whose rapes and beatings were viewed so publicly. This kind of isolation has serious long- and short-term impact.

Here is a summary of some of the pertinent research. What is presented in this chapter constitutes the tip of the iceberg. A Pew Internet survey by Lenhart (2010) found that typically girls are more frequently victimized. Ybarra and Mitchell (2004) found that 1 in 7 youth between the ages of 10 and 17 were exposed to sexual solicitation, 1 in 17 were harassed or threatened, and only a fraction reported these cases, while more than 63 percent reported being upset, embarrassed, or stressed as a result of these unwanted contacts.

Emotional distress. Abuse on the Internet creates emotional distress and psychosocial trauma; it has serious mental health consequences for teenagers (Ybarra et al. 2006). Studies have reported that 51 percent of students bullied at school are more likely to harass others in online environments, as are young people who experience high levels of depression or trauma in real life. Such young people also seek out close online relations to fill voids in their lives, further increasing their vulnerability to online exploitation.

More recently, in 2010, our study titled *Children's Experiences of Cyber-Bullying: A Canadian National Study* (Beran, Mishna, Heatherington, and Shariff 2010), found that children who were cyber-bullied were significantly more likely to experience risk behaviors, anger, physical injury, anxiety, eating problems, and drug use. Children may feel that their implicit sense of trust with an acquaintance has been violated just as they may feel that an explicit sense of trust with a friend has been broken. As with Ybarra's earlier findings, we found that children who were cyber-victimized were more likely to bully others than children who were not. Perhaps becoming a target of cyber-bullying creates an expectation among peers that harassment is normal, thus inviting reciprocating bullying behaviors in any form because "everyone does it." In the same report, our review of a range of research studies confirms that victims demonstrate the following behaviors: a fear of leaving home, plunging grades, loss of interest in school or dropping out, change in eating or sleeping habits, change in dress and appearance, an end to socializing with friends, and having suicidal thoughts. Hinduja and Patchin (2008) report that 20 percent of respondents in their study reported seriously thinking about attempting suicide (19.7 percent of females and 20.9 percent of males), while 19 percent reported attempting suicide (17.9 percent of females and 20.2 percent of males). (See also American Academy of Pediatrics 2009.)

Risk of criminal charges—sexting and child pornography. One Florida tragedy resulted when, after an argument with his girlfriend Jesse Logan, 18-year-old Philip Albert reacted by sending her nude photographs to 70 people, including her grandparents. Jesse committed suicide. As with the Canadian response in the Maple Ridge incident, the police in Florida charged Philip with distribution of child pornography. He now has a criminal record and cannot live near a school, although clearly he is not a pedophile and argued he was merely reacting to an argument with his girlfriend. Youth often fail to realize how important reputation and identity is, especially for girls.

Teachers have also been targets of pornographic jokes on social media that undermine their authority within the classroom, in some cases resulting in serious mental health problems. The foregoing illustrates a pattern whereby perpetrators continue the trend of dehumanization and victim blaming for some kind of "deserved" ridicule. What has changed with cyber-bullying is that perpetrators and their cyber-supporters insist that they did not mean to harm anyone. Most insist they were simply joking or making friends laugh. Hence, knowledge about the role of the bystander or cyber-lurker/voyeur and an understanding of the ways in which information is accessed, reviewed, saved, and distributed become essential from the perspective of regulation, policy development, and curriculum programming in schools and teacher education programs.

Private "venting" in public. On another level, young people also forget the "public" aspect of social media such as Twitter. For example, in early 2010 a McGill University undergraduate student attended a political meeting on campus and became increasingly agitated. He "tweeted" about how he wished he had an M-16 gun to kill everyone. When confronted by the administration, he said he was simply venting his frustration—tweeting felt like he was confiding in someone; whereas, in actual fact, he was publicly threatening to kill his fellow students without realizing the potential impact of his words. Similarly, high school students have insulted and threatened their unpopular teachers on social media, making false sexual allegations. When suspended, students often challenge the schools' actions, claiming freedom of expression, insisting that the schools breached personal privacy (Shariff 2008, 2009). These students thought they were having private conversations with friends without realizing, regardless of privacy settings, that this information can be accessed quite easily. This again is an example of the patterns we see as to the blurring of public and private realms as digital natives grow up with social media.

MISINFORMED PUBLIC PERCEPTIONS OF DANGER

Clearly the impact of cyber-bullying must be addressed; however, it is a fallacy to dwell only on the negative forms or "dangers" of information that are conveyed online. It is imperative to learn how digital media help people access and distribute socially responsible and supportive information as well. It is essential to talk about how we can engage social media such as Facebook, YouTube, Twitter, and mobile technologies to enhance digital citizenship. On a personal/professional level, I was recently shocked to see the cover of one of my books that has been translated into Portuguese. The original British version of *Cyber-Bullying: Issues and Solutions in the School, the Classroom and the Home* (Shariff 2008) shows a picture of a girl looking at a cell phone. The cover is relevant and in good taste. However, the Brazilian publisher Artmed decided to sensationalize the Portuguese cover of the same book for marketing purposes. The girl is replaced by a large skull and gloved fingers that make it look like something in between a "Casper the friendly ghost in skull" or some kind of horror movie in bad taste! The publisher's objective was to indicate the "dangers" of cyber-bullying. If they had read the book they would most certainly have noticed that I have never advocated this approach! I have, of course, insisted they remove it from the marketing cycle and replace the cover with one of which I approve, and they have agreed out of respect for my work. In a sense I felt subjected to identity theft. The Artmed cover constitutes a form of "information" that was intended for public distribution under my name without my consent, and that does not represent me at all. Of course I have learned my lesson and the next book contract I negotiate will always have a clause that says I must approve the cover before it goes to print.

The news media internationally has also thrived on sensationalized stories, reporting horrendous acts of cyber-bullying that begin in school playgrounds and continue online, sometimes resulting in suicide. Although there is no question that cyber-bullying is a very serious matter, many of these reports exaggerate the dangers and create moral panic among adults (most of whom are digital immigrants). The public is often led to believe that digital technologies are dangerous for children and teens (digital natives), especially girls (see Edwards 2005; Weber and Mitchell 2007). This in turn fuels concerns among parents and their lobbies, and teachers and their unions and policy makers, that kids are out of control online and that their access to social media ought to be curbed through filtering systems, zero tolerance punishments, and criminal sanctions. However, as most of the chapters in this book confirm, digital media are not in and of themselves dangerous. What *is* dangerous is a general lack of realization that digital natives do not distinguish greatly between their physical and virtual realities. They are growing up in a world submerged in technologies—a world where they are comfortable and at ease. Because of its infinite and fluid nature, rules, laws, and boundaries that served us well in the physical world no longer apply virtually to contain social interactions and civil behavior.

Girls and personal online information. Consider, for example, research by Weber and Mitchell (2007), who observe that social networking empowers teenagers, especially girls, to construct and produce strong and independent identities through online personal diaries that they describe as "public-privacy." Although this is an oxymoron, it reflects the way youth think about themselves and view their world. To enable courts to make informed judicial decisions that take into account the realities youth face in a contemporary digital age, it is important that the judiciary become informed about how today's teenagers—especially girls—perceive, understand, and live in real and virtual time and space. For digital natives, there is no separation of the two lives. Their known on- and offline identity and reputation is the most important aspect of their confidence. In order to be heard over the din of a million online voices, youth need to construct strong digital identities that pass the judgment of their peers on social networking sites. When an individual is identified and singled out for ridicule, her entire world falls apart because she knows that every time she logs into her online world, the embarrassment will persist. Weber and Mitchell explain that the trajectory from pre-adolescence to adulthood and social maturity is reflected in shared online conversations as pre-teens become sexually aware and intellectually mature and develop internal frameworks of moral and social responsibility.

Other scholars agree that while adults continue to view real and virtual space as separate, the digital identities of most young people are integral to, and inseparable from, their physical identities (Lankshear and Knobel 2005; Jenkins and Boyd 2006). Weber and Mitchell observe that pre-teen girls can include cuddly animals and images associated with younger children but also take photographs or videos of themselves in sexy poses and combine them with images that more closely resemble children's cartoons. They point out that to pre-teen girls, the word "sexy" can just mean "cute" in one posting and "sexy" in the most conventional adult sense in another. They note that girls' "public-private" diaries can contain photographs, downloaded music, popular culture examples, and a range of other information about themselves and friends that converge to create their identity, and through their online postings girls share ideas and gain a sense of belonging regardless of time and space. The communication is in a space they find safe. Therefore, when these online safe spaces are violated by cyber-bullying, identity theft, or unwanted sexual comments, insults, or advances, they no longer feel safe anywhere—in their real or virtual worlds. Such violations result in what some legal academics are referring to as "privacy harm."

PRIVACY BREACH OR PRIVACY HARM?

There is little clarity on the extent to which perpetrators can be held responsible for privacy harm and what that means in the Canadian legal context as opposed to definitions and court decisions that emerge from the United States. Calo (2011) provides a framework that has enhanced my understanding of online information that causes privacy harm in the context of cyber-bullying. Calo asserts that notions of online privacy can be better understood in terms of *subjective* and *objective* privacy *harm*. He argues that the law needs to evolve to recognize privacy harm as opposed to a continued focus on privacy *rights*. He describes the *subjective* category of privacy harm as the "unwanted perception of observation" (1) and *objective* privacy harm as the "unanticipated or coerced use of information concerning a person against that person" (1). In the case of cyber-bullying, creation of fake Facebook pages, sexting, unwanted postings of photographs on social media, and unapproved book covers like my own, Calo's framework is helpful in analyzing the impact of the emotional distress and fear that might occur when teenagers first have their information used against them; and even if it is taken down, the *subjective* privacy harm may come from a concern that if people know their identity they may be watched and harmed.

BLURRED LEGAL BOUNDARIES AND THE POLICY VACUUM

One barrier to improving digital citizenship is the growing policy vacuum. There is a lack of guidelines as to the legal risks, obligations, and stakeholder responsibilities to address cyber-bullying. As the foregoing examples and statistics demonstrate, notions of "public" and "private" and limits of free expression in virtual spaces are not easily defined. For youth, the process of growing up in a highly public and rapidly evolving digital environment can result in thoughtless violence, privacy breaches, and privacy harm (Calo 2011) for entertainment value at one end of the spectrum, or overreaction and moral panic by parents, law enforcement, or school officials at the other (see Cassell and Cramer 2008). As the lines between free expression, privacy, and safety become increasingly blurred in cyberspace, it is essential to inform the policy vacuum that currently fuels public concern about personal digital data that youth produce, share, and distribute—including photographs, videos, and related data—in an online public sphere accessible by an infinite audience. Public calls for increased legislation and regulation of digital content shared publicly by youth have risen to the forefront of public policy debates internationally. Courts, especially in Canada, are slow to keep up with the rapidly shifting technologies and reluctant to open up the floodgates to litigation.

Nonetheless, a slow but important shift is emerging in school board policies and corporate and legal responses that lean away from zero tolerance toward promoting social responsibility and digital citizenship. For example, President Obama held an all-day conference at the White House to encourage dialogue about youth and cyber-bullying (Calmes 2011). Facebook recently put out a call for research proposals that promote digital citizenship on its social network. This trend is welcome and long overdue. One way to support this trend is to identify the legal risks that come with cyber-bullying and inform the public about emerging legal issues and evolving legal responses. In other words, stakeholders need guidance and resources grounded in academic research to inform their policies and practices to reduce cyber-bullying and foster digital citizenship. The online environment provides substantial opportunities for free expression; however, the challenge comes in balancing free expression with public safety, privacy, protection of children, protection of reputations, supervision, regulation; and preservation of jurisdiction and authority.

NAVIGATING THE MINEFIELD

Policy makers, the judiciary, and legislators must learn to navigate the mine-field as new and rapidly evolving mobile devices, online games, and social networks are introduced. There is a rise in cases in the United States and Canada where students—suspended for cyber-bullying, gossiping, or joking about or demeaning peers or teachers—have accused schools of infringing on their constitutional rights to free expression (see Shariff 2008, 2009). Civil cases of defamation and libel are on the rise as individuals whose reputations have been ruined through identity theft, rumors, gossip, privacy breaches, and unfair comment fight back to set the record straight. Parents of students who are victimized, and teachers whose reputations and authority have been undermined, are often at a loss as to their rights to pursue perpetrators. In Canada, there are few precedents as to the possibility of success. There is a dearth of knowledge in this area, and few law schools, teacher preparation programs, or schools of information include curriculum content that address-es this important area of policy and practice. How do we fill this gap if the courts are really out of touch?

ARE COURTS OUT OF TOUCH?

A decade ago, I observed that American courts were largely out of touch with the real needs of threat assessment and the impact of cyber-violence. Judicial rulings on Internet threats under constitutional, civil, and criminal law at that time largely ignored and trivialized the complex and multi-faceted factors and the "real" harm caused by "virtual" threats. Judges tended to overlook the power hierarchies and gender considerations that can cause serious harm to female victims of cyber-bullying. More recently, however, American courts have begun to recognize the harm caused by threats, ruined reputa-tions, and sexual/homophobic harassment. Consider the case of D.C., an aspiring teenage musician from California. D.C. experienced significant im-pact from homophobic cyber-bullying. He had set up a web page to market his music, describing himself as having "golden brown eyes." This triggered a barrage of insults and threats posted on his website by school friends, who competed to see who could post the worst homophobic insults and death threats. The worst offender, R.R., who was sued for defamation, claimed that his expressions were "fanciful, hyperbolic . . . and taunting" and that he was irritated by the arrogance of the statement "golden brown eyes" (*D.C. et al. vs. R.R. et al.—Court of Appeal, State of California*, Reasons for Judgment, March 15, 2010:5). R.R. asserted his rights to free expression, explaining that he and his peers were just trying to have fun. D.C. suffered psychological harm and the Los Angeles Police Department asked him to withdraw from school for his own safety. His family had to relocate to another school in another district, causing considerable expense and time to the entire family. His film contract had to be delayed. Although he was not gay, people began to ask if he was gay.

The Court of Appeal ruled that libellous content, hyperbole, and "mere jokes" (18) are protected by the First Amendment; however, the banning of "true threats" is not unconstitutional. It is not necessary for speakers to *intend* the threat. It is a "prohibition from the disruption that fear engenders" (17). Limiting online threats protects from the "possibility that the threatened violence will occur" (17). Notably the court observed that the further speech strays from the values of persuasion, dialogue, and free exchange of ideas, and moves toward threats, the less it is protected (18). The impact on the victim, family, and perceived threat to safety must be considered. False information on sexual orientation caused reasonable people to believe it as truth— therefore its expression was deemed libellous.

Similarly, in a well-known case of sexual harassment, the U.S. Supreme Court in a controversial landmark decision, *Davis v. Munroe County Bd. of Ed.*, 526 U.S. 29 (1999), ruled that schools must recognize sexual harassment and the impact it can have on a student's emotional and physical health. In this case LaShonda Davis had been sexually harassed in the classroom for a period of five months without the school doing anything to alleviate it. The court ruled that the school created a "deliberately dangerous environment" in failing to protect LaShonda, resulting in a drop in her grades.

The serious nature and impact of virtual threats, breaches of privacy, and emotional harm caused to victims has also been recognized in Canadian courts at the provincial level:

- In the Quebec case of *Aubry v. Editions Vice Versa* (http://scc.lexum.org/en/1998/1998scr1-591/1998scr1-591.html), the circulation of private photographs was considered to be a civil law breach of the Quebec *Charter's* protections of "private life." The court ruled in favor of a 17-year-old girl, taking into consideration her social circle and precisely a "teenager's sensitivity to teasing by her friends" as foreseeable harm. In other words, a person's reputation can trump free expression in Quebec.
- A Supreme Court of British Columbia decision in the case of *R. vs. D.W.*, B.C.J. No. 627 (2002) was sensitive to the need for courts to consider "perceived harm" from electronic threats. In this case, 14-year-old Dawn Marie Wesley committed suicide after being bullied by her peers for 10 days and receiving a telephone threat. The court noted that in this case, "perceived harm" was as fatal as if the actual threat had been carried out and D.W. was convicted of criminal harassment even though she insisted she did not intend to kill Dawn Marie.

RETHINKING EXISTING LAWS AND REEXAMINING LEGAL FRAMEWORKS

In September 2009, Harvard University law professor John Palfrey testified before the U.S. Congress (http://judiciary.house.gov/hearings/hear_090930. html). Professor Palfrey urged lawmakers to consider problems of cyber-bullying and related Internet concerns more broadly and not to put sole blame on new technologies because most of the ways in which young people use digital technologies are positive. He noted that most young people, at least in the United States, do not distinguish between their "online" and "offline" lives. As a result, many of the positive and responsible behaviors that take place offline also happen, in one form or another, online. So, too, do many of the bad things that happen in everyday life also play out online. He argued that the law needs to provide incentives for technology companies to support and work to protect young users and harness their innovations. He suggested rethinking existing laws by reexamining legal frameworks toward reasonable enforceability.

CANADIAN POLICY VACUUM

All the concerns Palfrey raised resonate in the Canadian context too. There is a need to rethink existing laws and reexamine legal frameworks to make them congruent with the realities of the digital age. It is not as if the public is ignorant of the impact of cyber-bullying. Cyber-bullying has been a concern for at least a decade. It has been widely reported and sometimes sensational-ized by the media (Shariff 2008). In the last five years, there have been numerous academic conferences, and workshops for parents, teachers, and administrators such as the Canadian Association for the Practical Study of Law and Education (http://www.capsle.ca; *I Am Safe* conference, http://safe.ca/). Teachers' unions have also joined in, conducting surveys of members who have been cyber-bullied by students (Quebec Teachers Federation CROP Poll on Increase in Cyber-Bullying against Teachers, April 2011). Although many positive educational programs on digital citizenship and peace education have emerged, gaps in public policy persist. Our research repeatedly confirms that the public would greatly benefit from judicial guide-lines that are relevant and better suited to address the complexities of an evolving digital world, toward development and implementation of public policies and educational practices to reduce cyber-bullying and enhance digi-tal citizenship. Canadian academics, policy makers, legislators, and the judi-ciary are grappling with these emerging privacy dilemmas internationally.

DEFINING THE LINES OF DIGITAL CITIZENSHIP

Most cases of cyber-bullying and privacy breach involving Canadian youth in social media have been settled out of court. This is unfortunate because the Canadian public would benefit from knowing what legal options are available to youth, teachers, parents, and policy makers as they attempt to chart new directions in policy, programs, and practices to address cyber-bullying and online victimization. Parents and teachers would also benefit from knowing whether and how the law will protect their children/students from cyber-bullying and privacy harm if they are victimized online. A large step forward would entail recognition by the judiciary of factors that cause young people to want to remain anonymous, including the recognition that there is one identity on- and offline and that fear of privacy harm and perceived fear of actual harm that underlie such decisions are not trivial and can have devastating consequences on Canadian society.

In the cyber world there are no time limits, but there are infinite and interested audiences. There are, nonetheless, also limitless learning and leadership opportunities on social media that can create a sea change. Consider for example the political movements for democracy in the Middle East, all of which originated with social media. I have always argued that bans, filters, and zero tolerance are not helpful or productive. What we need to do is to engage all stakeholders in helping to define reasonable and realistic boundaries of responsibility and accountability and raise awareness of the serious impact of cyber-bullying and cyber-lurking/voyeurism, with a view to providing alternative online information that is entertaining but does not demean or dehumanize others. As my colleagues, the other authors in this book agree that digital media has significant potential for education and leadership toward making a sea change in social responsibility. As we have witnessed in the Middle East, young people can engage with social media in powerful ways to bring positive, democratic, and inclusive social change. The challenge lies in helping youth come to their own recognition of ethical and legal boundaries when encountering negative forms of online information, and fostering leadership among all stakeholders, young and old, toward social responsibility and digital citizenship.

Helping stakeholders analyze case studies, discuss and dialogue the emerging issues, and understand the impact of negative information searching and distribution behaviors of digital natives show great promise as a starting point from which to navigate these challenges. As evidenced by the recent launch of my website, Define the Line (http://www.definetheline.ca), established for exactly this purpose, stakeholders from parents, educators, policy makers, legislators, law enforcement officers, privacy experts, non-governmental youth organizations at the national and international level, mobile companies, and social media corporations are all seeking information that relates to their role. Informed stakeholders, especially youth, are more likely to take ownership of their information encounters if they understand the long-term impact on peers, themselves, and ultimately on society. As they grow up, digital natives need to be engaged in developing informed boundaries that guide online policy and practice in collaborative and cohesive ways. There is also a need for increased awareness, online interaction, and dialogue that will provide *digital natives* with a framework for thinking about their online information seeking and distribution activities, enabling the development of an internal set of values that recognizes the limits of online fun and entertainment at others' expense.

REFERENCES

American Academy of Pediatrics. (2009). "The Role of the Pediatrician in Youth Violence Prevention in Clinical Practice and at the Community Level." *Pediatrics* 124 (1): 393–402.

Artz, S. 2004. "Violence in the Schoolyard: School Girls' Use of Violence." In C. Alder and A. Worrall (Eds.), *Girls' Violence: Myths and Realities*. Albany, NY: State University of New York Press, 151–166.

Barak, A. 2005. "Sexual Harassment on the Internet." *Social Science Computer Review* 23 (1): 77–92.

Beran, T., F. Mishna, R. Heatherington, and S. Shariff. 2010. *Children's Experiences of Cyber-Bullying: A Canadian National Study*. Unpublished study.

Calmes, J. 2011. "Obama's Focus on Anti-Bullying Efforts." *New York Times*, March 10.

Calo, R. M. 2011. "The Boundaries of Privacy Harm." *Indiana Law Journal* 86 (3).

Cambron-McCabe, N. 2009. "Students' Speech Rights in an Electronic Age." 242 Ed. Law Rep. 493.

Cassell, Justine, and Meg Cramer. 2008. "High Tech or High Risk: Moral Panics about Girls Online." In Tara McPherson (Ed.), *Digital Youth, Innovation, and the Unexpected*. The John D. and Catherine T. MacArthur Foundation Series on Digital Media and Learning. Cambridge, MA: MIT Press, 53–76.

Chu, J. 2005. "You Wanna Take This Online? Cyberspace is the 21st Century Bully's Playground Where Girls Play Rougher than Boys." *Time*. August 8. Toronto: Ontario, 42–43.

Coloroso, B. 2003. *The Bully, the Bullied and the Bystander*. Toronto: HarperCollins Canada.

Edwards, L. Y. 2005. "Victims, Villains and Vixens." In. S. R. Mazzarella (Ed.), *Girl Wide Web*. New York: Peter Lang, 13–30.

Heckman, D. 2010. *Just Kidding: K–12 Students: Threats and First Amendment Freedom of Speech Protection*. 259 Ed. Law Rep. 381.

Hoff, D., and S. Mitchell. 2009. "How Do We Know What We Know?" In Shaheen Shariff and Andrew Churchill (Eds.), *Truths and Myths of Cyber-Bullying*. New York: Peter Lang.

Hinduja, S., and J. Patchin. 2008." Cyber-Bulling: An Exploratory Analysis of Factors Related to Offending and Victimization." *Deviant Behavior* 29: 129–156.

Jenkins, H., and D. Boyd. 2006. "MySpace and Deleting Online Predators Act." *MIT Tech Talk*. May 30. Accessed January 2012, http://www.danah.org/papers/MySpaceDOPA.html.

Lankshear, C., and M. Knobel. 2005. "Digital Literacies: Policy, Pedagogy and Research Considerations for Education." *Opening Plenary Address, ITU Conference*, October 20, Oslo, Norway.

Lenhart, A. 2010. "Cyberbullying 2010: What Research Tells Us." *Pew Research Center Internet and American Life Project*. http://www.slideshare.net/PewInternet/.

Mason, K. 2008. "Cyberbullying: A Preliminary Assessment for School Personnel." *Psychology in the Schools* 45 (4): 323–348.

Mayer, T. 2011. "McGill student investigated for hateful tweets: 'I want to shoot everyone in this room, …'" *The McGill Tribune* 30 (23:1), March 15.

National Center for Education Statistics. 2008. *Indicators of School Crime and Safety: 2008.* Accessed January 2012, http://nces.ed.gov/pubsearch/pubsinfo.asp?pubid=2009022.

Patchin, J., and S. Hinduja. 2006. "Bullies Move Beyond the Schoolyard: A Preliminary Look at Cyberbullying." *Youth Violence and Juvenile Justice* 4 (2): 148–169.

Patchin, J., and S. Hinduja. 2010a. "Bullying, Cyberbullying, and Suicide." *Archives of Suicide Research* 14 (3), 206–221. http://dx.doi.org/10.1080/13811118.2010.494133.

Patchin, J., and S. Hinduja. 2010b. "Cyber-Bullying and Self-Esteem." *Journal of School Health* 80 (12), 614–621.

Salmivalli, C. 2001. "Group View on Victimization: Empirical Findings and Their Implications." In J. Juvonen and S. Graham (Eds.), *Peer Harassment in School: The Plight of the Vulnerable and Victimized.* London: Guildford Press, 398–419.

Shariff, S. 2008. *Cyber-Bullying: Issues and Solutions for the School, the Classroom, and the Home.* Abington, Oxfordshire, UK: Routledge (Taylor and Francis Group).

Shariff, S. 2009. *Confronting Cyber-Bullying: What Schools Need to Know to Control Misconduct and Avoid Legal Consequences.* New York: Cambridge University Press.

Shariff, S., and A. Churchill. 2009. *Truths and Myths of Cyber-bullying.* New York: Peter Lang.

Thierer, A. D. 2007. "Social Networking and Age Verification: Many Hard Questions; No Easy Solutions." *The Progress and Freedom Foundation Progress on Point Paper No. 14.5,* http://dx.doi.org/10.2139/ssrn.976936.

Weber, S., and C. Mitchell. 2007. "Imaging, Keyboarding, and Posting Identities: Young People and New Media Technologies." In David Buckingham (Ed.), *Youth, Identity, and Digital Media.* Cambridge, MA: MIT Press, 25–48.

Ybarra, M. L., and K. J. Mitchell. 2004. "Online Aggressor/Targets, Aggressors, and Targets: A Comparison of Associated Youth Characteristics." *Journal of Child Psychology and Psychiatry* 45 (7): 1308–1316.

Ybarra M. L., K. J. Mitchell, J. Wolak, and D. Finkelhor. 2006. "Examining Characteristics and Associated Distress Related to Internet Harassment: Findings from the Second Youth Internet Safety Survey." *Pediatrics* 118 (4): e1169–e1177.

Chapter Ten

Systems

Jamshid Beheshti and Andrew Large

Today, information and communication technologies (ICT) are prevalent in the lives of young people in the developed world. These so-called digital natives, those born after 1989, who may "process information fundamentally differently from their predecessors" (Prensky 2001, 1) seem to be the dominant force in the technological drive. The term *digital natives*, however, may be controversial. Prensky (2012) and others have argued in favor of a new generation, the "net savvy" youth (Levin et al. 2002); digital children (Vandewater et al. 2007); the Google generation (Rowlands et al. 2008); generation M, for Media, MySpace, or the Millenials (Vie 2008); or generation V (virtual) (Marshall et al. 2009). Selwyn (2009) states, however, that "the overall tenor of these discursive constructions of young people and technology tends towards exaggeration and inconsistency" (370).

Many older colleagues point out that they rely extensively on ICT and, therefore, feel that they are as "plugged in" and "tuned in" as any teenager. Like some of the older adults, teens use the Internet for online shopping, downloading music, and sharing their personal information; 62 percent in the United States reported using the Net for finding and retrieving news and information about current events, and 31 percent reported that they search for health, dietary, or physical fitness information on the Net (Pew 2011).

Young people, however, do much more than text messaging and searching for information; they *live* in the digital world. They use social networking sites (SNS) to create personal spaces to store artifacts such as currency and familial possession as a means of self-expression. In an interesting study, Odom and colleagues (2011) interviewed 21 teenagers (12–17 years old) to solicit their opinions about their communication habits and to observe their behavior in everyday life. One 16-year-old stated, "I like to be logged in to my laptop and iPad so I know when something happens, like someone writes on my wall or a photo or tags me. . . . I want to see it around me. . . .way better than getting a text [message] or an email about it later . . . it keeps me up to date with everything going on" (1496). As Selwyn (2009) aptly points out, the use of ICT by youth should be viewed "as being subjected continually to a series of complex interactions and negotiations with the social, economic, political and cultural contexts into which they emerge" (371). (For a more detailed discussion see Thomas 2011; and the chapter by Abbas and Agosto, "Everyday Life Information Behavior of Young People," in this book.)

These interactions depend on many factors, among which is the user experience (UX) and user engagement (UE). In this chapter, we begin with a broad survey of popular technologies utilized by children and youth, followed by a look at methodologies for designing usable and engaging technologies with examples of empirically tested systems, and finally a discussion on user engagement.

CURRENT TECHNOLOGIES

The conventional view of individuals working in front of a personal computer may no longer be applicable in today's fast-paced lifestyle, where mobile or handheld devices are used effortlessly anytime and anywhere to produce and retrieve information for education and entertainment. Whereas desktop computers are fixed, stationary, and static, mobile technologies may be utilized in a variety of applications suitable for children and youth, who are always on the move. The data reported by Agosto and Abbas in their chapter in this book on "Youth and Online Social Networking: What Do We Know So Far?" show that 75 percent of 12- to 17-year-olds in the United States own cell phones, and text messaging (SMS) is common among 88 percent of them, with girls aged 14–17 on average exchanging about 3,000 messages per month. SNS such as Facebook with more than 750 million active users are also an important communication tool among youth. Just over 60 percent of 13- to17-year-olds have a personal profile on SNS, and despite the age restriction imposed by many sites, more than five million children under the age of 10 are SNS users (Consumer Reports 2011).

The worldwide smartphone market, which is capable of sophisticated operations and multitasking, grew by a whopping 63 percent from 2010 to 2011 (mobiThinking 2012). Thanks to the mobile technology, more recent data show a significant increase in volume of usage and text messaging in all these categories; in the United States just over 95 percent of 12- to17-year-olds are online, 80 percent of whom use social networks (Lenhart et al. 2011). The colossal increase in use of mobile technology has prompted one author to state, "What's the latest trend parents are using to toilet train their young child? Letting them use your iPad while on the potty. That is, as long as he or she delivers the goods!" (Orlando 2011).

Buckleitner (2009) identifies eleven types of mobile devices designed for and used by children, including phones, plug-and-play TV toys, tablet computers, laptops, electronic learning aids, portable gaming consoles, digital cameras, portable media players, and e-readers. These devices have opened new venues for mobile learning for children, ranging from physical exercise games to field trips and content creation (Rogers and Price 2009). However, the vast majority of the youngsters are still facing traditional methods of teaching and learning, with more than 90 percent of them sitting and working alone in the classroom (Norris and Soloway 2009). This situation, though, may be changing. The results of several experimental studies demonstrate the advantage of the application of mobile technology in educational settings over traditional methods (for examples, see Druin 2009). In a new paradigm shift, mobile technology alters some of the conventional methods of knowledge delivery in the classroom. Rogers and Price suggest that the technology "can be designed to enable children to move in and out of overlapping physical, digital, and communicative spaces" (2009, 5).

Seol and colleagues (2011) describe the Stanford Mobile Inquiry-based Learning Environment (SMILE), which allows elementary school students to develop multiple choice questions fairly quickly, collaboratively using mobile phones in the classroom. They concluded that the students not only enjoyed their experience but that they also created sophisticated questions with a wide range of complexity spanning different levels of Bloom's taxonomy. In another experiment SMS was used outside of the classroom to support mathematics education in the ninth grade. While the results of the study did not illustrate significant improvement over more traditional methods, both students and teachers expressed very positive perception toward the technology (Sorensen 2011).

The penetration of mobile technology in the educational context is reaching beyond the developed countries. For example, a mobile learning application for high school students in mathematics demonstrated its value over conventional methods in one of the Caribbean islands (Kalloo and Mohan 2011), and mobile phone cameras were utilized successfully in science studies in a school in Sri Lanka (Ekanayake and Wishart 2011).

WEBSITES AND PORTALS

Hundreds of websites have been created for children and young people, the purpose of most of which is commercial enterprise and entertainment. Buckleitner (2008) conducted an ethnographic study on children aged between two and eight and observed their behavior on the web. He concluded that the websites are highly commercialized, frequently entice children to click on undesirable options, invite them to "register" for rewards, promote consumerism, display logos and brand names, and use subtle branding techniques. He also observed that the websites vary widely in their quality, educational value, and suitability of content for young children. Fewer sites are designed for educational, informational, or edutainment purposes (for some examples, see Great Web Sites for Kids by the Association for Library Service to Children, American Library Association, http://gws.ala.org/). Considering that Google is by far the dominant force in the global search engine industry, capturing more than 82 percent of the market share (Netmarketshare 2011), and the vast majority of youth are using Google for searching and retrieval (Jochmann-Mannak et al. 2010), it is not surprising that very few children's search engines have survived the onslaught of this juggernaut.

Ask Kids (http://www.askkids.com), designed for those aged 6 to 12, is based on the Ask.com search index and has been in operation for some years. The main feature of the site is the *Answers*, which includes 16 top-level categories ranging from Schools and Libraries, to Weird Science and Gardens. Another survivor of the passage of time is Yahoo! Kids (http://kids.yahoo.com), which is a portal rather than a search engine. It includes many pre-defined categories such as games, music, movies, jokes, sports, horoscopes, and Studyzone. The portal relies on the Yahoo! Directory of websites developed exclusively for children. Bilal and Ellis (2011) conducted a study on Ask Kids and Yahoo! Kids and found that while both could retrieve results that overlapped with those from search engines designed for adults; both also found unique results that were not retrieved by other search engines.

KidsClick! (http://www.kidsclick.org), owned and maintained by the School of Library and Information Science at Kent State University, is one of the longest-standing search engines designed for children. In addition to a traditional keyword search box, it includes four additional search modes: Category Search, which includes 16 pre-defined top-level categories in a two-level hierarchical subject directory; an Alphabetical Search; a Quick Search for Digital Media, which consists of icons with labels; and a Dewey Decimal Search option consisting of DDC classes. The latter is linked to the second level of the hierarchical subject directory. Several newly created sites rely on Google's Custom Search to provide a safe search engine for young people, for example, Dib Dab Doo and Dilly too (http://www.dibdabdoo.com/), KidRex (http://www.kidrex.org/), and KidzSearch (http://www.kidzsearch.com).

Large, Beheshti, and Cole (2002) analyzed the results of their research on four popular children's web portals using focus groups to identify 51 attributes to construct an information architecture matrix. The attributes include the objective of the portal, the characteristics of the intended audience, content, interface, navigation, interactiveness, and retrieval tools, many of which are based on user-centered design. The matrix may be used for evaluating existing web portals, as well as for designing new ones to ensure that the portals' purpose, design objective, and design architecture are linked together logically, efficiently, and effectively. The researchers conclude that it is unlikely that even the best-designed portals currently on the market "can function equally effectively for all users, all content, and all needs. Design effort should be expended upon producing a set of ideals attributes (or tools) from which an optimal personalized portal can then be built" (837).

A number of informational sites have been developed to help both elementary and secondary students in their research for class projects. The *IPL2* (http://www.ipl.org), a merger of the Internet Public Library and Librarians' Internet Index (Abels 2011), comprises conventional keyword searching as well as five categories: Resources by Subject, Newspapers and Magazines, For Kids, For Teens, and Special Collections. The latter is a collection of eclectic topics, including Mobile Apps, Museums, Hurricane Preparedness, and Election. The For Kids option contains nine top-level categories ranging from Health and Nutrition to Sports and Recreation and Math and Science. The For Teens option, on the other hand, consists of 12 top-level categories designed to help teenagers in their research. A major feature of IPL2 is its reference service, which is provided by hundreds of volunteers. Awesome Library (http://www.awesomelibrary.org), maintained by librarians, is similar to IPL2, providing different options for children and teenagers. Another noteworthy site is the Library of Congress's Kids and Families portal (http://www.loc.gov/families), which includes such rich resources as the Performing Arts Encyclopedia and National Book Festival Webcasts. Collectively, these sites are representative of educational and informational portals currently available in the market for children and young adults.

OBSTACLES AND CHALLENGES

A body of research shows that children when seeking information under imposed tasks such as school projects encounter salient problems and challenges (Kafai and Bates 1997; Hirsh 1999; Large et al. 1999; Bowler et al. 2001). In a comprehensive review of the literature, Large (2005) concludes that children encounter problems in selecting appropriate search terms, move too quickly through the web pages while spending little time reading the materials, and have difficulty judging the relevance of the retrieved pages. More recent studies suggest younger children (under 12), even with increased exposure to the Internet and the technology, still face insurmountable obstacles in searching (Druin et al. 2009b). These obstacles have been categorized as search strategies, typing and spelling, and deciphering search outcome, which may result in disappointment and possibly abandonment of the search task. All the 12 participants in Druin and colleagues' study expressed their frustration while searching. The challenges of keyword searching for younger children is demonstrated by a seven-year-old, who expresses his exasperation when he states that he does not know how to spell the word "dolphins" (Druin et al. 2010).

Reiterating the results of the previous research, van der Sluis and van Dijk (2010) divide the problems facing children in interacting with retrieval systems into four salient groups. The first group deals with an insufficient mental model of the system leading to the use of natural language, repetitive keywords, and difficulties with Boolean operators. The second group covers vocabulary problems, which lead to choosing inappropriate search keywords. The third group, "chaotic search behavior," includes children's lack of attention to the search results and hence frequent looping and backtracking. The final group of problems deals with lack of skills and experience in relevance judgments.

It is probable that children receive very little guidance and assistance from adults to alleviate the problems and challenges that they face with information systems. A survey of 2,131 families in the United Kingdom shows that 68 percent of children aged 5 to 7 and 84 percent of youth aged 8 to 15 are likely to be left alone when searching the web (Ofcom 2010).

Torres and colleagues (2010) analyzed query logs on a children's portal to determine their search behavior on the web. The researchers' analyses show that long queries, which include a greater number of adjectives and verbs, result in poorer performance by children. In addition, query log analysis demonstrates that children tend to have lengthy sessions and more entries per session, which the authors propose may indicate lack of expertise in translating information needs to appropriate keywords. Torres and Weber (2011) in their analysis of the Yahoo! search logs found significant differences between those in the range of 19 to 25 years and those under 18 years old, but their analysis of log files showed remarkable similarities among age groups under 18 years old. The authors also found that young people tend to "click whatever is presented at a prominent position" (401). Another query log study of three children's search engines in Germany shows that children do differ from adults in their search behavior (Gossen et al. 2011); whereas the children's queries are more about finding sources of information on a topic, adults' queries tend to be more navigational or transactional such as finding websites or purchasing goods. Beheshti and colleagues (2010) analyzed some 92,000 transaction logs of a children's portal, and found that 83 percent of the users tend to prefer browsing through a subject taxonomy or alphabetical lists rather than keyword searching. The results of the analyses suggest that children seem to opt for browsing perhaps because it is less demanding cognitively, as it imposes an information structure that immediately restricts choice to a limited number of options (Borgman et al. 1995). Druin et al. (2003) conducted log analysis for the International Children's Digital Library and found that approximately 75 percent of the searches used the category search through browsing, and only about 10 percent used keyword search. Earlier studies on children's information behavior also corroborate these results; children are more at ease with browsing than keyword searching (Bilal 2002).

DESIGN METHODOLOGIES

In response to the obstacles and challenges faced by children and teens in their information-seeking activities, in the past two decades research in this area has shifted from systems to end users. While this is a positive change, until recently research was conducted by adults with little input from the target audience itself. As Hanna and her colleagues at Microsoft's Hardware Ergonomics and Usability Department commented, "Usability research with children has often been considered either too difficult to carry out with unruly subjects or not necessary for an audience that is satisfied with gratuitous animations and funny noises" (Hanna et al. 1999, 4).

In the mid 1990s, a paradigm shift in usability studies began to take shape, when researchers instigated young users' participation in the actual design process with the hope that the resulting information retrieval systems would become more adapted to their needs. Druin and her team (1997) began involving children in their design teams in 1997, when they developed Kid-Pad, a collaborative story authoring tool. Kafai and Bates (1997) conducted one of the earlier studies to involve children in the design process, when they recruited elementary school students to build a website directory for their colleagues. As more researchers involved children in the system design process, a need for adopting conceptual models suitable for children as designers arose (Large, Beheshti, Nesset, and Bowler 2004). The conventional user-centered methodology, where end users participated in the development of the system only at the testing and evaluation phase (Scaife and Rogers 1999), no longer sufficed as a model for the design process. As Bruckman and colleagues (2008) state, "To design for kids, we must have a model of what kids are. . . . We tend to think that we know kids—who they are, what they are interested in, and what they like. However, we do not have as much access to our former selves as many would like to believe" (806).

The models or methodologies applied in the design process may be divided into seven broad categories based on user involvement (Nesset and Large 2004). At the lowest end of the user involvement scale is User-Centered Design. The next model is Contextual Design, which utilizes ethnographic methods to determine how users work (Beyer and Holtzblatt 1999). In the Contextual Design methodology researchers collect data through observation in the user's own environment, and attempt to utilize these data as the basis for decision making in the design process. While Contextual Design does not involve users in all aspects of the process, the low-tech prototyping, pictorial diagramming, and other visual techniques used in the methodology may allow children to contribute to the end product. Learner-Centered Design is at the same level as the Contextual Design on the user-involvement scale. Proposed by Soloway and his colleagues (1994), the methodology is based on learning theories and assumes that everyone is a learner, and that learning cannot be detached from practice. The Learner-Centered Design focuses on the tasks that the system has to perform, the tools required to manage those tasks, and the interfaces for these tools.

Next on the user-involvement scale in the design process is Participatory Design proposed by Carmel, Whitaker, and George (1993), which is based on the principle that users know how to improve their work and are qualified to contribute to the development of new systems through their perceptions of technology. In this methodology, users are generally involved during the initial stage of the design process to help define the problem, and during the development of the product to help with evaluating it. In an attempt to address some of the challenges when working with children during other design methodologies, Scaife and colleagues (1997) introduced the Informant Design methodology, which views participants (for example children) as much more informed about learning practices than researchers. In this approach, depending on their knowledge, individuals participate at various stages of the process using different methods.

Druin and her colleagues incorporated some of the principles and techniques of Participatory Design and other approaches in the Cooperative Inquiry methodology, which was developed for a design process involving younger participants (Druin 1999). In Cooperative Inquiry children are treated as equal partners with adults in an intergenerational design team, where through training and cooperation the team members collaborate to design new systems. Adult participants need to be cognizant that children do not view them as authority figures in this setting, and they must be able to express their views freely instead of conforming to what adults expect of them. Techniques such as visual flowcharts, brainstorming, and interviewing are used to capture children's design ideas.

Large and his colleagues "in addressing whether intergenerational design techniques can be used to design a Web portal, found that no existing design methodologies fitted perfectly" (Large et al. 2006b, 65).

They adapted and incorporated a modified version of Cooperative Inquiry and User-Design from the field of instructional design (Carr 1997) in their research. The new methodology was called Bonded Design, because of a natural bond between adults as design experts and children as experts on being children. The new methodology also shares aspects of Learner-Centered Design in providing a learning environment for the team members, and borrows from Contextual Design the ideas of creating paper prototypes as well as developing a roadmap for each session.

Large and his colleagues utilized the Bonded Design methodology to design and develop a portal on Canadian history for grade 6 students, and a slightly revised Bonded Design methodology to design a portal for grade 3 students. Figure 10.1 shows diagrammatically the methodology. In the case of grade 6 students, the design team was composed of three adults as designers and eight children as users, who collaborated as equal partners in the process. The process consisted of several techniques undertaken iteratively over 13 sessions:

- As a first step, a needs assessment of end users was conducted to determine the portal's requirements and specifications. The team designed a questionnaire, which the student members of the design team administered among the entire grade 6 population in one school, to collect factual data regarding internet usage, library usage, and so on; to gather data about preferences such as graphics, animation, response time, and the like; and to "promote a team spirit among the design team members" (Large et al. 2006b, 73).
- During the Evaluation phase, the team assessed current systems (portals) in the market to identify their strengths and weaknesses.
- The Discussion phase consisted of examining and debating various elements of a portal such as search options, timeline, color, and so on.

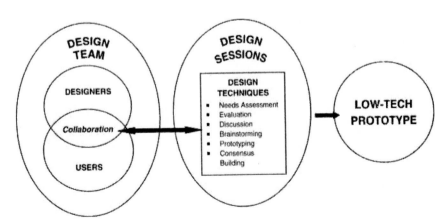

Figure 10.1. Bonded design

- In the Brainstorming session, children were encouraged to put forth their ideas and discuss them.
- Consensus building proved to be the most challenging phase of the process for the design team. While children were often enthusiastic about brainstorming and found it relatively effortless, due to lack of life experience and immaturity, they could not compromise easily on their own ideas to reach consensus.
- Consensus building resulted in mock-up prototypes drawn in PowerPoint that were presented to the team for further discussions.

At the end of the Bonded Design methodological process, a low-tech prototype was created, from which the actual portal, *History Trek*, was developed.

Regardless of the methodologies used, there is no doubt that the role of children is critical in the design process (Hanna et al. 1997). Their roles as users of the system, as testers in usability studies, as informants in the design process, and as partners are of the utmost importance (Druin et al. 2003).

EXPERIMENTAL SYSTEMS

Considering that children often use the same search engines as adults (Jochmann-Mannak et al. 2010) but differ from adults in their search behavior, a growing number of researchers have attempted to develop systems specifically for this group of users. The International Children's Digital Library (ICDL) began as an experimental project at the University of Maryland in collaboration with the Internet Archive funded by the National Science Foundation and the Institute for Museum and Library Services. Over several years, Druin and her colleagues used the Cooperative Inquiry methodology to design the system, with the goal of instilling in children through reading an understanding and a respect for diverse ideas, cultures, and languages. Currently the ICDL, whose target audience is 3- to 13-year-old children, consists of some 4,500 digitized children's books in 55 languages, with its ultimate goal of providing access to more than 40,000 books in over 100 languages (http://www.childrenslibrary.org). The website's colorful interface provides many choices and options for its users, including age indicator icons, icons that allow children to find books by their number of pages (short, medium, long), categorization based on the main characters of the books such as "Kid Characters" and "Real Animal Characters," and books by genre. The decisions for the design of these category browsers were based on children's abilities and expertise in information processing and motor skills, searching and browsing, and selection criteria (Hutchinson et al. 2006). An interesting feature of the interface is the application of the Boolean *and* operator, which is depicted visually by a plus sign (+) and is displayed along with icons that have been chosen to narrow the search results.

ICDL has been the subject of several research projects, among which is a study that shows age and gender are significant factors in search behavior in a digital library (Reuter and Druin 2004). The results of the study show that while younger children prefer interactive, simple interfaces, and opening books is their preferred search technique, older children favor more complex designs, but are more selective in choosing the books. Boys tend to submit more queries than girls, while girls choose more books. An international four-country study was also conducted on ICDL, with 12 children over four years (Druin et al. 2007). Using interview techniques and collecting book reviews and drawings, the longitudinal study showed that children from economically disadvantaged backgrounds benefited most from using the ICDL by improving their reading ability, while others developed a better appreciation for cultural diversity.

History Trek, a children's portal funded by a Social Sciences and Humanities Research Council of Canada grant, was designed by an intergenerational team over a number of years using the Bonded Design method as described earlier (Large et al. 2004). The portal includes approximately 2,500 links to English and French language sites on Canadian history deemed appropriate in content and language for elementary school students. Since its public debut in fall 2007, the site has had more than two million hits from around the world.

The bilingual portal offers several approaches to information retrieval: keyword searching, alphabetical search feature, scrollable timeline, a topic menu based on a hierarchical subject index to Canadian history using child-friendly terms, and an advanced search option, which allows a search to be restricted either to the title or assigned index terms of a site, or to phrase searching within the site title or description (Figure 10.2). A spellchecker in the English-language version of the interface was implemented and the portal also has a hyperlink to Google and to web portals (MSN and Yahoo). A link is provided to several web-based quizzes dealing with Canadian history. Portal personalization is offered through a "My Site" icon, allowing users to choose among four versions of the site mascot.

As with the ICDL, *History Trek* (see Figure 10.2) has been studied to determine the viability of its construct. Large, Beheshti, Nesset, and Bowler (2006b) used 12 focus groups comprising grade 6 and grade 3 students, and two operational field studies to evaluate History Trek and Kids Search Canada, a portal designed for grade 3 students. The study recruited more than 80 students. The results show that in creating a portal for children, the objective of the portal has to be defined clearly (informational, educational, or entertainment); a unifying design framework to incorporate all the features of the

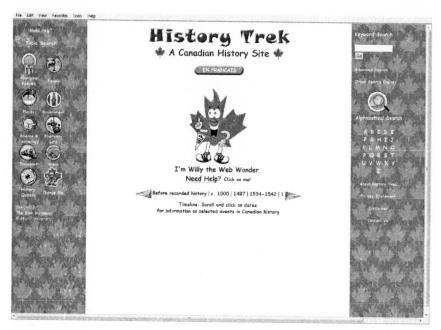

Figure 10.2. History Trek portal

portal should be used; a variety of information retrieval approaches should be included; browsing tools and capabilities including subject taxonomies should be integrated in the portal; spellchecking features should be included; colors and animation should be used for engagement, "but not at the expense either of clarity or operational usefulness" (Large, Beheshti, et al. 2006b, 10); search results should be displayed clearly with annotations; personalization features should be included; and ideally in-context help should be provided.

Researchers are also studying ways to improve existing systems for children and youth. For instance, acknowledging the difficulties and challenges in reading skills, De Belder and Moens (2010) describe a method for converting text intended to be read by adults to a simplified version for children. Others are focusing their attention on investigating the relationship between the digital landscape and children with disabilities, or developing systems that can accommodate disabilities such as attention deficit hyperactivity disorder (ADHD; McKnight 2010), autism spectrum disorder (ASD; Bilal 2010), and non-verbal children (Varona et al. 2008). User diversity, accessibility, and disabilities have been the subject of research since the 1990s (Laux et al. 1996) and continuing to date (for examples, see Langdon et al. 2012). Shneiderman (2000) suggests that a research agenda dealing with the "adaptability needed for users with diverse physical, visual, auditory, or cognitive disabilities is likely to benefit users with differing preferences" (87).

VIRTUAL ENVIRONMENTS

Digital natives often are well versed in using computer games, most of which now take the form of simulations, such as those designed for the X-Box 360 and the Nintendo Wii. According to a UK survey, teens' reliance on these devices to surf the web has increased significantly (Ofcom 2010). Recent reports suggest that virtual environments or worlds are one of the most popular modes of interaction on the web (Harris and Rea 2009). Computer simulations can take various technological forms, including virtual reality, augmented reality, and virtual environments. In the taxonomy of virtual reality, Milgram and Kishino (1994) identify a continuum that connects real environments to virtual environments. They define augmented reality as a display where real environments are augmented with virtual objects. Following Wilson and D'Cruz (2006), virtual environments (VEs) provide a computer-generated experience obtained by and through an interface that engages one or more of the user's senses, and almost always includes the visual sense. It gives a feeling of being within a three-dimensional space where the user interacts with objects and controls his or her movements. VEs can provide an interactive, stimulating learning environment (sometimes referred to as virtual learning environment or VLE; Pan et al. 2006), benefiting students in classrooms (Virvou, Katsionis, and Manos 2005; see also the chapter by Giovanni Vincenti, "Gaming and Virtual Environments," in this book). Summarizing the results of research, Hew and Cheung (2010) conclude that in K–12 and higher education, virtual worlds are utilized to facilitate communication among students for simulation of real world trials and procedures, and for experiential enactments.

Despite the demonstrated benefits in education, by far the vast majority of VEs have been developed for gaming. World of Warcraft is perhaps the best known and most used VE designed for adult gamers, while Habbo Hotel (http://www.habbo.com) is the most subscribed among the more than 250 virtual worlds constructed for teens. Habbo Hotel, founded in 2000, is an example of a thriving VE, boasting to be the "world's largest online community" with more than 200 million registered characters.

One of the few VEs designed for a wide range of purposes, including gaming, is the well-known Second Life (SL), launched in 2003 and intended for users 16 years and older. It now has about one million active followers. Communication in the SL virtual worlds is conducted through avatars, characters that can take the shape of a human, animal, vegetable, or mineral. Unlike many VEs, SL is used in educational and informational settings. An information archipelago in SL is allocated to Cybrary City, where more than 40 virtual libraries are situated. It is also the most studied VE among researchers. (For more details see the chapter by Giovanni Vincenti, "Gaming and Virtual Environments," in this book.)

Beheshti and Large (2006), in an attempt to investigate the efficacies of VEs for information delivery, have developed a non-immersive virtual reality library (VRLibrary) using the metaphor of a physical library with rooms, bookcases, and books. The library metaphor was chosen to capitalize on the navigational affordances of recognized artifacts (Shiaw et al. 2004) over reconstructing a new model in memory (Ware 2008). The library metaphor has been used in experimental projects for more than a decade, with different degrees of success (Beheshti et al. 1996; Pejtersen 1989; Rauber and Merkl 1999). In the VRLibrary, the user, just as in a physical library, can walk around the virtual library, move among the bookcases, scan the titles of books that are arranged on the bookshelves, select individual books, and open them. The difference is that the library is virtual and the books actually represent websites; when a book is "opened" it displays the contents of the website in a window. In this environment, users can utilize *search stations* (Figure 10.3) situated in different locations of the library to conduct conventional keyword and term searches, the results of which are displayed as red dots on a plan of the library. The user can then "walk" through the library to spot red arrows and dots pointing to the "books" found by the search.

VRLibrary contains about 1,500 links to English-language websites on Canadian history deemed to be appropriate in content and language for elementary students (and created initially for *History Trek*). The Dewey Decimal Classification (DDC) system was used to classify the websites and pro-

Figure 10.3.   Library search station

vide a structure and organization for the VRLibrary similar to that used in a typical public or school library. These features were added to the system based on the observations and results from previous experiments (Beheshti et al. 2005; Beheshti and Large 2006; Beheshti et al. 2007). While these studies showed that the VRLibrary may not be a more effective or efficient retrieval tool than conventional web portals, children reported that the environment is much more engaging and "fun."

USER ENGAGEMENT

Usability according to Nielsen (1993) is about how easy a system is to learn, its efficiency, memorability, error management, and user satisfaction. A few years after Nielsen's definition, the International Organization for Standardization (ISO) redefined usability as the "Extent to which a product can be used by specified users to achieve specified goals with effectiveness, efficiency and satisfaction in a specified context of use" (ISO 9241-11: 1998 (E), Definitions, 3.1). More recently, however, ISO has broadened this definition by adding another dimension, namely, the user's "perceptions and responses that result from the use or anticipated use of a product, system or service" (ISO 9241-210). This definition is derived from the culmination of research on the impact of Web 2.0, social media, and other ubiquitous technology on usability. The broader definition, referred to as the user experience (UX), describes the totality of experience of the user rather than focusing on narrowly defined task-oriented measures. In defining UX, Hassenzahl and Tractinsky (2006) suggest three facets that should be investigated: a beyond instrumental facet, which includes holistic, aesthetic, and hedonic factors; an emotion and affect facet; and an experiential facet. They conclude that "UX is a consequence of a user's internal state (predispositions, expectations, needs, motivation, mood, etc.), the characteristics of the designed system (for example, complexity, purpose, usability, functionality, etc.) and the context (or the environment) within which the interaction occurs (for example, the organisational/social setting, meaningfulness of the activity, voluntariness of use, etc.)" (95).

An important dimension of user experience is engagement, a first-person experience involving playfulness, fun, and sensory integration (Laurel 1993) that sustains a user's attention. O'Brien and Toms (2008) draw from theories of flow, aesthetic, play, and information interaction as well as the results of a semi-structured interview with 17 participants to define engagement: "Engagement is a quality of user experiences with technology that is characterized by challenge, aesthetic and sensory appeal, feedback, novelty, interactivity, perceived control and time, awareness, motivation, interest, and affect" (949). If engagement is the most important concept in human-computer interaction for the design of intelligent interfaces that are capable of adapting to users (Peters et al. 2009), then we can only assume that it is at least as critical, if not more so, for children and teenagers. Skinner and Belmont (1993) state,

> Children who are engaged show sustained behavioural involvement in learning activities accompanied by positive emotional tone. They select tasks at the border of their competencies, initiate action when given the opportunity, and exert intense effort and concentration in the implementation of learning tasks; they show generally positive emotions during ongoing action, including enthusiasm, optimism, curiosity, and interest. (Skinner and Belmont 1993, 572)

The opposite of engagement is disaffection resulting in passive, bored, depressed, anxious, and unenthusiastic children in the learning environment. Hence, in interacting with ubiquitous technology, and specifically with information systems, interfaces that are engaging will support and encourage children and young adults to be persistent while maintaining a positive attitude in an enjoyable environment to pursue their goals.

In an attempt to incorporate various theories and concepts, Sutcliffe (2009) describes user engagement (UE) as "how and why applications attract people to use them within a session and make interaction exciting and fun" (3). Sutcliffe suggests that UE is a complex psychological phenomenon consisting of three components: interaction, which explains the content that is conveyed; media, describing the means through which the interaction occurs; and presence, which describes and clarifies the representation of the user. While the combination of these three components results in an engaging experience, it is presence, without which excitement or arousal and flow may decrease significantly, that is most important. Presence, portrayed in virtual reality and virtual environments, constitutes a 2D virtual character or a 3D avatar representation of the user.

Only recently have HCI researchers begun to investigate the aesthetical aspects of interface design (Graves Petersen et al. 2008), be it 2D environments and characters or 3D virtual worlds and avatars. Aesthetics is a key concept in interactive technologies, and, therefore, in user engagement. Norman (2004) argues that aesthetics may be more influential in user preferences than is usability. Cawthon and VandeMoere (2007) suggest that aesthetics plays a crucial role in technology's overall attractiveness and its initial usage. While utilitarian considerations of the interface such as legibility may at times be in conflict with aesthetical qualities (Byron and Wattenberg 2008), there is no doubt that interfaces with highly rated aesthetics appeal provide high overall user satisfaction (Tractinsky et al. 2000; Lindgaard and Dudek 2003; Hartmann et al. 2008). In one of the few studies on visualizations for children, Large et al. (2009) found that the six criteria of aesthetics—balance, equilibrium, symmetry, unity, rhythm, and economy (as identified by Ngo et al. 2003)—were present in children's drawings of an ideal interface, suggesting that perhaps young people gravitate naturally to the principles of aesthetical design.

Research also shows that aesthetics is correlated with the use of metaphors and with "fun" (Sutcliffe 2009). The latter is particularly important in designing systems for children and teens. Fun is one of the many dimensions of a positive emotional state and of affect, itself an important variable in information environments for children (for an in-depth discussion see Nahl and Bilal, 2007). Three experiences may define fun: what is expected of the system and whether the system disappoints or satisfies, engagement in terms of time spent on the system, and endurability—what is remembered about the system and the desire to return to the system (Read et al. 2002).

CONCLUSION

In this chapter, we have reviewed the current systems and websites available for use by children and teens. We have assessed the potential challenges and obstacles facing the new generation when interacting with systems, and have provided a few examples of the experimental portals that researchers have constructed using one or more of the methodologies reviewed.

Despite all the studies on information systems and interfaces for children, more research has to be conducted on systems that can accommodate affective, cognitive, and physical experiences of this group of users (Bilal 2000). Bilal and Ellis (2011) found that search engines designed for children are "more effective on single-word queries than on two-words or natural language queries" (557). Considering that natural language (NL) search may be the preferred mode of information seeking for children, systems that can accommodate NL should be investigated, designed and developed. Another area for further study includes systems that can accommodate browsing to reduce cognitive loads of vocabulary recall and associated evaluative judgments. Systems that accommodate effective and efficient browsing can help children navigate through the labyrinth of broad terms and narrow terms to find information.

Recommender systems, such as an information filtering system, can also help children to avoid the problems they commonly encounter with keyword searching and vocabulary. After the initial search, the system can make recommendations based on past searches. Recommender systems have been used fairly successfully in the business world, such as Amazon.com, but their role, value, and effectiveness have not been investigated in ubiquitous information environments. On the other hand, children, like adults, may benefit from serendipitous and opportunistic discovery of information (ODI), rather than on a path imposed by the system. A number of researchers are currently engaged in studying serendipity and ODI (for examples see Erdelez and Makri 2011), but very few are focusing on children and young adults (Beheshti and Large 2011).

Ultimately, with the help of our young colleagues—that is, children and youth—we have to design and develop information systems that are fun. For this new generation, fun means engagement, and engagement means sustained behavior and involvement. These systems should afford the user presence (2D or 3D), be aesthetically appealing, use familiar metaphors, and provide options for natural language searching and recommender systems. Shneiderman (2004) aptly outlines the basic elements for developing fun interfaces as alluring metaphors, compelling content, attractive graphics, appealing animations, and satisfying sounds. By combining these elements using principles of aesthetical design, we can create engaging information systems for children and young adults.

REFERENCES

Abels, E. G. 2011. "Transforming the Internet Public Library into the ipl2 Virtual Learning Laboratory." *The Reference Librarian* 52 (4): 284–290.

Beheshti, J., and A. Large. 2006. "Preliminary Design Indicators to Desktop Virtual Reality Environments." *ASIST 2006 Annual Meeting, Information Realities: Shaping the Digital Future for All. SIG HCI Research Symposium: Human-Computer Interaction in Information Intensive Environments.* November 5, 2006, Austin, Texas.

Beheshti, J., and A. Large. 2011. "An Interface for Opportunistic Discovery of Information for Young People." Human-Computer Interaction Conference, Orlando, July 2011. Human-Computer Interaction. Users and Applications. *Lecture Notes in Computer Science,* 6764: 541–548.

Beheshti, J., V. Large, and M. Bialek. 1996. "Public Access Catalogue Extension (PACE): A Browsable Graphical Interface." *Information Technology and Libraries* 15 (4): 231–240.

Beheshti, J., A. Large, I. Clement, and N. Tabatabaei. 2007. "Evaluating the Usability of a Virtual Reality Information System for Children." *Information Sharing in a Fragmented World: Crossing Boundaries.* Canadian Association for Information Science 2007 Annual Conference, May 10–12, Montreal, Quebec.

Beheshti, J., A. Large, and C. A. Julien. 2005. "Designing a Virtual Reality Interface for Children's Web Portals." *Data, Information, and Knowledge in a Networked World. Canadian Association for Information Science 2005 Annual Conference,* June 2–4. London, Ontario.

Beheshti, J., A. Large, and M. Tam. 2010. "Transaction Logs and Search Patterns on a Children's Portal." *Canadian Journal of Information and Library Science* 34 (4): 391–402.

Beyer, H., and K. Holtzblatt. 1999. "Contextual Design." *ACM Interactions* 6 (January): 32–42.

Bilal, D. 2000. "Children's Use of the Yahooligans! Web Search Engine: I. Cognitive, Physical, and Affective Behaviors on Fact-Based Search Tasks." *Journal of the American Society for Information Science* 51 (7): 646–665.

Bilal, D. 2002. "Children's Use of the Yahooligans! Web Search Engine. III. Cognitive and Physical Behaviors on Fully Self-Generated Search Tasks. *Journal of the American Society for Information Science and Technology* 53 (13): 1170–1183.

Bilal, D. 2010. "The Mediated Information Needs of Children on the Autism Spectrum Disorder (ASD)." *Proceedings of the 33rd Annual International ACM SIGIR Conference on Research and Development in Information Retrieval: Workshop on Towards Accessible Search Systems*, 42–47. Geneva, Switzerland.

Bilal, D., and R. Ellis. 2011. "Evaluating Leading Web Search Engines on Children's Queries." In J. A. Jacko (Ed.), *Human-Computer Interaction: Users and Applications: 14th International Conference, HCI International 2011*, Orlando, FL: 549–558.

Bilal, D., and J. Kirby. 2002. "Differences and Similarities in Information Seeking: Children and Adults as Web Users." *Information Processing and Management* 35 (5): 649–670.

Borgman, C., S. Hirsh, V. Walter, and A. L. Gallagher. 1995. "Children's Searching Behavior on Browsing and Keyword Online Catalogs: The Science Library Catalog Project." *Journal of the American Society for Information Science* 46: 663–684.

Bowler, L., A. Large, and G. Rejskind. 2001. "Primary School Students' Information Literacy and the Web." *Education for Information* 19: 201–223.

Bruckman, A., A. Bandlow, and A. Forte. 2008. "HCI for Kids." In A. Sears and J. A. Jacko (Eds.), *The Human-Computer Interaction Handbook*, 793–809. New York: Lawrence Erlbaum Associates.

Buckleitner, W. 2008. *Like Taking Candy from a Baby: How Young Children Interact with Online Environments.* Accessed January 2012, http://www.consumerwebwatch.org/pdfs/kidsonline.pdf.

Buckleitner, W. 2009. "Pocket Rockets: The Past, Present, and Future of Children's Portable Computing." In A. Druin (Ed.), *Mobile Technology for Children*, 43–62. Burlington, MA: Morgan Kaufmann Publishers.

Byron, L., and M. Wattenberg. 2008. "Stacked Graphs—Geometry and Aesthetics." *IEEE Transactions on Visualization and Computer Graphics* 14: 1245–1252.

Carmel, E., R. Whitaker, and J. George. 1993. "PD and Joint Application Design: A Transatlantic Comparison." *Communications of the ACM*, 36 (4): 40–47.

Carr, D. 1997. "User-Design in the Creation of Human Learning Systems." *Educational Technology Research and Development* 45 (3): 5–22.

Cawthon, N., and A. VandeMoere. 2007. "The Effect of Aesthetic on the Usability of Data Visualization." *Proceedings of the 11th International Conference on Information Visualization.* Zurich: IEEE: 637–648.

Consumer Reports. 2011. "CR Survey: 7.5 Million Facebook Users Are under the Age of 13, Violating the Site's Terms." Accessed January 2012, http://pressroom.consumerreports.org/pressroom/2011/05/cr-survey-75-million-facebook-users-are-under-the-age-of-13-violating-the-sites-terms-.html.

De Belder, J., and M. Moens. 2010. "Text Simplification for Children." In *Proceedings of the SIGIR Workshop on Accessible Search Systems*, 19–26. New York: ACM.

Druin, A. 1999. "Cooperative Inquiry: Developing New Technologies for Children with Children." In M. Williams and M. Altom (Chairpersons), *Proceedings of the SIGCHI Conference on Human Factors in Computing Systems*, 592–599. New York: ACM Press.

Druin, A. (Ed.) 2009. *Mobile Technology for Children.* Burlington, MA: Morgan Kaufmann Publishers.

Druin, A., B. B. Bederson, A. Rose, and A. Weeks. 2009a. "From New Zealand to Mongolia: Co-Designing and Deploying a Digital Library for the World's Children." *Children, Youth and Environments* 19 (1): 34–57.

Druin, A., B. B. Bederson, A. Weeks, A. Farber, J. Grosjean, M. L. Guha, J. P. Hourcade, J. Lee, S. Liao, K. Reuter, A. Rose, Y. Takayama, and L. Zhang. 2003. *The International Children's Digital Library: Description and Analysis of First Use.* Technical Report. Accessed January 2012, http://drum.lib.umd.edu/handle/1903/1250.

Druin, A., E. Foss, L. Hatley, E. Golub, M. L. Guha, J. Fails, and H. Hutchinson. 2009b. "How Children Search the Internet with Keyword Interfaces." In *Proceedings of the 8th International Conference on Interaction Design and Children (IDC '09)*, 89–96. New York: ACM.

Druin, A., E. Foss, H. Hutchinson, E. Golub, and L. Hatley. 2010. "Children's Roles Using Keyword Search Interfaces at Home." In *Proceedings of the 28th International Conference on Human Factors in Computing Systems (CHI '10)*, 413–422. New York: ACM.

Druin, A., J. Stewart, D. Proft, B. Bederson, and J. Hollan. 1997. "KidPad: A Design Collaboration between Children, Technologists, and Educators." In *Proceedings of the SIGCHI Conference on Human Factors in Computing Systems (CHI '97)*, 463–470. New York: ACM.

Druin, A., A. Weeks, S. Massey, and B. B. Bederson. 2007. "Children's Interests and Concerns When Using the International Children's Digital Library: A Four-Country Case Study." In *Proceedings of the 7th ACM/IEEE-CS Joint Conference on Digital Libraries (JCDL '07)*, 167–176. New York: ACM.

Ekanayake, S., and J. Wishart. 2011. "Identifying the Potential of Mobile Phone Cameras in Science Teaching and Learning: A Case Study Undertaken in Sri Lanka." *International Journal of Mobile and Blended Learning* 3 (2): 16–30.

Erdelez, S., and S. Makri. 2011. "Introduction to the Thematic Issue on Opportunistic Discovery of Information." *Information Research* 16 (3). http://informationr.net/ir/16-3/odiintro.html.

Gossen, T., T. Low, and A. Nürnberger. 2011. "What Are the Real Differences of Children's and Adults' Web Search." In *Proceedings of the 34th International ACM SIGIR Conference on Research and Development in Information Retrieval (SIGIR '11)*, 1115–1116. New York: ACM.

Graves Petersen, M., L. Hallnäs, and R. J. K. Jacob. 2008. "Introduction to Special Issue on the Aesthetics of Interaction." *ACM Transactions on Computer-Human Interaction* 15 (3).

Hanna, L., K. Risden, and K. J. Alexander. 1997. "Guidelines for Usability Testing with Children." *Interactions*, September–October: 9–14.

Hanna, L., K. Risden, M. Czerwinski, and D. Alexander. 1999. "The Role of Usability Research in Designing Children's Computer Products." In A. Druin (Ed.), *The Design of Children's Technology*, 4–26. San Francisco: Morgan Kaufmann.

Harris, A. L., and A. Rea. 2009. "Web 2.0 and Virtual World Technologies: A Growing Impact on IS Education." *Journal of Information Systems Education* 20 (2): 137–44.

Hartmann, J., A. Sutcliffe, and A. De Angeli. 2008. "Towards a Theory of User Judgment of Aesthetics and User Interface Quality." *ACM Transactions on Human–Computer Interaction* 15 (4): 1–30.

Hassenzahl, M., and N. Tractinsky. 2006. "User Experience—A Research Agenda." *Behaviour and Information Technology* 25 (2): 91–97.

Hew, K. F., and W. S. Cheung. 2010. "Immersive Virtual Worlds in K–12 and Higher Education." *British Journal of Educational Technology* 41 (1): 33–55.

Hirsh, S. G. 1999. "Children's Relevance Criteria and Information Seeking on Electronic Resources." *Journal of the American Society for Information Science* 50 (14): 1265–1283.

Hutchinson, H. B., B. B. Bederson, and A. Druin. 2006. "The Evolution of the International Children's Digital Library Searching and Browsing Interface." In *Proceedings of the 2006 Conference on Interaction Design and Children (IDC '06)*, 105–112. New York: ACM.

ISO/IEC. 9241-11. 1998. *Ergonomic Requirements for Office Work with Visual Display Terminals (VDTs)—Part 11: Guidance on Usability*. Geneva: International Organization for Standardization.

ISO FDIS 9241-210. 2010. *Ergonomics of Human System Interaction—Part 210: Human-Centered Design for Interactive Systems (Formerly Known as 13407)*. Geneva: International Organization for Standardization.

Jochmann-Mannak, H., T. Huibers, L. Lentz, and T. Sanders. 2010. "Children Searching Information on the Internet: Performance on Children's Interfaces Compared to Google." *ACM SIGIR'10, July 23*, Geneva, Switzerland. Accessed January 2012, http://eprints.eemcs.utwente.nl/18231/01/Jochmann_Lentz_Huibers_Sanders.pdf.

Kafai, Y., and M. Bates. 1997. "Internet Web-Searching Instruction in the Elementary Classroom: Building a Foundation for Information Literacy." *School Library Media Quarterly* 25: 103–111.

Kalloo, V., and P. Mohan. 2011. "An Investigation into Mobile Learning for High School Mathematics." *International Journal of Mobile and Blended Learning* 3 (3): 59–76.

Langdon, P., J. Clarkson, P. Robinson, J. Lazar, and A. Heylighen (Eds.). 2012. *Designing Inclusive Systems*. London: Springer.

Large, A. 2005. "Children, Teenagers, and the Web." In B. Cronin (Ed.), *The Annual Review of Information Science and Technology*, 347–392. Medford, NJ: Information Today.

Large, A., J. Beheshti, and C. Cole. 2002. "Information Architecture for the Web: The IA Matrix Approach to Designing Children's Portals." *Journal of the American Society for Information Science and Technology* 53 (10): 831–838.

Large, A., J. Beheshti, and H. Moukdad. 1999. "Information Seeking on the Web: Navigational Skills of Grade-Six Primary School Students." *Knowledge: Creation, Organization and Use, Proceedings of the 62nd ASIS Annual Meeting*, 84–97. Medford, NJ: Information Today, Inc.

Large, A., J. Beheshti, V. Nesset, and L. Bowler. 2004. "Designing Web Portals in Intergenerational Teams: Two Prototype Portals for Elementary School Students." *Journal of the American Society for Information Science and Technology* 55 (13): 1–15.

Large, A., J. Beheshti, N. Tabatabaei, and V. Nesset. 2009. "Developing a Visual Taxonomy: Children's View on Aesthetics." *Journal of the American Society for Information Science and Technology* 60 (9): 1808–1822.

Large, A., V. Nesset, J. Beheshti, and L. Bowler. 2006a. "'Bonded Design': A Novel Approach to Intergenerational Information Technology Design." *Library and Information Science Research* 28 (1): 64–82.

Large, A., J. Beheshti, V. Nesset, and L. Bowler. 2006b. "Web Portal Design Guidelines as Identified by Children through the Process of Design and Evaluation." *Proceedings of the American Society for Information Science and Technology* 43 (1): 1–23.

Laurel, B. 1993. *Computers as Theatre*. Reading, MA: Addison-Wesley.

Laux, Lila F., Peter R. McNally, Michael G. Paciello, and Gregg C. Vanderheiden. 1996. "Designing the World Wide Web for People with Disabilities: A User Centered Design Approach." In *Proceedings of the Second Annual ACM Conference on Assistive Technologies (Assets '96)*, 94–101. New York: ACM.

Lenhart, A., M. Madden, A. Smith, K. Purcell, K. Zickuhr, and L. Rainie. 2011. "Teens, Kindness and Cruelty on Social Network Sites." *Pew Internet and American Life Project*. Accessed January 2012, http://pewinternet.org/Reports/2011/Teens-and-social-media.aspx.

Levin, D., J. Richardson, and S. Arafeh. 2002. "Digital Disconnect: Students' Perceptions and Experiences with the Internet and Education." In P. Baker and S. Rebelsky (Eds.), *Proceedings of ED-MEDIA, World Conference on Educational Multimedia, Hypermedia and Telecommunications*, 51–52. Norfolk, VA: Association for the Advancement of Computing in Education.

Lindgaard, G., and C. Dudek. 2003. "What Is This Evasive Beast We Call User Satisfaction?" *Interactive Computing* 15 (3): 429–452.

Marshall, B., M. Dark, J. Goldman, T. Hacker, and A. Smith. 2009. "Dark Web Patterns." In *Proceedings of the WebSci '09: Society On-Line, 18–20 March*, Athens, Greece. Accessed January 2012, http://journal.webscience.org/126/2/websci09_submission_28.pdf.

McKnight, L. 2010. "Designing for ADHD in Search of Guidelines." *IDC 2010 Digital Technologies and Marginalized Youth Workshop*. Accessed January 2012, http://www.divms.uiowa.edu/~hourcade/idc2010-myw/mcknight.pdf.

Milgram, P., and F. Kishino. 1994. "A Taxonomy of Mixed Reality Visual Displays." *IEICE Transactions on Information and Systems* E77 (12): 1321–1329.

mobiThinking. 2012. *Global Mobile Statistics 2012 Home: All the Latest Stats on Mobile Web, Apps, Marketing, Advertising, Subscribers and Trends* . . . Accessed January 2012, http://mobithinking.com/mobile-marketing-tools/latest-mobile-stats#phone-shipments.

Nahl, D., and D. Bilal. (Eds.) 2007. *Information and Emotion: The Emergent Affective Paradigm in Information Behavior Research and Theory*. Medford, NJ: Information Today.

Nesset, V., and A. Large. 2004. "Children in the Information Technology Design Process: A Review of Theories and Their Applications." *Library and Information Science Research* 26 (2): 140–161.

Netmarketshare. Google—Global Market Share on. Accessed January 2012, http://marketshare.hitslink.com/report.aspx?qprid=5&qpcustom=Google%20-%20Global&qptimeframe=M&qpsp=120&qpnp=25.

Ngo, D. C. L., L. S. Teo, and J. G. Byrne. 2003. "Modelling Interface Aesthetics." *Information Sciences* 152: 25–46.

Nielsen, J. 1993. *Usability Engineering*. San Diego, CA: Academic Press.

Norman, D. A. 2004. *Emotional Design: Why We Love (or Hate) Everyday Things*. New York: Basic Books.

Norris, C., and E. Soloway. 2009. "A Disruption Is Coming: A Primer for Educators on the Mobile Technology Revolution." In A. Druin (Ed.), *Mobile Technology for Children*, 83–98. Burlington, MA: Morgan Kaufmann Publishers.

O'Brien, H. L., and E. G. Toms. 2008. "What Is User Engagement? A Conceptual Framework for Defining User Engagement with Technology." *Journal of the American Society for Information Science* 59: 938–955.

Odom, W., J. Zimmerman, and J. Forlizzi. 2011. "Teenagers and Their Virtual Possessions: Design Opportunities and Issues." *CHI 2011, Proceedings of the 2011 Annual Conference on Human Factors in Computing Systems*, May 7–12, Vancouver, B.C., 1491–1500. New York: ACM.

Ofcom. 2010. *UK Children's Media Literacy*, March. Accessed January 2012, http://stakehold-ers.ofcom.org.uk/market-data-research/media-literacy/archive/medlitpub/medlitpubrss/uk-childrensml11/.

Orlando, J. 2011. "How Young Is Too Young? Mobile Technologies and Young Children." *21st Century Learning: Directions in Education, Early Childhood Education, Engaging Learning Environments*. University of Western Sydney. Accessed January 2012, http://learning21c.wordpress.com/2011/08/21/how-young-is-too-young-mobile-technologies-and-young-children/.

Pan, Z., A. D. Cheok, H. Yang, J. Zhu, J. Shi. 2006. "Virtual Reality and Mixed Reality for Virtual Learning Environments." *Computers and Graphics* 30 (1): 20–28.

Pejtersen, A. M. 1989. "A Library System for Information Retrieval Based on a Cognitive Task Analysis and Supported by an Icon-Based Interface." *SIGIR '89 Proceedings of the 12th Annual International ACM SIGIR Conference on Research and Development in Information Retrieval*: 40–47.

Peters, C., G. Castellano, S. de Freitas. 2009. "An Exploration of User Engagement in HCI." In Ginevra Castellano, Jean-Claude Martin, John Murray, Kostas Karpouzis, and Christopher Peters (Eds.), *Proceedings of the International Workshop on Affective-Aware Virtual Agents and Social Robots (AFFINE '09)*. New York: ACM. http://doi.acm.org/10.1145/1655260.1655269.

Pew Internet and American Life Project. 2011. *Trends Data for Teens*. Accessed January 2012, http://www.pewinternet.org/Static-Pages/Trend-Data-for-Teens/Online-Activites-Total.aspx.

Prensky, M. 2001. "Digital Natives, Digital Immigrants." *On the Horizon* 9: 1–5.

Prensky, M. 2012. *From Digital Natives to Digital Wisdom: Hopeful Essays for 21st Century Learning*. Thousand Oaks, CA: Corwin.

Rauber, A., and D. Merkl. 1999. "The SOMLib Digital Library System." *Lecture Notes in Computer Science* 1696/1999, 852: 323–342.

Read, J. C., S. J. MacFarlane, and C. Casey. 2002. "Endurability, Engagement and Expectations: Measuring Children's Fun." *Procs Interaction Design and Children*, 189–198. Eindhoven: Shaker Publishing.

Resnick, Mitchel, John Maloney, Andrés Monroy-Hernández, Natalie Rusk, Evelyn Eastmond, Karen Brennan, Amon Millner, Eric Rosenbaum, Jay Silver, Brian Silverman, and Yasmin Kafai. 2009. "Scratch: Programming for All." *Communications of ACM* 52 (11): 60–67.

Reuter, K., and A. Druin. 2004. "Bringing Together Children and Books: An Initial Descriptive Study of Children's Book Search and Selection Behavior in a Digital Library." *Proceedings of the American Society for Information Science and Technology* 41 (1): 339–348.

Rogers, Y., and S. Price. 2009. "How Mobile Technologies Are Changing the Way Children Learn." In A. Druin (Ed.), *Mobile Technology for Children*, 1–22. Burlington, MA: Morgan Kaufmann Publishers.

Rowlands, I., D. Nicholas, P. Williams, P. Huntington, M. Fieldhouse, B. Gunter, R. Withey, H. Jamali, T. Dobrowolski, and C. Tenopir. 2008. "The Google Generation: The Information Behaviour of the Researcher of the Future." *Aslib Proceedings* 60 (4): 290–310.

Scaife, M., and Y. Rogers. 1999. "Kids as Informants: Telling Us What We Didn't Know or Confirming What We Knew Already." In A. Druin (Ed.), *The Design of Children's Technology*, 27–50. San Francisco: Kaufmann.

Scaife, M., Y. Rogers, F. Aldrich, and M. Davies. 1997. "Designing For or Designing With? Informant Design for Interactive Learning Environments." In S. Pemberton (Ed.), *Proceedings of the SIGCHI Conference on Human Factors in Computing Systems*, 343–350. New York: ACM Press.

Selwyn, N. 2009. "The Digital Native: Myth and Reality." *Aslib Proceedings: New Information Perspectives* 61: 364–379.

Seol, S., A. Sharp, and P. Kim. 2011. "Stanford Mobile Inquiry-Based Learning Environment (SMILE): Using Mobile Phones to Promote Student Inquires in the Elementary Classroom." *Proceedings of World Congress in Computer Science, Computer Engineering, and Applied Computing*. Accessed January 2012, http://world-comp.org/p2011/FEC3167.pdf.

Shiaw, H., R. J. K. Jacob, and G. R. Crane. 2004. "The 3D Vase Museum: A New Approach to Context in a Digital Library." *Digital Libraries, 2004. Proceedings of the 2004 Joint ACM/ IEEE Conference* June 7–11: 125–134.

Shneiderman, B. 2000. "Universal Usability." *Communications of ACM* 43 (5) (May 2000): 84–91.

Shneiderman, B. 2004. "Designing for Fun: How Can We Design User Interfaces to Be More Fun?" *Interactions* 11 (5): 48–50.

Skinner, E. A., and M. J. Belmont. 1993. "Motivation in the Classroom: Reciprocal Effects of Teacher Behavior and Student Engagement across the School Year." *Journal of Educational Psychology* 85 (4): 571–581.

Soloway, E., M. Guzdial, and K. Hay. 1994. "Learner-Centered Design: The Challenge for HCI in the 21st Century." *Interactions* 1 (2): 36–48.

Sorensen, C. 2011. *Learning with Mobile Technologies: The Use of Out-of-Class Short Message System Text Messaging to Support the Classroom Learning of High School Algebra.* Unpublished dissertation. University of South Florida.

Sutcliffe, A. 2009. "Designing for User Engagement: Aesthetic and Attractive User Interfaces." In J. M. Carroll (Series Ed.), *Synthesis Lectures on Human-Centered Informatics.* San Rafael, CA: Morgan Claypool.

Thomas, M. (Ed.) 2011. *Deconstructing Digital Natives: Young People, Technology, and the New Literacies.* New York: Routledge.

Torres, S. D., D. Hiemstra, and P. Serdyukov. 2010. "An Analysis of Queries Intended to Search Information for Children." In *Proceedings of the Third Symposium on Information Interaction in Context (IIiX '10)*, 235–244. New York: ACM.

Torres, S. D., and I. Weber. 2011. "What and How Children Search on the Web." *CIKM '11 Proceedings of the 20th ACM International Conference on Information and Knowledge Management*, 393–402. New York: ACM.

Tractinsky, N., A. S Katz, and D. Ikar. 2000. "What Is Beautiful Is Usable." *Interacting with Computers* 13 (2): 127–145.

van der Sluis, F., and E. M. A. G. van Dijk. 2010. "A Closer Look at Children's Information Retrieval Usage: Towards Child-Centered Relevance." In *Proceedings of the Workshop on Accessible Search Systems Held at the 33st Annual International ACM SIGIR Conference on Research and Development in Information Retrieval* (SIGIR 2010), Geneva, Switzerland, 3–10.

Vandewater, E. A., V. J. Rideout, E. A. Wartella, X. Huang, J. H. Lee, and Mi-suk Shim. 2007. "Digital Childhood: Electronic Media and Technology Use among Infants, Toddlers, and Preschoolers." *Pediatrics* 119 (5): 1006–1015.

Varona, J., C. Manresa-Yee, and F. J. Perales. 2008. "Hands-Free Vision-Based Interface for Computer Accessibility." *Journal of Network and Computer Applications* 31 (4): 357–374.

Vie, S. 2008. "Digital Divide 2.0: 'Generation M' and Online Social Networking Sites in the Composition Classroom." *Computers and Composition* 25 (1): 9–23.

Virvou, M., G. Katsionis, and K. Manos. 2005. "Combining Software Games with Education: Evaluation of Its Educational Effectiveness." *Educational Technology and Society* 8: 54–65.

Ware, C. 2008. *Visual Thinking for Design.* Burlington, MA: Morgan Kaufmann.

Wilson, J. R., and M. D'Cruz. 2006. "Virtual and Interactive Environments for Work of the Future." *International Journal of Human-Computer Studies* 64: 158–169.

Chapter Eleven

The Future

Jamshid Beheshti and Andrew Large

Has the information behavior of children and youth changed significantly over the last two decades? In this book, we have attempted to answer this question from a variety of viewpoints.

SKIMMING AND MULTITASKING

Information behavior is a multifaceted phenomenon, which, with the advent of information and communication technologies, has evolved at a startling pace. Rowlands and colleagues (2008) observed that the new generation is "hungry for highly digested content," and its "information seeking behavior can be characterized as being horizontal, bouncing, checking and viewing in nature" (294). By horizontal they refer to the skimming activities of youth, so prevalent in their information seeking, be it at home or at school. Rowlands and his partners (2008) conclude that adults and youth behave similarly when seeking information; that "we are all the Google generation" (308).

However, as many researchers have indicated, there are differences between adults and children, even though both groups may use similar tools in their information behavior. Large (2005) and Bilal (2002), among other researchers, have concluded that the new generation lacks appropriate training and skills to transfer its information needs to effective search strategies, shows a strong preference for natural language searching, spends little time evaluating the retrieved information, and expects instant gratification with the search results. Younger children also face spelling and typing challenges that add more obstacles to their information-seeking process. In a follow-up experimental study to Rowlands et al.'s (2008), Nicholas and his colleagues (2011) imposed four tasks (pre-piloted questions) on 138 participants whose ages ranged widely among three generations: *X*, born 1973 or earlier; *Y*, born between 1974 and 1993; and *Google*, born after 1993. The results show that while the younger generation was faster in searching and retrieving the results, they viewed fewer pages and websites, and conducted fewer searches, resulting in less confidence in their answers to the task questions. The authors conclude that "there were profound and, possibly, concerning, differences between younger and older members of the general public in terms of their web behaviour" (42). One potential inference from many of these studies is that while the younger generation is technology savvy, it lacks the information and media literacy skills needed to make informed judgments on searching, selecting, authenticating, retrieving, organizing, synthesizing, and applying the information to create new knowledge.

Perhaps the biggest difference between adults and today's youth may be summed up by Bastian, a typical 14-year-old:

> My dad always gets really annoyed at me when we watch TV together as he says that I should only do one thing at a time, rather than 100 things at a time. It is not that bad, yes I am on Facebook, texting my friends, chatting to people, gaming, browsing the Internet, looking at YouTube clips, but I am still watching the show. (Rasmussen 2012)

This multitasking generation manages many activities simultaneously, but at a price. The success of Twitter is a manifestation of the skimming generation's approach to information, that is, short bursts of information delivered quickly, efficiently, and effectively. The surfing and skimming practices, however, may lack the deep level self-realization characteristics required in the information-seeking process (see the chapter by Bowler and Nesset, "Information Literacy," in this book).

CREATION AND PRODUCTION

Another generational difference is youth's longing to *produce* information as much as or perhaps more than to consume it. Evidence abounds: Facebook, YouTube, MySpace, and other commercial products' success attests to the new generation's desire to be actively involved in creating information, reliable or unreliable as it may be. While systems to assist children in their information-seeking endeavors are forthcoming, researchers are now contemplating systems that enable and empower children and teens to create their own content. In 2007, researchers at the MIT Media Lab with support from the National Science Foundation, Microsoft, Google, Intel, and others launched the Scratch programming language (http://scratch.mit.edu/) to provide an easy and accessible means for everyone, regardless of age and background, to produce their own interactive games, animations, and simulations

(Resnick et al. 2009; see also the chapter by Dresang, "Digital Age Libraries and Youth: Learning Labs, Literacy Leaders, Radical Resources," in this book). Since then, Scratch has been used by countless people, to the tune of some 1,500 new project uploads each day. The uploaded products are diverse, ranging from virtual tours to interactive tutorials and animated dance sequences, the vast majority of which is produced by children and teens between 8 and 16 years old (Resnick et al. 2009).

Harlan and colleagues (2012) concluded from observations of seven 15- to 18-year-olds that for youth to be engaged in production requires a certain degree of informed learning in the context under which they are operating. As they create content, they are constantly browsing and searching for information, making selections, evaluating, planning, reflecting, copying, modeling, and composing. It remains to be seen, however, if the results of their study can be generalized to other age groups and studies.

COLLABORATION

Youth's desire to create content also hinges on digital socialization. Contributions to digital participatory communities have become the norm, and an integral facet of the new generation's lifestyle. Content creation implies participatory activity and collaboration, which may signify another difference between adults and children, that the latter share freely their personal information with their peers. The digital interaction afforded through social networks, notwithstanding the dangers lurking on the Internet (see the chapter by Shaheen Shariff, "Defining the Line on Cyber-Bullying: How Youth Encounter and Distribute Demeaning Information," in this book), provide children and youth with personal gratification. Children exhibit a significantly higher level of learning, engagement, enjoyment, and motivation in collaborative environments (Webb and Palincsar 1996; Inkpen et al. 1999; Scott et al. 2003; Sluis et al. 2004). Experiments are now conducted on collaborative systems for children, including the tangible technology where physical artifacts are coupled with digital information. In many projects, augmented tabletop environments are used to show the efficacies of synchronous collaborative technology. For example, Hornecker and Buur (2006) tested a tangible interface on children in comparison with a physical artifact and a graphical interface in a gaming environment. The 2D graphical interface did not perform as well as the tangible tabletop interface, which closely resembled the physical artifact in engaging children and in encouraging collaborative activities. Rick et al. (2009) experimented with a multi-touch tabletop technology, where a horizontal display detects multiple concurrent touches to determine how children work together. They concluded after experimenting with 21 children between 9 and 11 years old that the tabletop technology facilitates collaboration through the shareable interface, and benefits learning.

This sense of collaboration and sharing may begin to blur and obscure the division between imposed tasks assigned by the school and everyday life information behavior. While social networks such as Facebook benefit children and youth in technological literacy, increasingly social networking sites are being used to support educational activities, and information and peer-to-peer resource sharing, providing an alternative to traditional learning management systems (Mazman and Usluel 2010; see also the chapter by Denise Agosto and June Abbas, "Youth and Online Social Networking: What Do We Know So Far?" in this book).

THE PARADIGM SHIFT

Does the new generation's behavior, then, signify a potential paradigm shift: brick and mortar libraries replaced gradually with virtual libraries, books with e-books, online public access catalogues (OPACs) with Google (and the like), and traditional reference materials with Wikipedia and similarly shared resources?

In this book, we have covered many aspects relating to the information behavior of children and young people, in an attempt to investigate and analyze the current situation and identify important issues in a potential paradigm shift. While we cannot predict the future, we can help shape it, and provide guidance and direction for future research.

Byrnes and Bernacki in their chapter, "Cognitive Development and Information Behavior," suggest that future research should focus on the relationship between the information behavior of youth and information overload, information processing capacity, and the methodologies to measure the capacity. The affective and cognitive aspects of information searching, and the differences in them between adults and children, should be investigated. Cole is also concerned about the dissimilarities between adults, older teenagers, and young children in their conceptualization of natural and social phenomena, and in their creation of relations between concepts and forming theories. In his chapter "Concepts, Propositions, Models, and Theories in Information Behavior Research," he advocates the development of metaphorical systems that can help young users in their theory formulation and concept construction. In the context of the new technologies and social networks, Agosto and Abbas also advocate more research on the differences between adults and youth in their information behavior.

In response to a potential paradigm shift, transformations are taking place across the spectrum of information and knowledge transfer and behavior. The brick and mortar libraries may be changing their roles from warehouses of organized containers of information to learning labs (see the chapter by Dresang, "Digital Age Libraries and Youth: Learning Labs, Literacy Leaders, Radical Resources," in this book), and librarians are increasingly taking the role of information and media literacy instructors. Bowler and Nesset, in their chapter "Information Literacy," observe that conflicting views exist on youth's multitasking and scanning behavior on the one hand, and the lack of in-depth reflecting and reviewing on the other hand. They suggest that new models of information literacy that incorporate social skills, cultural competencies, scanning, and contemplation and reflection should be investigated.

The paradigm shift is also of concern for Abbas and Agosto, who investigate youth's everyday life information behavior; Hanson-Baldauf, who writes about intellectual disabilities; and Shariff who conducts research on cyber-bullying. Abbas and Agosto conclude that youth's behavior, at least those who have access to information and communication technologies (ICTs), is dynamic and constantly changing, and factors that may affect this behavior, such as gender, should be examined. Hanson-Baldauf advocates more research on services and systems that would help those with disabilities, even though conducting research with these individuals may prove more difficult than other user groups. Shariff has a positive view about the advances in ICTs, and particularly social networks, while recognizing the dangers that children and young people may face in using them. The challenge lies in educating youth about ethical and legal boundaries, social responsibility, and digital citizenship.

Will the current information behavior models be applicable to the dynamic, ever-changing landscape of the new generation's information activities? Much research has to be conducted to determine the totality of factors and variables that may impact the information behavior of children and young people. And will the swift technological evolution remain static long enough to allow us to gain a snapshot of the new generation's information behavior? The challenge is perhaps clearer than will be our response!

REFERENCES

Bilal, D., and J. Kirby. 2002. "Differences and Similarities in Information Seeking: Children and Adults as Web Users." *Information Processing and Management* 38 (5): 649–670.

Harlan, M., C. S. Bruce, and M. Lupton. 2012. "Teen Content Creators: Experiences of Using Information to Learn." *Library Trends* 60 (3): 567–585.

Hornecker, E., and J. Buur. 2006. "Getting a Grip on Tangible Interaction: A Framework on Physical Space and Social Interaction." In *Proceedings of CHI 2006*, 437–446. New York: ACM Press.

Inkpen, K. M., W. Ho-Ching, O. Kuederle, S. D. Scott, and G. B. Shoemaker. 1999. "This Is Fun! We're All Best Friends and We're All Playing: Supporting Children's Synchronous Collaboration." In *Proceedings of the 1999 Conference on Computer Support For Collaborative Learning*, 252–259. New York: ACM Press.

Large, A. 2005. "Children, Teenagers, and the Web." *Annual Review of Information Science and Technology* 39: 347–392.

Mazman S. G., and Y. K. Usluel. 2010. "Modeling Educational Usage of Facebook." *Computers and Education* 55 (2): 444–453.

Nicholas, D., I. Rowlands, D. Clark, and P. Williams. 2011. "Google Generation II: Web Behaviour Experiments with the BBC." *Aslib Proceedings* 63 (1): 28–45.

Rasmussen, R. H. 2012. "Quotes from Children." Kids and Media. Accessed March 2012. http://www.kidsandmedia.co.uk/quotes-from-children/.

Resnick, M., J. Maloney, A. Monroy-Hernández, N. Rusk, E. Eastmond, K. Brennan, A. Millner, E. Rosenbaum, J. Silver, B. Silverman, and Y. Kafai. 2009. "Scratch: Programming for All 'Digital Fluency' Should Mean Designing, Creating, and Remixing, Not Just Browsing, Chatting, and Interacting." *Communications of the ACM* 52 (11): 60–67.

Rick, J., Y. Rogers, C. Haig, and N. Yuill. 2009. "Learning by Doing with Shareable Interfaces." *Children, Youth and Environments* 19 (1): 321–342.

Rowlands, I., D. Nicholas, P. Williams, P. Huntington, M. Fieldhouse, B. Gunter, R. Withey, H. Jamali, T. Dobrowolski, and C. Tenopir. 2008. "The Google Generation: The Information Behaviour of the Researcher of the Future." *Aslib Proceedings* 60 (4): 290–310.

Scott S. D., R. L. Mandryk, and K. M. Inkpen. 2003. "Understanding Children's Collaborative Interactions in Shared Environments." In *Proceedings of the Journal of Computer Aided Learning* 19 (2): 220–228.

Sluis, R. J., I. Weevers, C. H. van Schijndel, L. Kolos-Mazuryk, S. Fitrianie, and J. B. Martens. 2004. "Read-It: Five- to Seven-Year-Old Children Learn to Read in a Tabletop Environment." In *Proceeding of the 2004 Conference on Interaction Design and Children: Building a Community*, 73–80. New York: ACM Press.

Webb, N. M., and A. S. Palincsar. 1996. "Group Processes in the Classroom." In D. C. Berliner and R. C. Calfee (Eds.), *Handbook of Educational Psychology*. New York: Simon and Schuster Macmillan: 841–873.

Index

active learners, 49

Active Worlds, 156

aesthetics, 228–229

affective, 16, 24, 35, 36, 37, 40, 53, 54, 69, 70, 74, 76, 77, 78, 80, 229, 240

age changes, vii, 23, 24, 25, 31, 35, 36, 40

American Association of School Librarians (AASL), 46, 55, 103

American Library Association (ALA), 105, 110, 182, 215

American Society on Intellectual and Developmental Disabilities, 170

Android, 160

animation, 95, 219, 221, 223, 230, 238

Apple, 160, 186

apps, 160, 186

Ask Kids, 216

assignments, 2, 14, 15, 36, 40, 51, 52, 53, 84, 167

Associative Index Model (AIM), 11, 12

associative structures, 26, 27, 36

Australia, 50, 121, 144

Awesome Library, 217

Berry-Picking model, 18, 99

Big6, 48, 101

Bloom's taxonomy, 95, 215

Bonded Design, 220–222, 223

Brain Age, 152

browsing, 218, 229

Canada, 79, 121, 198, 199, 201, 202, 204, 205, 206, 207, 208, 209, 221, 223, 226

Care2, 117

CEGEP. *See* colleges

chat room, 77, 83, 133

chemistry, 158

Civilization, 148

Club Penguin, 156

cognitive development, vii, 23, 40, 72

cognitive load, 34, 40, 229

colleges, vii, 27, 29, 38, 39, 40, 46, 55, 108, 118, 179, 181

computer science, 154

conceptual framework, 3, 4, 13

conceptual knowledge, 25, 26, 28, 35, 56

Consortium for Citizens with Disabilities Housing Task Force, 175

constructivist, 29, 51

consumer, 59, 80, 84, 95, 96, 100, 119, 130, 160, 185, 215

Contextual Design, 219

Cooperative Inquiry, 220, 222

COTS, 148, 152

culture, 25, 45, 59, 77, 80, 93, 99, 109, 110, 111, 112, 145, 149, 153, 170, 183, 184, 204, 222

cyberbullying, 134, 135, 195–209

Define the Line, 209

declarative knowledge, 25, 35

demographic, 72, 77, 99, 135, 138

About the Editors and Contributors

June Abbas is an associate professor in the School of Library and Information Studies, College of Arts and Sciences, at the University of Oklahoma. Her research interests include children and youth's uses of technologies, their information use behaviors, and designing age-appropriate systems for youth. Dr. Abbas has published extensively on these topics, as well as the societal impacts of children and youth's Internet use on public libraries. She has also presented her research at state, national, and international conferences.

Denise E. Agosto is an associate professor in the College of Information Science and Technology at Drexel University. Her research and teaching interests focus on youths' social media practices, children's and teens' digital information behaviors, and on public library services. Dr. Agosto is widely published on these topics, and she is a frequent speaker at state, national, and international academic and professional conferences. The recipient of numerous teaching and research awards and grants, Dr. Agosto is currently serving as the principal investigator for *Libraries and the Social Web: Developing the Next Generation of Youth Information Services,* a research grant funded by the Institute for Museum and Library Studies.

Jamshid Beheshti is an associate professor in the School of Information Studies at McGill University, where he was the Director of the School for six years. He was also appointed as the Associate Dean of the Faculty of Education, and the Interim Dean of the Faculty. Dr. Beheshti is the principal investigator on a Social Sciences and Humanities Research Council of Canada grant on *Virtual Environments as an Intervention Agent in the Information-Seeking Process of School Students.* His areas of expertise are children-computer interaction, and information behavior.

Matthew L. Bernacki is a postdoctoral researcher at the Learning Research and Development Center at the University of Pittsburgh and a member of the Pittsburgh Science of Learning Center's Metacognition and Motivation thrust. He received his PhD in educational psychology at Temple University and completed prior graduate training in experimental psychology at Saint Joseph's University in Philadelphia, Pennsylvania. His research investigates how self-regulated learning theory can be applied to learning with educational technology. His recent work examines the metacognitive and motivational processes that underlie students' learning from hypertexts and intelligent tutoring systems.

Leanne Bowler is an assistant professor at the School of Information Sciences, University of Pittsburgh, where she is responsible for the specialization in children and youth. Dr. Bowler received her PhD and two master's degrees (MLS, MEd) from McGill University, Montréal, Canada. Her dissertation explored the landscape of adolescent metacognitive knowledge during the information search process. Her research interests lie in the area of children's and youth information behavior, with a focus on new media literacies. Topics that Dr. Bowler is currently exploring include the metacognitive knowledge needed to navigate new media, health information on the Web for teens, and design-based research with young people. Dr. Bowler teaches courses about design-based research methods, new media literacy, technology for young people, children's literature and media, and early literacy and language development.

James P. Byrnes received his PhD in developmental psychology from Temple University in 1985. Prior to his return to Temple as professor in the Psychological Studies in Education department in 2004, he held academic appointments at the City University of New York (postdoctoral fellow), University of Michigan (visiting assistant professor), and University of Maryland (assistant, associate, and full professor). He has served as vice dean of the College of Education at Temple, vice president of the Jean Piaget Society, and associate editor of the *Journal of Cognition and Development*. He has published over 70 works on various areas of cognitive development, but his most recent work has focused on developing two comprehensive models: one on academic achievement and the other on adolescent decision making. The model on academic achievement has been specifically designed to provide insight into ways to eliminate or substantially reduce gender, ethnic, and racial gaps in achievement. The model on adolescent decision making has been designed to provide insight into ways to decrease the level of unhealthy forms of risk taking in this age group.

Charles Cole has been a researcher-writer in the information science field for nearly 20 years. In the last decade, he has expanded his interest in information need to designing information retrieval systems based on why and how humans naturally search for information when they are in a construction-of-a-focus phase of performing a task. With Amanda Spink, he has edited two books in information science: *New Directions in Human Information Behavior* (2006) and *New Directions in Cognitive Information Retrieval* (2005). A third book, *Information Need: A Theory Connecting Information Search to Knowledge Formation*, was published in 2012. Dr. Cole received his PhD (information science) in 1994 from the University of Sheffield, his MLIS from McGill University in 1989 and his BA (history-geography) from McGill University in 1978. He completed a two-year postdoctoral fellowship at Concordia University in 1999. He is currently researcher, affiliated member, at the School of Information Studies, McGill University. He is also a consultant (Colemining Inc.).

Eliza T. Dresang holds the endowed Beverly Cleary Professorship in Children and Youth Services in the Information School at the University of Washington. She received her PhD in 1981 from the University of Wisconsin–Madison School of Library and Information Studies. She worked with the Cooperative Children's Book Center, and as the director of Library Media and Technology for the Metropolitan School District at Madison, and taught at Florida State University, where she was the Eliza Gleason Atkins Professor in the College of Information. She has written widely on *Radical Change Theory*, and the paradigm shift in reading behavior of children due to digital technology.

Dana Hanson-Baldauf is a PhD candidate from the School of Information and Library Science at the University of North Carolina at Chapel Hill and is a LEND Trainee with the Carolina Institute for Developmental Disabilities. She received her BS and MS from the University of Kansas in special education. Her dissertation research explores the everyday life information experiences of young adults with intellectual disabilities. Dana's interest in disability information studies is both professional and personal. She is a former middle school special education teacher, a proud coach for the Special Olympics of Orange County, North Carolina, and has an older sibling with an intellectual disability. Dana would like to acknowledge Dr. Sandra Hughes-Hassell (UNC-SILS), Deb Zuver and Donna Yerby (UNC-CIDD), and T. J. Smithers for their kind support in the drafting of this chapter.

Andrew Large is CN-Pratt-Grinstad Professor of Information Studies in the School of Information Studies at McGill University, and currently associate dean (research and graduate students) in its Faculty of Education. His research interests lie in the areas of information retrieval, interface design, and usability, especially in the context of children as users. He has published and spoken widely on these and other research themes, and is co-editor of the quarterly journal *Education for Information*.

Valerie Nesset earned her MLIS (2002) and PhD (2009) at McGill University in Montreal, Canada. Currently, she is an assistant professor at the University at Buffalo (SUNY). Her main research interest is in the intersection of information-seeking behavior and information literacy, specifically with elementary school–aged children. She also conducts research into website and web portal design for children, as well as in indexing and abstracting.

Shaheen Shariff is an associate professor in the Department of Integrated Studies in Education, Faculty of Education, at McGill University. She is an international expert on legal issues that have emerged in relation to online social communications such as cyber-bullying, free expression, privacy, libel, and criminal harassment. Her research and teaching are grounded in the study of law as it impacts educational policy, pedagogy, and practice. She is also a member on the board of directors for Kids' Help Phone, and is the spokesperson for an upcoming UNICEF report concerning the online safety of children. She was invited to participate on a United Nations panel on cyber-hate chaired by Secretary General Ban Ki Moon and has served on an international advisory committee working with UNESCO and CIDA and the International Institute for Educational Planning to develop a toolkit for use globally in drafting teacher codes of conduct. She was also recently a panelist with the (U.S.) First Amendment Center's online symposium, which featured her scholarship on the legal implications for educational institutions in relation to policy issues around cyber-bullying.

Giovanni Vincenti is a lecturer for the Department of Computer and Information Sciences at Towson University, in Towson, Maryland. He received his doctorate of science in applied information technology from Towson University in 2007. He has been teaching undergraduate and graduate courses for several years, letting him develop his interest in instructional technologies that range from simple learning objects as a supplement to in-person instruction, all the way to the utilization of virtual worlds in the classroom. He has been collaborating for years with James Braman, co-authoring several published works including the edited volume titled *Multi-User Virtual Environments for the Classroom: Practical Approaches to Teaching in Virtual Worlds*. Vincenti and Braman are also leading e-learning projects for the Institute of Computer Sciences, Social Informatics, and Telecommunications Engineering (ICST). In addition, Dr. Vincenti serves as a consultant to companies and universities that focus on online learning.